THE BLACK WHITE
DIVIDE IN
AMERICA
... STILL

Communication is the beginning of understanding. In *THE BLACK/WHITE DIVIDE IN AMERICA ... STILL* authors Marlin Foxworth and Ralph Gordon present compelling viewpoints on the most challenging issues facing this country. This uniquely formatted treatise provides a thoughtful forum for the resolution of myriad social, political, and economic race based problems which we must resolve. I recommend this book to anyone seeking enlightenment on the issue.

— *ELIHU HARRIS*
Chancellor, Peralta Colleges, Alameda County, California
Former Mayor, Oakland, California
Former Assemblyman, California State Legislature

Marlin Foxworth and Ralph Gordon have written an important and instructive challenge to white Americans: the Black/White Divide remains a major source of inequality and suffering. Foxworth was an urban school district superintendent three times, and this book's uncovering of the reality of school life in the 21st century is particularly unsettling because so many White Americans seem to think that because they heard of a given issue being raised in the media that somehow it has been "dealt with." Our next U.S. Secretary of Education would do well to start by reading this book — but since that is unlikely, you need to read it and take its ideas and insights to your local school board.

— *RABBI MICHAEL LERNER*
Editor of Tikkun Magazine www.tikkun.org and
national chair of The Network of Spiritual Progressives
wwwspiritualprogressives.org, and author of the 2006 national bestseller
THE LEFT HAND OF GOD: TAKING BACK OUR COUNTRY FROM THE RELIGIOUS RIGHT

Cornel West wrote that, "A fully functional multiracial society cannot be achieved without a sense of history and open, honest dialogue." But, to paraphrase Jack Nicholson in *A Few Good Men,* "America 'can't handle the truth." We spend enormous sums claiming to fight crime, poverty, the achievement gap in our schools and a host of other social manifestations of the American racial divide without ever confronting the core issue ... racism. Foxworth and Gordon slap us in the face with the reality of America's racial dilemma. Theirs is a scholarly, thoughtful but sobering work that should cause each of us to examine our individual and collective complacency. This is a call to action that America cannot afford to ignore.

— CLAUDE EVERHART
Former Deputy Mayor, San Francisco, California

In 1920, W.E.B. DuBois wrote of "the veil" that separates Blacks and Whites and renders both unable to see themselves and one another clearly. Foxworth and Gordon in 2008 use another construct, the "divide," to show how inability to see one another clearly has led to structural separation of Blacks and Whites in American society. In almost a century since DuBois' powerful writings caught American consciousness, Foxworth and Gordon remind us with anecdote and analysis that the "divide" still exists. It is vital that we be so reminded. This is a book that should be required reading for all who cherish a just society.

— NORMA S. REES, PH.D.
Past President, California State University, East Bay

The authors have raised the discussion of the black/ white divide to new heights. Both Foxworth and Gordon use intellectual arguments punctuated by a sobering realism that America will not realize the meaning of its constitutional mandate of equality until it faces the truths that the racial divide is not a "card" to be played during egregious disagreements.

THE BLACK/WHITE DIVIDE IN AMERICA ... STILL is neither a textbook, nor an insider book to be read by only professors and intellectuals. It's a must read for all who wish to understand why, and how to begin eradicating the walls of a perilous divide.

— OLDEN HENSON
City Council Member, Hayward, California

THE BLACK/WHITE DIVIDE IN AMERICA ... STILL is not allegorical. In their book, Marlin Foxworth, Ph.D. and Ralph Gordon have described the "divide" in clear, unambiguous terms. They make it plain that the "divide" is the product of a society, its structure and education system that continue to operate with the culture, needs and methods of dominant America as its primary focus. The authors analytically note a multiplicity of ongoing negative consequences resulting from that perennial reality. Equally important is their thoughtful prescriptiveness for ending those consequences and replacing them with equality. This book is a must read for those who want and are willing to help create it.

— RANDALL B. LINDSEY,
Co-author Cultural Proficiency: A Manual for School Leaders, (2nd Ed.)

The authors of *THE BLACK/WHITE DIVIDE IN AMERICA ... STILL* leave the readers naked, speechless, without protection, as they denounce the forces that perpetuate racism in America. What they have written is a manifesto that demands to bring to consciousness the injuries inflicted by those living in the "upside of the divide" on those of different skin and cultures. The authors are adamant and, like MLK, they leave us with a profound sense of hope that one day we may "eliminate the divide." To those who tolerate the divide, I say, "Ya, basta!"

— *HECTOR E. MENDEZ, LCSW*
Executive Director of La Familia Counseling Service Hayward, CA

Authors Marlin Foxworth and Ralph Gordon delineate so very clearly the structural elements of the racism that persists in America today. They shine needed light on the nuanced ways that destructiveness has been modernized. Major in that modernized collection of racist tools is indifference. They explain how so many born into the privilege of the dominant culture substitute their self-proclaimed good intentions for the racist results bludgeoned on those of us not provided that same privilege. They also point out that many Americans, but not yet enough, who are not on the receiving end of racism — but want it to end — are willing to help make that happen. The prescriptiveness of this book is needed if America is to become what it says it is but has not yet become. Written in a way that all of us can read it, this book paves a road to a real land of equality.

— *PAUL COBB*
Publisher, The Post, Oakland, California

THE BLACK WHITE DIVIDE IN AMERICA ... STILL

The Inherent Contradiction In Partial Equality

MARLIN FOXWORTH, Ph.D.

and

RALPH GORDON

REGENT PRESS
Berkeley, California

ISBN 13: 978-1-58790-142-3
ISBN 10: 1-58790-142-0
Library of Congress Control Number: 2008923333

Cover by Paul Veres
Text Design & Production by Mark Weiman

MANUFACTURED IN THE UNITED STATES OF AMERICA
REGENT PRESS
Berkeley, California
www.regentpress.net
regentpress@mindspring.com

NOV 2008

To my beloved bride, Kathi.
And to all those who have encouraged
and supported me as a writer –
even before I knew that I was one.

— *Ralph Gordon*

More thanks than I can describe go to my wife, Barbara,
for never needing makeup to highlight the love in her eyes nor a
microphone for making clear the truth in her voice nor a request for
having my back when I've gotten negative, even hateful, responses when
addressing some of the issues in this book. That she *is* serves alone as
reason enough for me to have written in this book as I have.
And thanks to our son, Kazi, for knowing so very early in his life what
must be faced in this still divided country and for having
the courage to do so relentlessly.

A special thanks goes to Fred Katz, my Professor of Anthropology,
for seven different classes and an internationally known jazz and
classical musician who played for President Roosevelt twice in the White
House and was asked by President Kennedy to score the music for a
film on disabled children. He played with the Chico Hamilton Quintet
and worked with magnificent singers like Carmen McRae, Tony Bennett
and many more. I could knock on the door of his house and walk in
without waiting for an answer. He taught me that humility was strength
and that earning a degree was, at best, only a step in the process of
learning that should never be allowed to end.

Deep, abiding thanks goes to Dr. King, Cesar Chavez,
Mohandas Gandhi, Sojourner Truth, Harriet Tubman, Malcolm X and
so many more who have been my teachers, without knowing they have
been and without us ever having met.

— *Marlin Foxworth*

FOREWORD
Dr. J. Alfred Smith, Sr.

PROFESSOR TED PETERS SAYS that because of radical evil in society, we sugar coat our garbage, cover our unwholesome motives, and use violent acts against others with a veneer of goodness. In spite of our moral fragility there is human freedom which opens the door for building human community on the principles which Thomas Aquinas calls the four cardinal virtues: temperance, justice, prudence, fortitude and the three theological virtues of faith, hope and love. Both Marlin Foxworth and Ralph Gordon are masterful communicators, not only in unmasking the depth of our denial of cancerous racism which erodes unity in the community, but they open the door to the dawn of opportunities for making America's creed the Nation's deed.

Both of these men write from the empirical foundation of different perspectives. One writes as an educator, the other writes from his broad experiences in the business and corporate world. But, from different angles of social location, they accurately explain the nature of our postmodern dislocation while revealing their highest hopes for the discovery of what Martin Luther King, Jr. called "The Beloved Community" and what Howard Thurman called "The Search for Common Good." In sharing with the readers their unfortunate encounters with racism, it is evident that the terrain of their souls was not polluted with anger, bitterness, hostility, or pessimism. I am happy, because Foxworth and Gordon both have strong hope in the positive possibilities of humanity. They do not agree with Oxford University Professor Richard Dawkins, who believes that our selfish genes determine our aggressive behavior, as if we are in a genetic chess game where each gene seeks to check mate all competitors. Racism and human selfishness for Foxworth and Gordon are not biological in the survival of the fittest doctrine of social Darwinism.

These two men are deeply committed to their belief that human behavior can be spiritually motivated to love others as equals in value to themselves. These two men believe that unless we come together we shall come apart.

For the sake of the sacred in each of us, for the preservation of human dignity, for the promotion of human protection against violence in personal and public life and for the eradication of racial injustice and war as a tactical weapon to resolve political disagreement, I challenge each of you to establish a study group to read and discuss the living, giving ethics of two men whose lives are dedicated to the ethics of The Prince of Peace.

Dr. J. Alfred Smith, Sr. is Senior Pastor at Allen Temple Baptist Church in Oakland, California.

INTRODUCTION

Ralph Gordon

THE ROAD TO COMPLETING this book has been a fascinating one for Marlin and me. Our friendship began a few years ago, when we were introduced at our place of worship — Oakland, California's Allen Temple Baptist Church. Allen Temple, with a few thousand members, is the largest Black church in Northern California. Some even refer to it as a mega church — despite the existence of truly gigantic churches (with over 10,000 members each) in Southern California and elsewhere. These worship environments can be disorienting, impersonal and overwhelming for some. So, it is particularly rewarding to establish and maintain such an enduring friendship in such a large-scale setting.

We connected in the men's fellowship of the church. Some will refer to this as "bonding" — either in a positive or in a denigrating way. For those who would tease men who bond, our message is: Not to worry. Men who are comfortable with themselves, and with one another, won't be swayed. They will stay focused on the task at hand: improving relationships with like-minded brethren, thereby setting the stage for improving themselves. So it has been for Marlin and me. And, our connection has an added element of being special.

We have defied the odds of a society that has erected and so well maintained a wall — a divide — between people of different ethnic backgrounds, particularly with differences of color. A person from outer space could land on earth, in America, watch our media and conclude that people only cross the racial line in "buddy movies," sports and other somewhat surreal venues. But, neither Marlin nor I allow media constructs to dictate how we will think, live or interact with others. Our connection with one another, born in a church, is secure — despite the larger differences (cultural and ethnic) between us.

Ours is a tale of two citizens. We have arrived at this point along different paths: he, from sunny, sprawling and laid back Southern California and me, from the seasonal, congested and more intense Northeast; he, a career educator, primarily in public schools and me, a career technology sales guy. Did we really have to have a whole lot in common to connect? Was it the fact that we are both blessed by our marriages to beautiful and smart women? Who knew? So, here is the man from Philly, a guy who has come into warm and sunny California from the relative cold of the Northeast, teamed up with an educator from Southern California — connected and engaged in dialogue about the world we live in.

At a certain point, our friendship and dialogue moved into in-depth and intense discussions at a restaurant's breakfast table. One of us was suddenly out of a job. And, we agreed to meet more regularly, dine and discuss what was going on in the world. Here, we dissected politics, job issues, family values, spiritual perspectives and numerous other topics.

As in Europe, Californians tend to meet in restaurants for more than just the satisfaction of a physical need to eat. It's more of a social experience: dining. When I lived back East, I remember that it was not the usual custom to tarry in a restaurant — even for a group gathering. After all, there was always a need to expeditiously clear the table for the many others who were waiting for it. Lingering was almost considered to be rude. The task was to eat your food, enjoy pleasant yet *efficient* conversation (if possible) and then move on. No such mandates seem to exist here, on the "Left Coast." Here, we often schedule a breakfast, lunch or dinner solely for the purpose of a social gathering. In this way, the consumption of the meal almost becomes secondary. Such was the case for Marlin and me. The breakfast was just a vehicle for us to have a regular, one-on-one fellowship, to commiserate about worldly matters and to maintain an atmosphere where sympathy and empathy could be offered to the one who was unemployed. These breakfast get-togethers began to comprise a rich crucible for the development and exchange of ideas and to determine that the perspectives of the two diners with the disparate backgrounds were very much in synch with one another.

Just as a morning meal literally "breaks the fast" from the prior day, this dialogue is intended to help others rid themselves of the taboos with which so many Americans are plagued: a sense that it is not okay to talk about racial issues with someone of another skin color. On the contrary, open and honest inter-racial communication can be the catalyst for infinitely better understanding. It can be the bulldozer to knock down negative stereotypes that are held and reinforced — on both sides of the color line. It can be the bridge over the troubled waters of the Black/White divide.

For us two men, at our breakfast get-togethers, the concepts flowed forth abundantly. A repository was being built. Yet, our feeling was that there was not a substantive amount of literature available to reflect our views — particularly the contrast and intertwining that we represent. So, we had to do something to fill this void. Fortuitously, we discovered that we each have a passion to write. Ah ha! The idea for a joint book project was born. We would write a book, engage our passion and fill a void all at the same time. This text represents the culmination of that effort — born at a breakfast table and developed thereafter.

We hope and trust that you will be stimulated, enriched and perhaps enlightened by your reading of this book. We know that you might not agree with all of our perspectives. That is okay. Nevertheless, we hope that your thoughts will be stimulated and perhaps even provoked. Perhaps you will be moved to action by two men who went from a breakfast table to a computer keyboard and then to a manuscript in search of a means of communicating about and lobbying for a successful effort to bridge the *Black/White Divide*. Better yet, let's eliminate the divide — for good. We're working to do so. Won't you join us?

INTRODUCTION

Marlin Foxworth, Ph.D.

THE BLACK/WHITE DIVIDE IS ... STILL.

Its building blocks are variously structured and modernized. Just as a major weapon for securing social dominance around the world has been transformed from the sword in the early 1600s to the cluster bomb in the early 2000s, so too with the tools that maintain the *Divide* and the methods for justifying its sustenance.

Historic Talk, Historic Inaction

Accepting what is as what must be cleaves what should be from what will be. There is no social cry, particularly from the upside of the *Divide*, about the fact that the *Divide* continues to exist. There is no widespread American societal dialogue about the inevitable momentousness of social structure. There is no ongoing, analytical, media covered, academia considered, fiscally appraised, legislatively demanded, spiritually insistent discourse about the edifice of dominance and subordination in American

Society and the inevitable consequences deriving from it. Instead of the intensely needed all-generations, every-socio-economic-class, all-cultures, country-wide dialogue about that dominance and subordination and its most profound manifestations, e.g., disproportionately high benefits on one side of the *Divide* and disproportionate negative consequences on the other, there is annual, mostly superficial talk on Dr. King's birthday about "how much was accoumplished during the civil rights movement." However, there is woefully little significant consideration of having gone almost nowhere since. When it comes to addressing the *Black/White Divide* as a country, we are skilled at doing nothing of lasting, constructive consequence.

Look at the size and number of African American ghettos. There is never news that America has changed its socio-economic-cultural practices and, as a consequence, ghettos are regularly being transformed into the kind of communities with the social and material benefits that would prompt many in the dominant culture to move there. Look at the contributions of African Americans to the wars fought, all, ostensibly, to protect the "American Way of Life." Is there not more willingness in America to have African Americans give their lives for that *way of life* than there is for America to insist on the equal inclusion of African Americans in it?

The Commitment To Write About The Divide And Its Structural Elements

My commitment to writing this book arose from a team appraisal of the *Black/White Divide* today in contrast to it in the 60s. My head, heart, stomach, soul and I conferred about the hope in the 60s that the *Black/White Divide* would end then. Next, the five of us discussed the *Divide* today and how it is buttressed by clever social methods that garner very little analysis or active opposition and face no ruggedly supported alternative. The

other four on the team were unanimous in their directive
to me to add analysis and prescriptions for a letter of
invitation to hope.

Then we talked of the issue with our brother, Ralph
Gordon. His conference with his team, structured identically the same way as mine, was over in seconds. Then
there were 10 of us ready to address the issue! His team
directed him as mine had me. We needed to define elements of the *Divide* and the support of it in so many
ways, including social indifference. What of the historic
fellowship of the *Divide* and America's economic structure? What are major perceptions of the *Divide* and how
is it that responsibility for it is so skillfully placed at
the feet of those who walk on its downside by those in
America who don't? The language of the *Divide* needs to
be seen for its commercial prowess and spin, for how it
structures perceptions of what hasn't been sufficiently
accomplished to make it appear like it has, e.g. integration. What of the generalizations of socio-cultural categories of people, by people with little or no direct experience
of those they generalize and of the realities they face, who
have the power to produce socio-economic consequences
out of those generalizations? Does America not provide
more schooling and training about perceptions of the historical diminishing of the *Divide* than it does education
about its contemporary size, structure and persistence?
What are the contemporary offspring of the rage in the
50s and 60s about the *Divide*? If America's dominant religiosity is about morality, why do so many bell towers
serve to call so many people on so many Sundays to services silent about the *Divide* ... and the immorality that
shapes it? What of the leaders who shaped hope about
overcoming the *Divide* and were killed for doing so? And
what about ... ?

Weapons from other eras have been collected throughout history as heirlooms by dominant cultures. They are

polished and displayed. The human damage they've done gets trivialized or lost in the glow of the glory they symbolize from having defeated *them.* What is seen socially, how it is seen and how it is displayed in most communication media are powerfully determined by the dominant culture. That capacity to shape the significance of what is seen manifests itself in a variety of ways along the *Divide.* Physical beauty, for example, is only skin deep. Standards of beauty, however, are deeper. Close your eyes. Let your mind picture the faces of the women who are African American who you know as celebrities given frequent attention in dominant culture media. How many of them leave their hair as it is naturally? ... Do you have the number yet? You don't need a calculator do you? Is there an internalized message about looking like what you came from, about the standard of beauty you have been given? What wounds have been inflicted by the hot iron? Is its burn not more than skin deep?

America was a country with an economic system until some time in the 90s. Now America is steadily moving closer to being an economic system with a country. Power has always been secured in the U.S. via the acquisition of money. It is just more so now than ever before. Human worth in America is determined more today than ever by access to and possession of material wealth than it is by the fact of human life itself. Being on the upside of the *Divide* means more: more safety; more material wealth; more health care; more schooling; more travel; more political support; more access to governmental decision makers and power; more chances of getting more of more and more. Being on the down side of the *Divide* provides *more* also: more reason to have less hope in the social system you're expected to support.

Most who inflict the spiritual, social and economic disease of racism on others are usually in denial that they have done so. Some don't deny it. They just don't care, even seeing their bigotry instead as justified and needed opposition to those appraised as unwilling to do what they must to be solid Americans. Racism has been defined too long in contemporary society as intentionally applied bigotry. It is still here in that form. However, its more widespread manifestation is that same bigotry as effect, regardless of intention, melded with the social power to create and sustain social subordination of other sociocultural categories of humans. The absence of prejudicial intention is rendered often by an individual as evidence that s/he is not racist. The depressingly limited willingness in public education to seriously, unrelentingly and intensely address the gap in the indicators of academic success between students who are African American (called "Black") and students of the dominant culture (called "White"), extant in public education — without excuse or justification — since its beginning, is a classic example of racism as effect. It is manifested in denial, indifference or the perpetuation of programs or practices that provide evidence of good intentions but change nothing academically. Such is a mainstay for the *Divide*.

There is a conviction in Dominant America that unless there is evidence that a perennial problem for a social category of Americans is a result of intention on the part of those with the power to create and/or perpetuate the problem, i.e. those on the upside of the *Divide*, it isn't their problem. Good intentions, usually in the form of charity, are provided for addressing the symptoms ... never the cause.

The transition of America's public schools from segregated enclaves to what are labeled "integrated schools" functions to hide from view the reality that segregation still exists in not as easily discernible, multifarious ways. Data, for example, makes it so clear about which sociocultural-economic categories of us disproportionately go to college and which disproportionately drop out of high school. Again, absent intentional contributions to the disparities in this data, an "Oh-Well" response finds justification in the upside of the *Divide*. Programmatic governmental response functions as a conduit for good intentions but never for the radical systemic changes needed. President George W. Bush's "No Child Left Behind" initiative, ostensibly intended to end the gaps in the indicators of academic achievement by socio-cultural group, is a classic. Not thoughtfully constructed, never thoroughly set in motion, depleted of its original funding, "headed" but not led, charitable but not focused on social structure, it is more "proof" of good intentions than it is a tool for real social change. Its effect is the same as indifference. Oh, well!

A major, big time sustainer of the *Divide* is the belief that *race* is a scientific reality. Racism's existence is predicated on the conviction that there are races other than the singular human race. Research makes it so clear that such is not the case. Races (plural) do not exist. Culture is a reality, one universally applicable, with no exceptions. Concentrating on *race* rather than on social structure and on the function of culture as a critique of and approach to a social system is concentration on what isn't rather than on what is. The effect of such a focus is the same as indifference. Oh, well!

There is also denial that a major structural element of racism — and therefore of the *Divide* — is having the aggregated societal power to negatively effect the lives of whole socio-cultural categories of people. There may be prejudice, even bigotry, but without that collective power it is not the same as racism. It is one thing to be part of — intentionally, consciously or not — the exercise of cumulative power that creates social categories under the rubric of "them" and denies "them" some or many benefits of a social system. It is another thing to think badly of or demean individuals, whether or not they deserve it, that are of a socio-cultural category of people that history and your own experience have told you denies you and yours those benefits. Prejudice can hurt individuals in the country, those who exercise it and those at whom it is aimed. It is like punching someone today because s/he looks like the person who cut too closely in front of you on the freeway yesterday. An individual face is damaged ... but so is the fist and individual who used it. No good can come of it. Racism is a systemic element of American society. It damages a whole country, everyone in it, those who exercise it or ignore its exercise and those in receipt of its invidious consequences. Like with war crimes, there are those whose lives are brutalized and/or ended ... but there are also those whose souls are scarred because they ignored the violence, consequently doing nothing to end it and therefore contributing to its continuance. There is no one in a society where racism exists who isn't damaged by it.

A Village of US or a Village of Social Practicality

So ... in my travels I kept seeing a Village of Social Practicality where the causes for the *Black/White Divide* in American reside. Stripped of their contemporary garb, the Reasons living in that village look like their ancestors who first moved there in 1619. Unlike their ancestors, though, these 21st Century Reasons in residence are skilled at using a proclaimed absence of evil animus to shield their contributions to the perpetuation of the *Divide* while denying, even to themselves, that it is being done. The *Divide* they have remodeled structures a separateness today as effective as the one then.

The *Chamber of Reasons* in that *Village of Social Practicality* provides the rationale and justification for the production, maintenance and modernizing of the *Divide*. As with those who came before, each generation of *Reasons* calculates and prescribes the socio-political-material lucre for one side of the *Divide* and the means for justifying and sustaining what must be always less on the other. In that, they perennially contribute to the variance in hope between one side of the partition and the other. Although those *Reasons* lack sufficient exposure, they are a continuing part of the structure of America. They parent and raise the resistance to those who wish free access for travel back and forth across the *Divide* because they assume — almost always correctly — that the intention of many of them is to break it down, challenge the *Reasons* in residence at the historic *Village of Social Practicality* and demolish and replace it with the *Village of Us*. They make sure the passageways some have attempted to build across the *Divide* are seen by the majority of those in power as undeserving of economic, governmental and political sustenance and, therefore, are not sustained. They fashion and hold onto a constitution of results that is 180 degrees out of face with both declared intentions and the premise upon which this nation's constitution is structured. Simply put, their actions and inactions — not their words — show that they hold the foundational truths of America's constitution to be not self-evident.

The path that must be traveled across the *Black/White Divide* to the new *Village of Us* is curvy — to say the least. Different people take different roads in a search for that new village. Sometimes the lanes narrow to one and the risk of collision rises. The intersections of some paths come at sharp bends in the road, where oncoming traffic gets hidden in the shadows of old *Commonsensical Trees*. There are no yellow traffic lights to warn you or red lights to tell you to stop when others may be moving across your path. There are ruts in the road, too, caused by the crashes of many who have attempted to drive the full distance. Some have been forced off the road into a pit of fatal consequences. An abounding number of individuals even turn around and head back home after they have driven through the *Village of Social Practicality,* heard the voices of *Reasons* living there and concluded that the destination is unreachable or no longer impor- tant or that the visit to the other side may be too costly, too uncomfortable, even dangerous.

There are those on the side of the *Divide* with po- litical, social and economic dominance who see no need to travel across the *Divide* for an inquisitive stopover, let alone to search for a new village where all other cul- tures are not subordinated to theirs. There is nothing in what they picture of the other side, where those they call *"them"* might live, or of the exploration that ema- nates from driving back and forth across the border of disconnection that attracts them, even for a short trip. Why go someplace where your neighbors don't look like you, where it may be less secure? Why spend time going somewhere else when what you need for prosperity is al- ready where you live? Surely, if "those people over there" want the same, they can drive over to where we live to get it. Certainly the implied invitation is a cousin to good intentions. Given that lack of attraction to the other side for some, they perceive anyone from their side of the *Di- vide* who would travel over it in search of a new village as, at best, an irritant, someone who wastes energy for a trip that isn't needed. At worst, those irritants are seen as threats to the sustenance of the benefits in the *"home"* side of the *Divide.*

The forms of racism and the *Divide* it has built are most often, but not always, more subtle than they were in the 60s. The consequences, though, are as profligate. The need is to end that *Divide* now, to shape a society without it. The absence of sufficient commitment to do so, derived from either the belief that it cannot happen or disinterest because no benefit is seen in doing it, is the stuff of its sustenance. The desirability for ending the *Divide* is not to be confused with a call for assimilation.

If a *Divide-Less America* is to be braced and buoyed, each of us needs to be culturally who we are and constructively prideful about those from whom we have come, from whom or with whom the meaning in our lives was shaped principally. In each of our cultures, though, and in the ones that will come, there needs to be an unbreakable and irremovable conviction that each human is only that, usually wonderfully that, sometimes horribly that, not differently that. Although our methods for pursuit of life's meaning may be nuanced, we are not.

The *Black/White Divide* is.

What you read in this work is a view of the *Divide* from two of us who were raised on opposites sides of it. Our long years of travel over and around and through it, though, found us parked one day, looking at it together. Each chapter contains what we have agreed are major components of the *Divide*. We wrote separately about each of those factors first and talked later about what we had written. The anecdotes you will read in this work are of influential, sometimes pivotal, experiences each of us has had with the *Divide*. They shaped, most often profoundly, our perceptions of things needing to be done about the *Divide* and of prospective life in a society without it. There are many more stories we could tell. However, *WAR AND PEACE* has already been written.

The fact that you are reading this is most assuredly an indication that the topic is of concern to you. Please accept the invitation from Brother Ralph Gordon — my brother — and me to assess what the two of us have written of our experiences with the *Divide* and of the analysis and prescriptions that come from them. The *Divide* can continue to be sustained ... or confronted and ended. There is in that consideration a challenge for each and every single one of *Us*. As soon as possible after reading the last word on the last page of this work, you are urged to answer for yourself what would be done about ending the *Divide* if it were left up to you.

So ... the *Black/White Divide* is. Will it be so for those who will refer to *Us* as ancestors? Or will there be constant gladness about residency in the *Village of Us* they have inherited?

The *Black/White Divide* is.

CHAPTER 1

FROM PHILLY TO THE DIVIDE

Ralph Gordon

ASK THE AVERAGE man or woman on the street this question: "What is the most pressing problem in America?" The respondent will very likely say the major issue is the economy, the energy crisis, the threat of terrorism or even the possibility of persistent, escalated and/or further military conflicts with other nations. For many people, however, it is quite clear that the issue that is most pervasive and enduring in the United States is the arena of relations between the races. The sizable and increasingly vocal presence of multiracial persons in our diverse society challenges simplistic notions about race. The lines of color are still very clearly drawn in this society. At times, even the old "one drop of blood" rule seems to define who a person is and how that person will be treated. My personal experience bears this out.

It was not my choice to come into this world and to then define myself by a racial classification — particularly not in a derogatory manner. Color-conscious and negative labeling was thrust upon me as I grew up in American society, in the very large city of Philadelphia, Pennsylvania. From its Greek etymological roots, Philadelphia bears the nickname "City of Brotherly Love." However, while growing up, I found out that this moniker was not particularly reflective of how things actually functioned in the metropolitan town that locals, natives and fans affectionately and intimately refer to as "Philly."

Philadelphia, Pennsylvania — a/k/a "Philly" — could not and should not be confused with the town of Philadelphia in the southern state of Mississippi. In terms of the Black/White divide, the Deep South can be closer to the proverbial deep end than it is to the Northeastern U.S. The Philadelphia of the South has the infamous distinction of being the site of the 1964 lynching murders of three dedicated civil rights workers: James Earl Chaney, Andrew Goodman and Michael Schwerner. These young men had the boldness and the bravery to work in an exceedingly hostile region on behalf of disenfranchised (mainly Black) citizens in the State of Mississippi. The fate of these civil rights workers was the opposite of "brotherly love." These men — one Black and two White — exemplified the multiracial composition of the struggles in the 1960s for ethnic equality. (Note how long it took for even one of their killers to come to justice.) This Philly of the South is difficult to compare to the Philly of the North. Yet, some who grew up in and still reside in South Philly — as my hometown's south of Market Street area is known — might beg to differ.

Some time ago, South Philadelphia was popularized by the actor Sylvester Stallone in his *Rocky* movies. His character's training run through South Philly's Italian Market area is now an iconic cinematic image. However, this romantic notion of the community is not held by all who come from or have ventured into this part of the city — especially not its citizens of color. Although I was born in North Philadelphia and raised in West Philadelphia, I was well acquainted with the safety and security need to be very careful in wide areas of South Philly. Decades later, flashbacks recur as I venture into the area to procure South Philadelphia's most notable product and its most replicated export: the cheesesteak. Even though I'm a native, sometimes I can almost feel the same chill as those civil rights workers of the 1960s, venturing into the Deep South.

The interracial makeup of the civil rights workers, in many instances, constituted an early on bridging of the Black/White Divide. Viola Liuzzo, an earnest White mother from Detroit, who was murdered (in 1965) for daring to go down South and help people of color, deserves a mention in this posthumous hall of fame and shame: a victim of vicious perpetrators of hate. The Ku Klux Klan murderers surely saw Liuzzo and the other White civil rights sympathizers as being "nigger lovers": the horrible epithet that caused some to lose their lives, especially in the Deep South.

All of these things aside, racism is neither defined nor confined by geography. So, there was no shortage of examples for me to observe and internalize all over the Philly of the North. Still, it was evident that when people communicate openly and honestly, regardless of their differences, very good things can happen. Genuine understanding and peaceful coexistence can be manifested.

The Philadelphia of my youth and adolescence was overshadowed by a Gestapo-like police department. These days, upon hearing so much about the abuses of law enforcement agencies like the police departments of Los Angeles (LAPD) and New York City (NYPD), I can only chuckle — with images of "Philly's Finest" never too far from my mind. Police power was taken to a violently abusive and capricious level by the bull-headed and single-minded police commissioner of those turbulent times:

Frank Rizzo. This so-called "cop's cop" dominated Phila-delphia as its chief of police and then as mayor. Rizzo's reign of terror managed to deter many outsiders from visiting the city. Case in point: Rizzo's overblown predic-tions of possible mayhem in Philly scared off many thou-sands of potential visitors to the city's bicentennial cel-ebration in 1976. It was as if Genghis Khan had achieved legal status as the ruler of the town.

Living under Frank Rizzo's rule of Philadelphia was often an exercise in survival — particularly if you were Black. Racial classification is not a choice. Despite the Black pride movements of the late 1960s and early 1970s, Rizzo's regime endeavored to make Blackness a veritable curse. Fortunately, the whole of the citizenry did not go along with the despotic leadership of this misguided man. He was denied a direly sought after exemption from the term limits that were in place — preventing him from running for a third term as the city's mayor. Thankfully, Philly was saved from an almost unending shadow of one man's tyrannical presence. There was reason to hope. The city — and I within it — breathed a sigh of relief and moved on to some sense, sensibility and civility in a post-Rizzo era.

My psyche was shaped as I observed people of my skin color aligning themselves with what was obviously a racist regime. It was clear that all whom I had thought of as brothers and sisters were not truly kindred souls. Here were people of color who had blithely and perhaps blindly supported an obvious racist. In the meantime, others across the color line — White people — demon-strated that they were in harmony with the best in all of us: that they were committed to "justice for all," that promise of America's Pledge of Allegiance. It became clear that I would need to be more circumspect in determining who was really my brother or sister.

Although there was no Phillyish Ward Connerly

(fighting against progress for his own people), there were Judas-like traitors just the same. Jewish people have referred to those who so vigorously reject their own cultural heritage as "self-hating Jews." There must be a category that can properly be labeled and reserved for "self-hating Blacks." It behooves one to be able to recognize and to diagnose these folks who would betray and help to deter the progress and security of their own kind. Identifying these people relatively early has enabled me to form my alliances not simply along color lines but in synch with those who share principles of racial equality and justice. These unions often are formed across the color line as I consider people by who they are and by what they do — not by the hue of their skin.

Today, there are many who defy any simplistic classification by skin color. As the melting pot of American society increases in its variety, a whole segment of multiracial people defies categorization. Consider Tiger Woods: he has strongly identified himself as a multiracial human being, largely due to the Asian ethnicity of his mother. Yet, America regards this golf champion primarily as a Black man — a so-called African American — who has broken the color line in a heretofore "lily-White" sport. Woods' stunning and historic accomplishments, on the golfing greens and in the advertising world, almost pale next to his perceived identification as the first Black — yes, Black — mega champion of golf. No matter what the pursuit or achievement, America has a propensity for first looking at the color of a person's skin.

I'm certainly no Tiger Woods; yet, all too often, I can sense the curious stares when I step into certain environments. The looks aren't always hostile. At a minimum, they are quite curious. One can feel the stereotyping judgments before they are spoken aloud. It is the type of thing that could make a person angry, on a daily basis. But, I concluded long ago that it would drive me mad if

I allowed these things to bother me with any degree of regularity. Like so many others, I've built up a tolerance — only allowing a limited number of offenses to break through my *shield*, to the extent where a response or reaction is warranted. My reactive nature is also tempered as I realize that so many people actually mean no harm. They just don't know any better. How could I help things by lashing out at those whose worst sin might be a case of naiveté?

A more significant reason for not engaging in frequent acts of backlash is the knowledge that there are so many who are with me — with *us* in a walk for better human understanding and interaction. How could I honestly face these people and join with them in the fight against injustice if I had a hair trigger reaction for any and all perceived slights? Of necessity, I have happily been moved to develop a longer running fuse before allowing myself to move to another, more visceral level of response. My attempts at a noble level notwithstanding, there are still those who see me simply as a Black man, subject to whatever limits their perceptions may hold.

Despite this chromatic preoccupation, there is a large and growing population of those who would be enlightened in their views. Those who will look beyond skin color toward that famously proposed paradigm: the content of the character; those who will not take the simplistic and misguided route of buying into stereotypes and then staying with the resulting misconceptions. There are many who yearn for a more peaceful and less color-conscious nation. There are those who long for a country where the "all men — and women — are created equal" statement becomes a fact rather than just a cliché.

Some will argue that this is all academic. They will say that race is not really a defining factor for the human condition. Scientifically, this can be argued to be true. But, a society lives by mores and norms that are not so easily or logically explained. Our interactions with one another are not based on scientific realities. They are based upon social constructs. So, to challenge the notion of race on a scientific technicality misses the mark and falls far short of actually facing and dealing with the real problem.

Human beings interact with each other based on a variety of social constructs — falsely built or not. To act as if these concepts do not exist would be unrealistic and potentially damaging and even dangerous. On the contrary, a race-neutral policy is the shrewdly built ruse of Ward Connerly, his anti-affirmative action backers and others of like minds — who act as if skin color no longer matters in America.

There is no question that the peoples of the earth have much in common basically and scientifically. Yet, culturally and otherwise (via these aforementioned social constructs), they deal with one another in peculiar ways — sometimes for the better, sometimes for the worse. America is not unique in using color as a determinant for these interactions. But, as Kenneth Stamp cites in his book, THE PECULIAR INSTITUTION, this nation has a knack for taking something — namely slavery — that has been around for a long time and morphing it (or "warping" it?) into something uniquely devious, destructive and damning. America has a strong need for a cleansing in this arena.

Communication is often the fountain where understanding takes a sip and then is refreshed and strengthened. Just as some will claim particular items as "guilty pleasures," I stake out the area of communication as a place where I am proud to obsess. We, the authors of this book — after feeling, identifying and then nurturing a kinship in earlier contacts — experienced such a communicative connection and awakening in a long series of breakfast discussions. Though our skin colors are different, we found that our perspectives are very often solidly aligned. The idea for this tome was born over eggs, toast and coffee — and concepts and beliefs that were cut from a very similar cloth.

Marlin and I have found that our greatest differences lie not in how we were racially born or in how we are ethnically classified. We are better defined by other facts. Marlin is a Southern California native who has a strong background and training as a professional educator and administrator. On the other hand, my life is filled with the specter of the Northeastern U.S. (Philadelphia) and my background in the business world, in general, and high technology sales, in particular.

Actually, I come to this writing with more than just the "specter of Philadelphia." In Philly, one learns to live with harsh weather changes, an intense pace of life (rivaled or perhaps exceeded by the near neighbor of New York City), deep national history and a heavily concentrated population. Residents of the Northeastern U.S. typically possess a perspective of the "Left Coast" that is at once bemused and confused. Non-California denizens think that earthquakes are the daily worry of Golden State residents. But, once you live in California, you recognize that a shaking earth is not our biggest fear. No, that distinction belongs to the perennial villain that emanates from a relatively dry climate and wooded terrain: *fire.*

As a transplant from the East Coast, I've also discovered that California is hardly the "promised land" when it comes to race relations and sensitivity. Yes, it superficially has more tolerance than is found in a number of other areas of the country. But, it hardly is a paradise. Even here in the Golden State, there is much work to be done. Perhaps two guys from a breakfast table can help to move things along. In so doing, they — *we* can even help ourselves.

Each of us brought his own sense of upbringing and

personal and professional experience to the table. What we found was a rich harmony — over breakfast. I pray that our meeting of minds, and its literary output, will help to shatter falsely held, preconceived notions and stereotypes.

I know something about stereotypes. It is ridiculous to live for more than half a century, achieve success in the corporate arena, get married and have children and grandchildren and then have someone of another ethnic group ask you if you're a basketball player — just because you're over six feet tall. Honestly, am I truly to be impressed by such an inquiry? On one hand, it might be considered flattering to simultaneously carry an AARP card and to be asked if I'm an athlete. Yet, it's an indication that height and brains are not perceived to be coexistent in a Black man's body — at least not by a sizable portion of today's society.

Fortunately, there are many, White Americans who do not subscribe to such atavistic notions. We hope that this book will enlist their support and assistance in helping to overturn the misconceptions of many others in the populace. We hope that these writings will help to move others progressively along the line of enlightenment — racially speaking, in particular, and humanely, in general.

On the contrary and by the same token, many Blacks lump all Whites into one conceptual category. Simplistic thinking is just that: plain, simple, shortsighted and stupid. It would be great if we could all evolve beyond our thoughts of slotting people according to their skin color. Two men of common values, from both sides of the color line, are working to rise to that challenge. Our common sense of the value of human beings is just one of the many things that bind us together — particularly in this writing endeavor. Our goal is to share both the separateness of our paths and (more importantly) the common thread of our humanity — and our togetherness as brothers —

yes, brothers — striving for justice for all people.

In this text, two men — one Black, one White — discover a profound resonance in our views of issues affecting so many of us. The idea was to put these thoughts on paper and into a book, and to share them with interested and concerned readers; and people who also seek a better understanding of what ails us — and, to sincerely (and sometimes painfully) probe for cures. Hopefully, this text can help others reach a better level of racial understanding. More of us can then be agents of change in a country that sorely needs all the help it can get with this major issue.

CHAPTER 2

THE BUMPY ROAD TO THE VILLAGE OF US

Marlin Foxworth, Ph.D.

THE LICENSE FOR MY TRIP and the undeniable need to take it came in the Fall, 1962. I was in the last semester of my sophomore year at San Fernando Valley State College (now California State University, Northridge). I was 19 years old and had come back to school after taking a semester out for six months of active duty in the National Guard. I had met Bob Russell, one of a diminutive number of students who were African American. I don't remember how we met. We just did. In the course of an informal conversation, he told me of the bigotry he repeatedly encountered in trying to get an apartment near school. Being a Journalism major, I wrote both an article and an editorial on the problem for the October 19, 1962 issue of the student newspaper, the *Valley State Sundial.*

Green Lights and Cross Traffic

In the article, "Housing Closed to Negro," I quoted Bob many times. "I have been given several excuses," he said, "as to why there were no apartments available. Some people came right out and said they didn't rent to Negroes. I called one man on the phone, told him that I was a Negro and that I was looking for an apartment near school and he said he would call me back. He never did."

Bob pointed out that he had been staying with friends not far from campus and he walked into the house to find a gathering of neighbors there. He said, "They were discussing how my staying would affect the neighborhood property value. When I walked in they looked at me as though I were a monster from outer space. But," he added, "after we talked for awhile they realized I was alright." Bob also pointed out that he learned of an apartment near campus that did not discriminate against "Negroes."

The fact of writing the corresponding editorial, "Segregation Knows No Limit," was indelibly influential in the path provided me to travel. In that editorial I pointed out, "Segregation and all its rotten facets have not only permeated the State of Mississippi and the town of Oxford but the strongholds of the great 'liberal' State of California." I likened Bob's experience to having " … a bitter taste of the brew distilled from the toxic fruit of the segregation plant." I insisted the issue was part of " … the wholesale prostitution of basic American principles." As part of the editorial close, I wrote, "Only when the laws of the land insure the freedom of all people, and not a select few, can the final cure be realized."

Around lunchtime the day the paper came out I walked into the cafeteria. I saw several males I had met on campus who were of the dominant culture and I approached the table where they were sitting. As soon as I came up to them, they all looked at me and said nothing. Then one asked, "What the hell is wrong with you?

I suppose," he spat out, "you want my sister dating a nigger next!" He, by his hateful statement and they, by their silence, defined their values enough to show, with all the clarity needed, that we were already traveling different paths, heading for a different place. My relationships with them terminated at the end of his question. I didn't like what I felt but had no sense of personal loss. I did not want to stay there and join them in a lunch of vitriol. I did, however, want to head back down the road I had begun to travel. It was clear they weren't interested in even a short junket to where they saw me headed.

James Farmer, the leader of the Congress of Racial Equality (C.O.R.E.), was to give an address at the college a little later that day. I strolled across campus with a fellow journalism student to the hall where Farmer was to speak. I hoped I might meet him and ask him a few questions before I had to go on to my next class. We waited for a few minutes but he had not yet shown. "I have to get to class," I reluctantly said to my fellow student. "Please ask Mr. Farmer what he thought of the editorial."

A man who was African American was standing next to us. "Are you talking about the editorial in today's student paper?" he asked. I turned to face him and matter-of-factly answered, "Yes."

"It was pathetic," he snapped back. He said something about being on Mr. Farmer's staff and something else about the editorial excusing racist behavior. The pain from his assessment of my work diminished my focus and shut down my voice. I could say nothing in response and just walked on to class.

Doing the article and editorial to expose and oppose racism was righteous. I did not doubt it then. I do not doubt it now. However, I also stated something in that editorial that contradicted that righteousness. It came in the section in which I asked where the "accusing finger" should point. "Certainly," I had written in response to my own question, "not at the apartment owner. He, himself, is caught in the biting jaws of the modern economy and social conformity." This statement was an unwitting but pitiful endorsement of racism. My good intentions to the contrary could not change that.

By amalgamating blunt honesty and a quick slap in the face of my journalism for a teaching method, that gentleman from C.O.R.E. proved, in seconds, to be one of the best professors I ever had. In effect, because the lightness of my skin shielded me from being on the receiving end of it, I excused a practice for which there was no excuse. I had said in essence that bludgeoning another's citizenship rights, humanness and soul is acceptable as long as it is done passively, under economic and social pressure. The truth that the "professor" so quickly put forth was that social or economic pressure never could be justification for demeaning or contributing to the diminishing or destruction of the quality of life of another of Us. That lesson was, in effect, both a green light to continue on the road I had begun to travel and fuel to do so. Unfortunately, the truth in his appraisal of my editorial is challenged or ignored in America's society just as much — even if a touch more subtly — today as it was in October, 1962. It has been challenged or ignored by individual, social, political and systematized institutional denial and sheltered from needed analysis and massive, corrective social action by the substitution of proclaimed good intentions for results throughout America's history. Such is a classical contribution to the sustenance of the *Black/White Divide*.

That night or the next, I got a phone call at my parents' house. I was still living with them. The person on the line gave no name. It was clear from the tone in his voice that he was older than I. He told me he had read my editorial and he did not like what I had written about discrimination against Negroes. We argued a little but he did most of the talking. Without a specific threat, he very calmly warned me that I better back off my stance against prejudicial treatment of Negroes or I could be facing some serious consequences. He hung up with that warning in place. I was not hurt but was a little nervous.

The furor over my editorial didn't last long. No physical violence came my way. Then it was Fall of 1963. The March on Washington led by Dr. King had only been over a short time. I remember hearing no talk of it at school. It seems to have been seen primarily as a historical fact rather than as propulsion to action. A small rise in the enrollment of students who were African American was slow in coming. The activism against racism that might have coincided with that change in enrollment was not yet in swing. Nothing to date had fused the backbone of the Civil Rights Movement in the South into the spine of campus life at Valley State.

The Gift of Light, Love and Respect

I was at a Valley State football game one night that Fall. It was halftime. Like many in the bleachers, I stood to stretch, talking to an acquaintance about nothing in particular. I was scanning down the bleachers aimlessly when the stadium lights beamed a sharp focus up to me. Several rows below, also standing and chatting, was a stunningly beautiful woman. The richness of her brown skin gave status to the light. A message about the calmness of her climbed all the way up to where I was standing. That she also had a beautiful figure certainly obliterated any distractions and stabilized my gaze. The second half started. The game ended. She was gone. I forgot the score, who won, who lost. I remembered her.

I didn't see her again for months. It was February, 1964. Dante Green, who his friends called "Danny," and I were sitting at a table in the corner of the college cafeteria. I could see both entrances from where I sat. She entered the room and I shut up for a few seconds. Danny was talking but I wasn't paying attention. "Danny," I interrupted, "see that woman who just walked in?" He turned in the direction she was walking and acknowledged that he did. "She is soooo good looking," I said to him ... while still looking at her.

"She's alright," he contended.

"You better get your glasses fixed," I shot back. She turned along the aisle a couple of tables away from where we sat. I got up to introduce myself but she stopped at another table, obviously to greet some people she knew. I sat down. She left that table in about 30 seconds and started walking again. I got up once more. She stopped yet again to talk with others at another table. I sat down in a different empty chair. I couldn't catch up with her until she was outside. When she stopped and turned in response to my greeting I knew what the stadium lights had told me was right. The distance from her in the bleachers that night, though, had kept me from seeing her eyes and knowing how they talked for her. This day's afternoon sun made it all clear. I introduced myself and asked if she would consider going out with me.

Her name was Barbara. She said she didn't go out during the week, "unless I'm bored." She was a student who lived and worked in the dorm and I was welcome to call her there.

I did.

Our first date was the night of the last game of the season for Valley State's basketball team. I was a senior and had gone out for the basketball team in the second half of the season. There were only five games left by the time the coach decided to let me suit up. I didn't play in the first four. A friend, his date and I rode together to pick up Barbara at the dorm and then we all traveled across campus to the gym. At halftime of the freshmen game I got up and told Barbara that I would see her after the next game. "Where are you going?" she asked in veiled shock. "Well," I answered, "I wear those shorts and that funny shirt without sleeves and before the next game and at halftime I'll run up and down the court. During the game I'll sit on the bench and get splinters in my butt." She understood.

The game was against Long Beach State. As I had in the other four games, I was getting splinters in my behind. I was sadly contemplating my college basketball career ending without having played in a single game when the coach called a time out. There was a minute and 48 seconds left in the fourth quarter. Even though I was only six feet tall and a guard, he put me in as a forward. So very near the last few seconds, the ball was on our end of the court. Bob Russell, about whose experience with racism I had written the article and editorial, was the center on our team. The NCAA had outlawed stuffing the ball. Bob hung in the air, the ball in his hand, inches over the rim and he was a tick away from dropping it through the net when he saw that I was open. He brought the ball back down from a sure two points and passed it to me. I put up an 18-foot jump shot ... and missed it by about a yard. The other team ended with the highest score but, granted the benefit of hindsight, it was clear that Bob and I didn't lose.

It was his passing the ball to me when he didn't have to that remains an ineradicable tattoo of hope on my soul, a clear symbol of the reciprocal insurgency of respect. Bob, perhaps without knowing he had, shinned more light on the path.

A House Is Not A Home

Months later I talked with a friend who had graduated from Valley State the previous June about sharing a two-bedroom apartment where he was about to move. Barbara and I had been dating for months and I asked her to go with me to see it. I knocked on the manager's door and we waited for a reply. When he opened the door and stood before us I told him that I was going to be moving into one of the apartments and asked him if we could check it out. He looked briefly at us and said we could not see the apartment. We left to the sound of his shutting door.

Either that night or the next, the mother of the "friend" called me at home and said she and her husband thought it was not in the interest of their son for he and I to be living in the same apartment. Shielding the malignancy of her request with an assuaging tone, she asked me to understand. Oh, I did! My "friend" never contacted me again, nor I him. Over the decades I have forgotten his name. I remember him only with sadness for what he had done to himself. Without knowing he had done so, he freed me from living with the thinly veiled bigotry he had inherited from his parents and had sanctioned for his own soul.

Back Then, Here Now

I graduated from college in the summer of 1965. In August of '65 the accumulative, historical, physical, emotional, spiritual and economic bashing of people in and around South L.A. shaped and triggered the Watts Rebellion. The destructive anguish in it was multi-faceted. Primary in the destruction were the approximately 35 violent deaths of people in Watts for which there is official admission.

Prior to graduation I had been teaching and coaching part time in a parochial elementary school. I went to the pastor after the explosion in Watts and asked him if there wasn't something that could have been done and should be done from the pulpit to address the issues at the base of what had just occurred in Watts. "No," he very quickly replied. "It would embarrass the Negroes in our church."

The commitment in the leadership of that church to do nothing was one of the most profound messages I had ever heard. The causes of explosions in the soul of a community and in the souls in that community could not be addressed in the interest of avoiding embarrassment that was assumed would occur. The proffered faith seemed to be an itinerary for the Sweet By-and-By and the pastor a travel agent for the trip. There would be no travel through the trash and ash and body strewn streets of the Here-and-Now. *My* soul beat my body out of the pastor's office.

The destruction in the rebellion came from the destruction before the rebellion. Back then Watts was an island of fiscal despair surrounded by a mainland of economic hope — but the bridges to get there were extremely difficult to find. Back then poverty was disproportionately visited on people of color. Back then there was disparity by socio-cultural-economic categories in the indicators of academic success in our public schools. Back then that disparity disproportionately demeaned those of us who were African American and Latino. Back then churches that responded to the demeaning resulting from racism were, themselves, a minority. Back then a U.S. President who attempted to support the civil rights, including voting rights, of citizens who were Black was an oddity in that role. Back then, throughout most brands of institutional officialdom, self-proclaimed good intentions were regularly proffered in place of concerted efforts to end racism in its multiple variations. Back then none in the ranks of officialdom made clear that the tragedy was not that there were approximately 35 deaths or more — even many more — in the Rebellion but that there was one death and its tragedy was repeated approximately 35 times — or more. The trip on this bumpy road was beginning to show me what traveling around all the other curves since has verified: Back-Then is Here-Now. It has not left. It has only modified slightly in form.

Love and Relative Love

Barbara and I dated for three years in a constant world of stares. Our incomes would have risen considerably if we could have been paid for the eye muscle exercise we provoked during that time. Being watched that way was an ongoing reminder of the troubled world in which we loved each other. It also was a message that being alert was necessary given that such stares could transform into physical action against us. The alertness remains today, stationed, though, just beneath consciousness and a globe away from paranoia. The stares that tug our consciousness to the surface are usually the ones that are too long and almost invariably come in communities that are of the dominant culture and noticeably distanced from large African American populations.

It was about 1:30 a.m. on New Year's Day in 1967 when I proposed to Barbara. Yes, she said, "yes." I dropped her off at her apartment and picked her up in the early afternoon to take her to a party at her parents' home. As soon as we got there I asked Barbara's mother, Cora, and her father, Joe, if they would come out on the front porch because there was something I had to tell them. Obviously wondering what was going on, they stepped past the front door and waited for me to explain.

I said, "I asked Barbara to marry me." Cora, with eyes widening, wanted to know instantly what Barbara said. "She said yes," I answered confidently.

"Gosh," Cora responded with a little wonderment, "she must really love you!"

"Yes, she does," I answered in a tone intended to question subtly how she could think otherwise.

"Now, that's real good," Joe said. Even though the wedding was to take place July 1, 1967, exactly six months away, it was clear to me I was "family" from that moment.

Within about two weeks I took Barbara to my mother's

apartment. With the three of us sitting in her living room, I said, "Mom, I wanted to tell you I'm engaged." "Oh," she responded with a little surprise, "to whom?" She asked the question with Barbara sitting only feet away. There were only the three of us in the room. I quelled the anger I felt at the question and its apparent assumption that I might bring one woman with me to tell my mother that I was engaged to a different one. I turned a little toward Barbara and pointed to her. "To Barbara," I answered gently. "Are you ready to get married?" mom asked. I said, with a little more diligence, "Do you mean 'do we have to get married?' No, we don't have to get married! Am I ready to get married? Probably not. I'm just here to tell you that I'm going to."

We were out the door in a matter of minutes. In the walk to the car I said to Barbara, "Don't ask me how I know because I don't know how I know ... but my mother won't be at the wedding." She asked anyway. I couldn't answer it. The wedding was almost six months away. My mother had gall bladder surgery the day before the wedding, which was July 1, 1967, and couldn't make it. Across the years since then she told me a few times that I had misinterpreted her absence from the wedding and that it was only because of surgery that she wasn't there. She even moved in with us for a few months during the 90s. When we talked on the phone after that, she frequently and graciously asked how Barbara was doing. The coincidence of her surgery and our wedding, though, remains an heirloom in Barbara's and my family.

Barbara and I began looking for a place to live about two weeks before the date of our wedding. We drove to an address in nearby Van Nuys, California, in the hope of renting an apartment we had seen advertised in a newspaper. Barbara was a little tired and waited in the car while I walked to the office of the apartment complex. The manager, a woman with a British accent, informed me that there was an apartment available in the building next door and asked me if I would like to see it. I told her I most certainly did and said I would like to stop on the way to get my fiancé who was waiting in the car.

We stopped for a second at the car. There was a moment of silence as Barbara stepped out the door. The manager looked at her and caustically asked, "Are you at all colored?" She then quickly indicated she did not rent apartments to *colored* people. We calmly but resolutely insisted that she show us the apartment or that she would face legal trouble. She showed us. We saw the apartment and said we would get back to her. We didn't. We simply wanted this manager of the Bigotry Arms Apartments to feel as much discomfort as possible as a consequence of treating us as though we were neither real live human beings nor citizens of California and America. We were able to rent an apartment not far from there soon after that encounter.

We got married in Oxnard, California. Our wedding party included Barbara's brother, Joe, my two brothers, Bob and Mike, and a mix of friends, African American, of the dominant culture and Latino. None of my other relatives came, even though several of them lived close by. The demands of the job or being on vacation were given as reasons by two of them, I assume honestly so. As was the case with relatives of Barbara's who didn't show, the rest of my relatives — with one fascinating exception — have said nothing over the years about their absence.

That one exception was the husband of one of my relatives. He took the position that people with light skin should not marry those with dark skin. Although I cannot remember the family source, I so very clearly remember another relative telling me that the assessment that it was inappropriate for Barbara and I to marry was derived from this person's assessment of the section of the bible about the family of Ham.

Very soon after our first anniversary, I got a call from the "friend" Barbara and I had double dated with before. He had been in the wedding party and I hadn't seen him and had talked with him only once since the day of our wedding. I was glad to hear from him and excitedly asked him how he was doing. "I'm not doing too well," he responded. My heart sank a little. I pressed him for an explanation. "I'm getting married," he answered. "I'm confused," I pushed back at him. "You should be doing great."

"Well," he responded hesitantly, "my fiancé's parents don't ... ah ... don't like Black people very much and ... well ... we didn't invite you to the wedding." For seconds only, anger and sadness vied for control over my response. "We don't need to come to your wedding" I replied, letting neither feeling show much. "But I have a question to ask you. Didn't you tell me awhile ago that your fiancé has a couple of kids from another marriage?" He acknowledged that such was the case. "So," I posed to him, "this is what you are going to teach your kids? Have a good life." The good-byes were quick and softly spoken. I have not seen or heard from him, nor him from me, since 1968. Even though the world of work and even some positive social realities have me driving regularly across the *Divide,* I don't know what his address is over there. I tossed the kind of address/phone book that would provide such information.

The Slam of Dominance and the Need to Know

In 1969 Barbara and I were living in an apartment near the intersection of 89th Street and Normandy in South L.A., not far from where the Watts Rebellion had erupted a few years before and not far from where there was a community explosion many years later in response to the violence visited by some L.A.P.D. officers on Rodney King. Suggestions abounded at the time that the number of deaths in the 1965 Watts Rebellion were far greater than 30-something identified in official reportage. In fact, a next-door neighbor, a mechanic for the L.A.P.D. told me he tried to get into Watts during the rebellion and in the drive there counted about 30 bodies at the intersection of Manchester and Broadway, which is near but not in Watts. Accurate? Who knows? What were the real geographic boundaries of the rebellion? What was the actual number of humans killed in it? Why is what went on in Watts that August officially called a "riot" but not a "rebellion"? Questions remain about the accuracy of governmental accounting of lost life and of its characterization of the rebellion.

While we lived in that apartment, Barbara and I had our only child, a son, on January 16, 1970, two-and-a-half years after we got married. We named him Kazi, which means "work" in Swahili. We just liked the name. Through discussions with both of our families, it is pretty clear that Barbara and I have passed on to Kazi an ancestry that is Scottish, Irish, English, Spanish, French, Italian, Mexican, Chinese, Cherokee, one other Native American culture, and African American, by way of Jamaica and probably elsewhere. Yet, whenever anyone asks him what he is — and it is almost always people who are of the dominant culture who do so — his answer is simple: "I'm African American." The answer derives not just from his features. He found love and social perspective and wonder and joy and intelligence and prideful history and hope in African American culture via his life with us, experiences on his own and the influence of Barbara's parents and brother, Joe. What's more, it was either that no one in our families who was primarily attached to any of the other cultures was still living and known to us or, with the primary exception of my sister, those who were showed neither consciousness about or interest in African American culture or the history and the constancy of the racism visited on those of it. Essentially, then, each other culture is ancestral happenstance. None, by itself, has been an active influence in his life.

In aggregate, obviously, the European cultures are the major structural subsets of dominion in America since its founding. Kazi's travel back and forth across the *Divide* made that clear to him early on. For him as a young man, being an object seen through the prism of that dominant culture, which at its collective best manifested tolerance for but has never been more than superficially inviting of African Americans, has been much like taking the same course repeatedly ... but taught by multiple instructors. Jim Crow may no longer fly but other caustic birds of prejudice, his relatives, do.

The Staying Power of History's Malevolent Idiocy

Kazi, when he was eight or nine years old, was playing one day with a boy who was of the dominant culture, about the same age, who lived in our neighborhood in northern California. That young man, with serious curiosity, asked Kazi, "Are your balls brown too?" The young man's younger sister, with serious curiosity, chimed in, "Do you have a tail?" This occurred in the late 1970s — not the 1670s.

A fellow elementary student repeatedly called Kazi "nigger" and would snatch the ball he played with at recess and throw it away from him across the playground. Kazi informed him that he better quit or he would hit him. The student didn't quit. Kazi did hit him, knocking him down. A teacher then got involved. She took Kazi and the other child to the principal's office. The principal literally flipped a coin to see which of the two would apologize first to the other but she did nothing to deal with the issue that precipitated the combat.

When Kazi was in the fifth grade a different student persistently called him "nigger." Kazi finally let me know that he had asked the young man to stop over and over and over again and that he did not. He told the teacher about it and she did nothing. When I confronted the teacher, she explained that she had a bad ear and it was into that one that Kazi probably had spoken. "I'm sure that's what happened," I responded. "But," I continued insistently, "I have a question. Did you hear me?" Instantly at the end of her affirmative response, I asked, "And it stops now?" She, of course, guaranteed me that it would.

When I saw Kazi at home that evening I told him I had talked to his teacher about the issue and that he, not the teacher, was the problem. "Why are you saying that?" he wanted to know so badly. "Because," I explained, "you were talking in your teacher's 'nigger' ear. You need to talk in her 'peckerwood' ear." We laughed because if we had not the pain of what that experience with the teacher had prophesied for the future would have soared to the surface. We laugh about it today, because decades have permitted the sorrow to lessen and give way to the zaniness of my response.

The pattern stayed the same over the years. He attended Morehouse College in Atlanta, Georgia. There, once, some young men who were of the dominant culture swerved their car at the one in which Kazi was ridding with friends and repeatedly screamed "nigger" at them. In California, while an assistant manager in a business that was part of a growing electronics game franchise, Kazi was told by the manager, a young man of the dominant culture and the son of the owner of a few of the company's chains, that the Ku Klux Klan was originally a good organization. Also in California, while an assistant manager in a coffee house, Kazi put on some of the music the company made available to play for customers during business hours. The music was African. Shortly after it began to play, the young man of the dominant culture who was manager asked Kazi if he was "feeling his ethnicity." Then the manager, with his hands tucked under them, began flapping his arms up and down, mimicking the clucking of a chicken. And there was the time when ... and then ... and after that there was ... and ... and ... ad nauseam. These things didn't occur before the Civil War or the Emancipation Proclamation: they happened after the March on Washington and the Civil Rights Movement, during the time of much talk about "celebrating diversity."

Much like a well-trained martial artist, Kazi has learned to both anticipate and step aside from the punches of such malevolent idiocy ... yet without striking back in kind. The spirit, history and values at the base of Morehouse College certainly helped in that regard. He has learned well how to negotiate around the obstacles provided by the *Divide*. He, along with his friends, including one who is of the dominant culture, face, leap over, joke about and are conscious every waking hour about the separateness still part of America.

Indifference to Indifference

Fifteen years after Barbara and I were married my mother invited me to attend a family reunion at the home of the relative whose husband saw it to be wrong for light skin and dark skin people to marry. My answer was uncomplicated: "No." She then asked me to do it for her. With that request, I agreed ... but stipulated, "If any one of 'em comes up with racist crap, I'm out the door ... after I get in their face." She accepted the stipulation.

This relative's husband made a most feeble attempt at apologizing shortly after my arrival. It took the form of him asking me to step into the other room and telling me that some people aren't very good at apologizing. I internalized his apology but only at the depth it was given.

I went alone on this visit and on a few stopovers there to visit my mother after she moved in with these relatives. Barbara and I both knew that without genuineness being tucked into that old, insubstantial apology and it being rendered directly to her, her presence would be met with tolerance at best. My interactions with them were always pleasant, the discussions never deep, never inclusive of any bastardizing of the bible or of the segregationist message sent to Barbara and me so many years before. These individuals and I remain "family" in technical fact but not in spirit.

At my last visit to this cousin's house shortly before my mother died, I witnessed irony's step into all of this. A daughter of this cousin and her husband willingly bore a child of a father who is African American. I was so glad to see that grandchild treated lovingly by her grandparents, the same people who would not come to the wedding of Barbara and me, never apologized for the bigotry at the base of that decision and never even greeted Barbara and Kazi when given the opportunity to do so. How well a child can teach, even without having gone to college to secure the credential to do so! Maybe a change came also from years of unavoidably experiencing humanness manifested in an increasing number of cultures where they live. Yet ... ?

These "relatives" and Barbara, Kazi and I were at the house of another cousin immediately following my mother's burial in January, 2004. We were there for a few hours talking with many of mom's friends and other extended family members. During those hours within the confines of the same house and its yard, thirty-six and a half years after Barbara and I were married, there came from this relative and her husband not only no apology to Barbara for the bigotry expressed but no greeting for Barbara and Kazi and no acknowledgement of their existence. Such provided no hurt for the three of us. It did provide *italics* and an <u>underline</u> for the *persistence of bigotry, denial of responsibility* for it and *indifference to* any *human damage* it might create — even for the humans who enacted it. Such, indeed, was clear *indifference to indifference.*

What One's Soul Knows

My sister, Sandra, lived in Addis Ababa, Ethiopia for seven years. She always stayed in poor communities, living sometimes in mud huts. She asked me some questions on the phone during a brief visit back to the states, before returning to Africa. My first inclination was not to respond because we both already knew the answers. She quickly made clear that the purpose of the questions was to tug some family history back up on the table for further consideration. Our father, an only child, was from Selma, Alabama. He left there, when he was 16 years old, on his own. He had almost nothing to say about his experience in the South except that he had one friend who was Black with whom he used to box. Kids of the dominant culture often called Sandra "nigger lips" or "liver lips" when we were growing up because her lips were more African than European looking. We have the same parents. There is a Foxworth, Mississippi, to the west of Columbia, where Foxworths who are African American and Foxworths of the dominant culture live and Foxworth is hardly an African name. And, my sister reminded me, there is the disinclination of most family members to initiate or participate in discussion about the prospects of Africans being in our not too distant past. (That disinclination might magnify in consideration of the research findings about the origins of us all being in Africa.)

With the above back up in the light, Sandra asked me, "Well, are you drawing any conclusions?" My answer was simple: "Yes, sister, I draw the same conclusions you do."

Neither of us needed official verification of African Americans in our family's ancestry in the U.S. Her experiences and mine here and her's in Africa had told us so much about what we needed to know about who and what we are. Such was the case whether or not we could find documents that proved it. Yet, despite the typical "American" denial that skin color is important in contemporary American Society, it is used every tick of the clock in our country in making assumptions about who and what someone else is and how s/he might see or interact with who and what we've identified ourselves to be. Color is a key on Dominant America's calculator for equating distribution of economic-political-social wealth, the social interest rate for maintaining it and the degree of access to its federal reserve. That dominant culture use of color, coupled with the refutation of doing so, has structured one of the most historically significant vilifications of humankind, in America or anywhere in the world. The consciousness of humans not of the dominant culture about the negative significance so many in it attribute to *their* color is one of the most historically significant survival tools known to humankind, in American or anywhere in the world.

Over all these years there have been times, albeit not many and not often, when people who have identified themselves as African American and who know me — but not well — have sent messages to me of disapproval that are clearly shaped by experience with the *Divide*. Usually, they are subtle, never direct, never verbal, almost always in an environment that is African American, when issues pertinent to the realities of the *Divide* are being addressed. It sometimes takes the form of shaking the hands of others in the room with brown skin in a way different from how mine is shaken. There is the refusal to look me in the eye when sitting across the table from me at meetings, even during long ones. There is that occasional silence in response to a point I've made about dealing with an issue of racism and then the quick move onto someone else's point of view and the discussion that follows it.

I also have heard so many times through my decades

in public education leadership roles that many in the profession who are of the dominant culture perceived me as "too Afro-centric." The perception was never communicated directly to me by the persons who held it. It usually followed a session I initiated on dealing with racism and bigotry and their persistent, negative consequences on public education's academic success rates for students who are African American and Latino. The information about that perception of me always came from someone else who wanted me to know, usually so that I could protect myself. The names of those who perceived me that way were never given. Nor did I ever ask for them.

What the Hell is Wrong With You?
Who the Hell Do You Think You Are?

In the process of scouring the *Divide* in public education and trying to address its destructive results, the message to me, given in silence or indifference but not vocally, from many who are of the dominant culture with whom I've worked — but certainly not all — is this: "What the hell is wrong with you?" In the same context, the message, comparably rendered, from many who are African Americans with whom I've worked — but by no means all — is this: "Who the hell do you think you are?" It is through the perception of the lightness of my skin that some of the dominant culture conclude I should know better than to take a position that racism is still epidemic in our society and that we should unite, irrespective of culture, to end it. It is through the perception of the lightness of my skin that some African Americans conclude I cannot really know about racism and what to do about it because there is no way I could have experienced being on the receiving end of it.

The need to place me in one "racial" category or another showed up in a variety of ways along this bumpy road. Perhaps the most summarily revealing are two headlines, for two articles, in two different newspapers, in two different parts of California, about two different presentations I made on dealing with racism. In the Sunday, September 24, 1989 issue of *The Times,* a newspaper serving Contra Costa County, California, the headline for the article about my presentation read, "Discrimination Issue Remains Unsolved, Black Educator Says." In the January 20, 1992 issue of *The Sun,* a newspaper serving San Bernardino County, California, the headline and sub-headline about my presentation read, "King is Honored in County: A White School Superintendent Strikes a Chord With His Mostly Black Audience." In each case, the apparent need for an editorial assessment about my "race" became a judgmental filter through which the substance of the article was passed.

The Crumbling Structure of the Road to Us

Over those years until now, the bumpy road to Us has been altered deceptively. Its crumbly pavement and potholes haven't been fixed. There has been, instead, a successful effort by the Department of Unethical Transportation to funnel traffic on the Bus of Social Equality down a deceptively smoothed over path away from the Village of Us. The toll fee for access to the fast lane on the road away from Us gets paid only with a Social Express Credit Card issued by the Bank of Dominant America. Given the speed of those allowed access to that fast lane, the facades of equality along the side of the expressway are often misperceived for being real, permanent facilities, cemented into America's foundation. A turn down an off ramp, coupled with purposeful focus, however, will make clear that what has been built beside the road is for looks only. The modern Community Center for Equality, for example, has a foundation made of a melding of social mud and political quick sand and walls structured by the old, very thin plywood of socio-political deception, windows that minimize the penetration of light with the hazy fumes of indifference, an air conditioning system that pumps out the smog of profit over people, a floor dangerous to walk on because of the political spin wax with which it is polished, a cracked and fallen shelf on which the truth of equality once had been stored ... and no meeting room in which *We* can discuss and organize what *We* must do together to get back on the road to the *Village of Us*, a place made of all our cultures and of the joy in knowing it.

Hopefully, *We* will get back on the road before the heat of inequality along the *Black/White Divide* sparks another rebellion bigger than all the others before it combined. Hopefully ... *WE* ... will ...

CHAPTER 3

VARIED PERCEPTIONS OF THE BLACK/WHITE DIVIDE

Marlin Foxworth, Ph.D.

ABRAHAM LINCOLN'S OPPOSITION to slavery emanated from his perception that the nation would remain divided if the practice didn't end. He did not effect the abolishment of slavery because of a conviction that people of African heritage, the enslaved, merited entitlement as "us," as real citizens. The official end of the institution of slavery was not ever followed with a socio-legal-economic-educational system with built-in means for operational self-correction that would be triggered when the entitlements of citizenry were not delivered to all. Despite the constructive and healing intentions of many in the dominant culture who found slavery to be the evil it was, the end of it was not a function of corrective action following a national audit on moral values. Ending slavery was primarily a means for removing an impediment to that expansion of benefits for those who already were getting most of them.

Ongoing Modernizing of the Divide

Obviously, since its beginning with slavery in 1619, America's *Black/White Divide* has been sustained by legal and social adjustments and manipulations. The major subsistence of the *Divide* was transformed after the Civil War from slavery to servitude and after that to legalized, multi-faceted segregation that lasted nearly 100 years, almost through the 1960s. Adherence to the laws of slavery was altered to extralegal support of a social system that was differently named but just as demeaning. The informal segregationist system after the 60s has in it an unconstrained, usually unspoken and generally not admitted endorsement of the social structure that enables the dominant culture to keep *them*, African Americans, categorically in *their place* and to sustain dominion of Dominant America along the *Divide*. That is done by the intended action of some but much more by the melding of unconsciousness with indifference — despite supposed good intentions to the contrary. That is so despite the wish of many in Dominant America that it not be so.

From the 1960s to the present, the *Divide* has been ratified via subordination and extra-legal, de facto segregation of African Americans. Rather than being physical, that segregation plays out in the absence of equal access to America's multiple social benefits, e.g., higher education, income, etc. The official physical and, if perceived as needed by those doing the subordinating, violent constraints of the subordinated were altered after the 60s to constraints not as frequent, no longer legal, not as often violent and sometimes less visible on the social horizon. The openly enacted and vicious police response to civil rights demonstrators in Birmingham, Alabama, in 1963, for example, elicited greater consciousness and more intense reaction than did the veiled but vicious treatment of many African Americans in Oakland, California in 2002 and 2003 by a group of policemen called the "Riders."

Double standards for upholding or applying the law remain here in the early 21st century. A classic example of that social duplicity comes from the reality that often people who are African Americans and convicted of a crime are given longer prison sentences than are people who are of the dominant culture convicted of the same crime. It is an ongoing and profound contribution to the *Divide* that an excessively high percentage of African American males will experience some time in jail and that today's prison population in America is approximately 50% African American while African Americans comprise less than 14% of the nation's population. There is no excuse for any crime, particularly when it is violent. It is reasonable to conclude, though, when crime is disproportionately a function in any community that those residing in it, especially the individuals committing the crimes, have little to no expectation or hope that a productive, materially sufficient life will accrue to efforts at participation in and adherence to the rules of the prevailing socio-economic system — particularly when its major benefits are posited predominantly, if not exclusively, outside the community.

Another perceptual element of the *Divide* is imbedded in that statistical disproportionality. The consequent view, even for some living in the area, is that urban communities that are African American are insecure and perilous. A conceptual kinship is fashioned between "African American" and "dangerous." That perceived tie between culture and threat blocks long and intensely needed focus on the *universally human*, not *culture or "race" specific*, response to systemic, historic, present day and anticipated second-classness. The contribution to the *Divide* here arises from the exclusivity of the focus on the inexcusable, e.g., the murders in urban communities that are African American. Excluded is the absolute need for a national grasp of the *human* consequences inevitably produced by the continuity of being *them,* every second, of every minute, of every hour, of every day, of every year, of every century, since being forced to come here. Yes, there is profound courage and insightfulness in rising above those consequences during every tick of the clock, on every day, in each calendar, for all those years and decades and centuries. Yes, while being perennially *them* is not and cannot be justification for crime, it is a major variable for some in low appraisals of self and of those categorized socially or culturally with you. Is it not a universal *human* reality that such low appraisal, most particularly that of self or *us*, is treated sometimes with a matching level of self-respect — including none?

Various responses to the *Divide* wend their way through an aggregation of innumerable social issues and elements, e.g., art, civil rights, culture, education, employment, entitlement, health care, housing, human rights, income, inter-group relations, language, law enforcement, legislation, media, politics, religion, spirituality, voter initiatives and, even, the future of this democracy. Indeed, even unconscious tolerance of inequality removes equality, but not privilege and aggregate social power, also for those in the social stratum demonstrating the tolerance. An ongoing effort at Democracy cannot be constructively and indefinitely sustained without a collective recognition that the notion of *equality for some* is the antithesis of Democracy.

Four Perceptions of the Divide

Both the sustenance and continuation of the *Black/ White Divide* and of efforts to overcome and/or end it are couched in theme and variation of four general perceptions of it. Attached to those perceptions are the analysis of the *Divide's* structural components and the correlative prescriptions for maintaining it and modernizing it as needed, or accepting it but assisting those most negatively impacted by it, or adapting to it under the assumption that even though it should end it is not likely to, or ending it and creating an *Us*, structured of real *equality* and all of our *cultures*.

Sound System — What's Wrong With *Them*?

First, there is the perception that the American social system, including its politics and economics, is sound and that anyone who does not glean from it the multiple benefits it produces has her/himself to blame. That blame is often generalized beyond its individual application to social categories of people with which an "unsuccessful" individual in focus is perceived to have primary affiliation. The individual and the category of humans with which that primary cultural alignment is noted — or assumed — are summarily categorized as *them* by those who benefit from being located in the upside of the *Divide* and are not of *that* culture. In that context, it is a dominant cultural view that *they* need to get *their* act together like *we* do instead of continuing *their* complaining. Activism on changing this "sound" system is seen variously, then, as anything from an inexcusable, wrong minded social irritant to un-American activity that merits curative social and, when politics are right for it, governmental response.

High-level concern about violations of the legal tenets of the system occurring in the communities where *they* live and intense policing in them are not just the consequence of "rational" concern about crime and crime rates. Ignorance or indifference about flaws in the social system and *their* perceptions of them parent a dominant cultural view that *they* are both the exclusive source of the problem and the singularly needed locus of its resolution — if there can be one for *them* at all. The continuance of the *Divide* is fueled, in part, by doubt about *their* commitment to overcoming *their* difficulties and lethargy about *them* doing so, as long as the problem stays in *their* communities.

While this first perspective has it that *they* who are to blame for not doing what is possible to be successful within this sound system, compassion for the human discomfort *they* are believed to have created for *themselves* is sometimes seen as legitimate. Charity for *them* is a frequently — but not widely — called for iteration of that compassion. The charitable content, program focus, goals and delivery system manifestations are most often created by those with the compassion for *them* but without essential experience with the realities in *their* communities. Despite a very long history of the same practice, there seems to be insufficient concern by the charitable who hold this first perspective that no cure has been found for the social disease regarded as needing that compassionate treatment. These compassionate, sometimes "faith-based" initiatives focus on what are historically and unceasingly perceived as symptoms of social ineptitude in the same, non-dominant socio-cultural categories of humans, including African Americans particularly. That compassion is programmatically expressed rather than addressing the social structure that inevitably benefits the dominant culture most, including the *compassionate,* and produces the separateness for which there is denied responsibility or tolerance in *compassionate* circles. The continuance of the charitable programs depends on both the availability of funds and on there being neither substantial reduction in compassion nor a conclusion by those with the money that it needs to be spent elsewhere.

Another sustaining element of the *Divide* flowing from this *first* perception is the sometimes appropriate conclusion that in African American communities there is an appraisal of people of the dominant culture as *them.* An important distinction in this *theming* of others leaps out from the dominant, collective, systemic, material, political power to effect social limitations and other negative consequences for the *them* perceived. Yes, given conflict germinating from the *Divide,* there can be harm done to an individual of the dominant culture perceived by someone African American as one of *them.* However, even if there were a collective desire to do so, it could not be effectively systematized, institutionalized and generalized to the majority of the dominant culture's population because there is insufficient economic, political and social power in African American communities to do so. The absence of collectivized power to do so often coexists with a spiritually and experientially based disinclination to do unto others what they have done or allowed to be done harmfully unto you and yours. Ironically, in this context, the collective absence of hammering back is fueled for so very many by the spiritual strength to not do so because it is perceived as wrong.

This *first* perception of the *Divide* is a continuous and major sustainer of it. The inalterable and centuries old insistence that *they* are the exclusive source of *their* multifaceted difficulties is a denial that the American Social System, like all others throughout the world and its history, has inevitable social consequences. As much in denial in this perspective is the near universal reality to date that one socio-cultural group dominates in any society when there are more than one. Dominance can have no existence without subordination. Effective subordination in this context comes in the form of categorizing *them* as "inferior," evidenced by what is perceived as *their* general, historical, group refusal to take advantage of the perks of the social system. The exceptions among *them* are seen as confirmation of the soundness of the system and the refusal of most of *them* to be constructively of it.

This downward view of *them* from the loft of dominance fashions the de facto definition of "inferior" as those who believe or perceive or respond to *our* social structure differently than *we* do. Inferior life for *them* is not seen necessarily by all who have this perspective as the inalterable consummation of *their* construction as humans but rather as the consequence of *them* getting collectively what *their* behavior has asked for collectively. Treatment of *them* as inferior is manifested in the major social structure elements put in place by the dominant power to service its own multiple human, social, cultural and economic needs and desires and is sustained by those of that power who have come after and who continue to perceive the system as working satisfactorily. Legal, social, economic functions fashioned from this perspective sustain the *Divide* because of the thus far impenetrably protected dismissal by those deriving the most from the system of the remotest possibility that America's social structure contributes to the *Divide* at all.

Stalwart System with Correctable Glitches

Second, there are those who view the American Social System as reliably stalwart but not without correctable glitches. However, given its steadfastness, it only needs to be tweaked occasionally. Tucked into this take on American Society is also the less bold view that *they* are what need to be worked with and on so *they* can overcome *their* problems. Unlike in the first perception, this one identifies lack of success with the system as a function of debilitating and impeding circumstances, some recognized as historically extant in communities on the down side of the *Divide*. When *they* are not making it in the system satisfactorily, then, there are a couple of prospects for corrective solutions. New ones are to be culled out from a perceived supply of creative possibilities or current options and the right one or combination employed to effect needed correction(s). These actions are designed to help people rectify *their* internalized dysfunctional adjustments to the social impediments they face. That the "corrective" actions taken never excise the problems from the socio-cultural categories of the individual citizens to which they are applied and never institutionalize the equity or equality professedly intended is not taken, most particularly in Dominant America, as an indication that the structure of the social system itself might need to be altered.

This *second* perspective melds, in effect, with the *first*. Despite programmatic and even heartfelt efforts to care for the wounded, it is often perceived that the wounds are self-inflicted exclusively. When not seen that way, there is no mechanism for identifying what created this type of social bomb and what sets off its historically repeated explosions. Like an occupying force in another country, it may be honored for providing hospitalization for the wounded but many will see it more for the insensitivity and destructive consequences of its presence.

The *first* and *second* perspectives hold sway in the determination of the social and governmental action or inaction in the face of the downside experiences of the *Divide*. These perspectives are inalterably fixed in the conviction that the American social structure is the hope for ending the *Divide* and is either not a contributor to it at all or, at least, not a major contributor.

Talk of Equality and Its Absence in Fact

The *third* perspective is the result of analytical appraisal of discrepancies between the governmental and political verbiage on equality and the unending and powerful presence of its absence. When there is social equality, individual differences in the acquisition of systemic benefits can be attributed rationally to variance in human interest in, focus on and skill and tenacity for employing the available social mechanisms for accessing those benefits. Socio-cultural group differences in benefit acquisition, however, cannot be ascribed to individuals. This perspective concludes that perennial variation by socio-cultural group in receipt of the quantity and quality of social benefits is a function of a social structure absent of needed, built-in and functional corrective apparatuses and, therefore, in need of alteration.

This perspective is comparable to that of a mechanic assessing a car built with plastic brakes. Such a car in motion necessarily will make trouble at some point for those on the same road and, ultimately, for its driver and passengers. That will be so no matter how much comfort those who travel in the car derive from its interior and seemingly smooth ride. What happens to all involved, including those in the crosswalk in front of the car, when its brakes melt?

Lani Guinier, Harvard Law School Professor and a President Clinton nominee for Assistant Attorney General for Civil Rights in 1993, makes a case for this perspective throughout her book and in its title: THE TYRANNY OF THE MAJORITY: FUNDAMENTAL FAIRNESS IN REPRESENTATIVE DEMOCRACY. She addresses the inevitability of consequences in social structure, America's specifically, in her analysis of electoral procedures. "When groups identify collective interests and vote them," she points out, "elections become winner-take-all. Minorities — whether defined by race or geography or income or what have you — wind up losers." Every bit as pertinent to analysis of the *Divide* is her argument, "That it is not merely a question of whether, on matters of substantive justice, minority rights trump majoritarian democracy. Instead, we ought to question the inherent legitimacy of winner-take-all majority rule."

Her analysis speaks tangentially to the irrelevancy of good intentions in light of social structures having inevitable consequences. In this case, one of those inevitable consequences is the existence and continuance of the *Divide*. Guinier states: "My claim is that disproportionate majority power is, in itself, so wrong that it delegitimates majority rule. As Alexis de Tocqueville recognized, 'The power to do everything, which I should refuse to one of my equals, I will never grant to any number of them.' The problem according to attorney Ed Still is that majoritarian systems 'create winners who take all rather than winners who share in power, thus making politics into a battle for total victory rather than a method of governing open to all significant groups.' Because they do not necessarily recognize the salience or intensity of minority interests, winner-take-all majoritarian systems do not give minority groups a reason to support the ultimate bargain or to believe the outcome is public-regarding or legitimate."

"Beyond this, I would argue that majority rule is unfair in situations where the majority is racially prejudiced against the minority to such a degree that the majority consistently excludes the minority, or refuses to inform itself about the relative merit of the minority's preferences. This is because the claim that majority rule is legitimate rests on two main assumptions that do not hold where racial prejudice pervades the majority: (1) that majorities are fluid rather than fixed; and (2) that minorities will be able to become part of the governing coalition in the future."

Guinier finds that it is through those two assumptions that justification for winner-take-all majority rule is fashioned. She identifies the flaw in the assumptions with the following:

"Simply put, racism excludes minorities from ever becoming part of the governing coalition, meaning that the white majority will be permanent. Because it excludes minorities from joining the majority, racism also renders the majority homogeneous, comprised of white voters only. The permanent, homogeneous majority that emerges obviously does not virtually represent the interest of the minority. To the contrary, such a majority will 'marginalize' or ignore minority interests altogether. Therefore, racial polarization in the electorate and in the legislative body destroys the reciprocity/virtual representation principle and buries it within racially fixed majorities, thereby transforming majority rule into majority tyranny."

If, as Guinier indicates, the "majority" remains a homogeneous socio-cultural group, what does that say of the inclination among the more liberal in the dominant culture to "celebrate diversity?" Without an active focus on fashioning a social structure without dominance and subordination, is not that willingness to celebrate the multiplicity of cultures, including the many "minorities" in America, tantamount to "compassionate conservatism?" It says, in effect, let us demonstrate our collective fondness for our multiple cultural iterations while doing nothing effective — or at all — to end the inequality visited on them by our social structure. Does that not help conserve the structure? Is this not a case of the make-up of intention hiding the acne of effect?

This *third* perspective, while an elemental sine qua non for ending the *Divide* and fashioning a multicultural *Us* in its place, is seen for the threat it is to the perpetuation of the disproportionate systemic benefits of and for the dominant culture. It is seen from that loft too as oppositional to American social and economic structure rather than for its foundational conviction that the system needs to be altered, even radically, but not replaced with a system of an entirely different nature. It also indirectly challenges the justification of socio-cultural-economic group good intentions as a rational nullifier of inevitable negative consequences of the America Social System.

The Divide as an Element of American Social Structure

The *fourth* perspective is an intermingling of the following: the *Black/White Divide* is an element of American Social Structure; whether or not it ever can be corrected remains to be seen; there is no likelihood that will occur; and the only means for dodging or overcoming the racist consequences of the *Divide* is to respond to social environment with analysis and adaptability. That perspective is taken as being *realistic* by those having it based on the assumption that the social structure that is, with its gaps between the talk about and production of equality, has to be and will continue as is for the foreseeable future. The conviction that individuals not of the dominant culture lack the collective power to alter a societal structure is taken in this perspective as equally "realistic." Consequently, there are two choices for response to a social framework not fashioned with a solid and consistent system for the delivery of equality — and the equity needed for it — in social benefits to you and those of your primary cultural. 1) You can fight the system and, most likely, lose or 2) analyze it and what you have to do to not only survive but also garner some benefit from it and act accordingly.

In their book, CRACKING THE CORPORATE CODE: THE REVEALING SUCCESS STORIES OF 32 AFRICAN-AMERICAN EXECUTIVES, Price Cobbs, M.D. and Judith L. Turnock write about the *Divide*, without calling it that, and about the consequences of entitlement and the lack of same in American corporate culture. That analysis has applicability every bit as pertinent to the realities of the *Divide* at large as to its manifestations in corporations. "For those with a feeling of entitlement, a sense of belonging," they write, "adapting to that culture is relatively painless. The problems for newcomers, especially outsiders, when they first encounter this new culture begin at the visual level. Minorities and women clearly do not fit the mold. Lacking both the traditional outward appearance and knowledge of the language, imagery, and symbols of the culture, they have to work to make themselves feel they fit in and to make it appear to others that they belong. With so much new data to process, the possibility of thriving there, of receiving and interpreting the culture's messages, initially seems remote." They proceed to describe a multitude of utilitarian tactics used by some African Americans who became successful corporate executives.

Like the *first* perspective, this *fourth* one holds that the African American individual is the source for overcoming blockage to "making it" in American social structure. Unlike that *first* perspective, though, this one does not conclude the individual is the source of the impediment. However, the individual can contribute to the racist effectiveness of the multi-faceted *Divide* by not being sufficiently introspective and self-actuating in surmounting its chronic presence. Cobbs and Turnock, their corporate focus again applicable to the *Divide* in general, write, "The debate between success or failure, happiness or sadness, satisfaction or disappointment, easy or difficult, risky or safe, winner or loser, is resolved in the head and heart of each individual ... Specific situations don't cause problems; it's how you see them and how you deal with them."

This *fourth* perspective guides the lifting of individuals *of* a socio-cultural category but not *the* category out of the *Downside* of the *Divide*. By itself, the sub-title of the Cobbs, Turnock book descriptively makes the case: THE REVEALING SUCCESS STORIES OF 32 AFRICAN-AMERICAN EXECUTIVES. It is not "The Revealing Success Story of African America." The current success stories in African America would qualify well for several, long and even inspiring shows of *The Survivor*. Actions resulting from the "realistic," practical and individualistic applicability of this *fourth* perspective bring otherwise denied quality of life to many African Americans and hold sway over what is seen as the "unrealistic," impractical and collective move to change a social system. Without such a movement, however, variations of *The Survivor* will likely be all that can play out on the televised *Downside* of the *Divide.*

A Needed Fifth Perception of the Divide

There is in all this, though, a needed *fifth* perspective. It ensues from an amalgamation of multiple considerations regarding the *Black/White Divide.* The *Divide* is shaped and sustained by social structure. Working to adapt to the *Divide* and consequently become an exception to the rule accepts, at least for the time being, the existence of the rule. Individual efforts to overcome the consequences of the *Divide* make sense individually but cannot function effectively to change the system that needs to be overcome. Avoiding collective and cross-cultural pursuit of ending the *Divide* and constructively replacing it with a cultural-socio-economic structure with equal and, when necessary, equitable benefits, because doing so is categorized as "unrealistic," is tantamount to contributing to the persistence of the *Divide* and its negative consequences. "Race" is a determinative variable in structuring America's social stratification and status assignments. Any effort to unite "races" and structure "positive race relations" is doomed to defeat because "race" is founded not in science but in social conviction about inevitable and inalterable separateness among humans categorized as the kinds of it.

This *fifth* perspective requires defiance of a major mathematical principle: 100% is the total of anything. From this *fifth* perspective, the necessary total for overcoming the *Black/White Divide* and replacing *Us-and-Them* with only *Us* is 200%. That total requires that the initiatives and actions of perspectives *three* and *four* be energized by the same collective heart, shaped into the same body politic and be based on the foundational value that there are no *others* in American Society, only *Us* ... in every single cultural iteration with which *We* have been or will be gifted. The focus is to have a 100% devoted to adapting to the social structure and overcoming the impediments inherent in the *Divide* as long as it remains, without relinquishing the sustenance from and for *Our* primary cultures. The focus requires another 100% devotion to altering the structure of our society economically, legally, socially and spiritually so that particular socio-cultural groups are never again kept down by it. The *fifth* perspective would also defy a structural element of language, i.e., there will be *up* for all socio-cultural groups ... without *down*. Any variance in accessing social, including material, benefits will be in a much narrower range of them and a function of individual choice, e.g., choosing to take on an employment responsibility different in requirements and corresponding pay than another one. The variance will *not* result from a *social structure* that tolerates fluctuation in access to those benefits by socio-cultural group. The elements of each 100% approach are to be applied simultaneously, despite the contrariness each may posit to the other.

This *fifth* perspective does not see the *Black/White Divide* and its debilitating consequences for communities that are African American as the primary or exclusive result of intentionally active dominant culture racism, although it is still bountiful. Indeed, active, on the surface, in your face, I'll-get-your-kids-too kind of racism is probably less a part of American Society now than ever. This perspective does see racism as the effect of the power role in the *dominance* and *subordination* relationship between two cultures with radically different points of origin and collective experiences in American Society. In defining racism as effect, despite the nature of intentions, this perspective sees the need to immediately end the acceptance of the proclaimed good intentions prevalent in the *dominant culture* as an acceptable denial that racism exists or is any longer having open-ended, attenuating effects on those on the receiving end of it. This *fifth* perspective also finds racism to be ruinous over the long haul even for those who are not subjected to its most palpable and sinister consequences. The assumption here is that all cultures and all in them in a society without such a *Divide* will benefit and end up being the foundation elements of a culturally collective model for the world that so many in the *dominant social stratum* seem to think America is now.

Michael Lerner and Cornell West, in their book, JEWS AND BLACKS, both analytically and prescriptively address racism and anti-Semitism. "It would be naïve," they note, "to believe that these problems admit of easy solutions." The applicability of that assessment of difficulty so clearly applies to overcoming the *Black/White Divide*. Just as applicable to facing the *Divide* is their rejection of " ... any strategy for healing that separates the ethical, psychological, and spiritual dimensions from the economic and political."

The two of them also insightfully simplify such sociocultural conflicts in America and the anticipation of addressing them. "Inflicting pain," they note, "takes hardly any time at all; healing it may take decades." Lani Guinier begged the question for ending the Dominant/Subordinate — *Black/White Divide* when she wrote, " ... democracy in a heterogeneous society is incompatible with rule by a racial monopoly of any color."

The task now is to be analytical about the structural elements of the *Divide* and prescriptive about what to do to create an American *Us* joyous about *our* multiple cultural iterations rather than tolerant of them. The effort requires of us the conviction that what has been and is does not have to be. It requires the conviction that dreaming is not only not antithetical to reality, it is the parent of it at its best. The need for analysis of the structural elements of the *Divide* and prescriptions for our 200% focus will be demanding. We must choose what we want or keep what we have, despite its never-ending, destructive human costs. It is not a matter of whether we *can* create the structure to sustain *Us. Will we?* Will ... *WE?*

CHAPTER 4

STRUCTURAL ELEMENTS OF THE RACIAL DIVIDE

Ralph Gordon

THE RACIAL DIVIDE is firmly entrenched in American culture. Of course, this is a matter that is denied by many. Some use devious means as they slyly and deceitfully claim that the United States is a color-blind society. Others wishfully and idealistically think that everything is just fine in the racial arena. Still others sit in indifference and could care less about this issue. Yet, all are affected by the fact that this is not really "one nation, under God, indivisible, with liberty and justice for all." The full promises of the Pledge of Allegiance have not yet been kept. Those dreams have not yet been realized. The racial divide is firmly entrenched in American culture. And, its perpetuation is facilitated by a number of structural elements.

This divisive fact of life requires a lot of help to stay in place. Some of these elements are on the surface and require no undue probing for their discovery. Other components are more subtle — and, in some cases, sinister. With a serious analysis of the racial divide, it becomes clear that it is necessary — even vital — to speak to the makeup of these structural supports for the divide and the elements in our society. One realizes that the racial divide does not just exist as a matter of course. No. It requires intentional efforts and structures for it to survive and thrive. Although it is easier and (perhaps) more comfortable to simply look at the racial divide in a tangential fashion, without really examining what it is actually comprised of, overcoming racial divisiveness requires a far better understanding of the obstacles to progress.

First, we have to acknowledge the fact that few if any persons or organizations (outside of virulently racist groups) will admit to being in existence for the purpose of deliberately keeping Americans divided on the basis of color. Ostensibly, all entities will have a set purpose that appears benign and even noble on the surface. Yet, a firm scratch of those surfaces can reveal objectives that are on a far different track. Here are a few examples of societal elements that aid in keeping the races firmly divided.

The "conservative" intelligentsia are well served by an increasing number of think tanks. These entities are significantly funded and deeply rooted as purveyors of ideologies for right-wingers. The brilliant use of think tanks, by "conservative" forces, includes the expenditure of vast amounts of money: on research, on "conservative" staffing etc. Lots of time is invested and many sharp minds are employed as these organizations carry out their strategies to maintain a racially separatist status quo. The think tanks skillfully even use Black persons — like Shelby Steele (a spokesperson for the Stanford-based Hoover Institution) — to spout their philosophies and programs. "Conservative" think tanks take firmly entrenched positions. These stances make it clear that the preaching entities are not satisfied with an image of just studying issues. No, they speak so authoritatively that they can move to shape policies for the perpetuation of the racial divide.

For example, someone strategically came up with the idea of mounting an assault on affirmative action, quotas, "preferences" and the like. Then, funds were made available for the traveling act of Wardell Connerly to hit the road — following his successful championing of California's Proposition 209 (against affirmative action in the state's collegiate system). The "conservative" think tanks can very effectively deploy such strategies via seemingly scholarly research, papers and posturing. Then, operatives — such as Connerly — can move forward with the confidence and knowledge that they are on a course of probable success. "Conservative" think tanks, and other entities, have mastered this technique. As with many other key strategies (political or otherwise), so-called liberals have not yet sufficiently mastered the effective use of think tanks.

From the ivory tower of the think tank intelligentsia, we descend to look at neighborhood impacts. At this level, insurance redlining has long been a way to imprison poor people by taking away their ability to be recompensed for their losses. If you cannot recover on your claims for property losses, you will become further mired in the depths of poverty. From time to time, one hears of a determined insurance commissioner who will wage the battle against such practices. But, these situations are notable by their exception. In the meantime, poor people — usually those of color — continue to pay a lot more for coverage, only to receive a lot less. The disparity in insurance coverage leads to a further separation of the races. As poor Blacks are locked further down in aggrieved neighborhood and environmental conditions, they face an increasing divide between themselves and others in our society.

The sinister — not benign — intent of those who would widen the racial divide is manifested by keeping the lowest and the least among us "in their place." Then, the law enforcement people are expected to maintain the necessary control over those who are locked in to particular areas. This is the segregation of our times. Perhaps surprisingly, it is a result that is in evidence more often in the northern states than in the Deep South of yesteryear. Insurance companies deftly deal with the chasm that results from the widening racial divide.

Insurance firms claim that they must make the tough decisions as to where risks are the greatest and then price their products and services accordingly. This is not simply a risk management proposition. It has been shown that often such decisions are made on a presumptive basis — when the scientific and/or empirical data are not in evidence and not even on their way. The result of the discriminatory pricing causes egregious costs for those who can least afford them. Hence, the racial divide is coupled with an economic chasm. Such is the by-product of the divisive elements.

It might be diagnostically simple if insurance redlining (and other forms of institutionalized discrimination) were limited to those at the bottom rungs of the economic scale. But, that is not the case. Our capitalist system and its denizens are understandably caught up with the economic status of citizens — and make judgments accordingly. However, American society has a preoccupation with skin color — regardless of the financial position of a person. If economics were the sole determining factor, wealthy Blacks might never experience racism or discrimination. Whether it is a Black celebrity trying to hail a northbound taxicab in mid-town Manhattan or golf superstar Tiger Woods being insensitively and inaccurately teased about eating "soul food" (by perennial golfing prankster, Fuzzy Zoeller), the list of infractions is long and enduring. Redlining is a deleterious practice that has its foundation in skin color, not in economic status.

Another form of redlining emanates from the real estate community. This represents a move from the legalized segregation of old to the de facto system of today. There would not have been a need for neighborhood integration efforts had not certain residential areas been deliberately maintained as racially divided enclaves. The "partner in crime" for this form of neighborhood resistance is the activity of the realtor. The practice of "steering" has long been used to dissuade potential homeowners of color away from certain locales. This method directs certain people — primarily Blacks — from even seeing available properties in particular areas. The realtor who does this ensures that the buyers pose no integration threat to a neighborhood that ostensibly wishes to remain "lily white." A number of the residents may have wanted to keep the area this way. But, the realtors are co-conspirators when they deliberately keep non-whites out of certain neighborhoods.

Even when real estate agents don't do such damnable things, people of color sometimes have moved in only to find deeply ingrained neighborhood resistance. My wife and I haven't had a cross burning on our lawns (thank God!). But, we know what it is like to see simmering resentments from neighbors who wonder (not too subtly) what you're doing in "their" neighborhood. I wish that I had a dollar for each person who asked us the intriguing question: "How did you find this area?" It is as if the neighborhood was a well kept secret from folks of color and we somehow broke the security code. Perhaps there was a breakdown in the effectiveness of the "steering" real estate agents. Some who utter this coded and probing question may believe that they mean no harm. And, perhaps they don't. But, for the recipient of the insulting remark, this sad attempt at territoriality is more than just a mild irritant.

My mind still rumbles with the memory of a neighbor who thought that I was … Well, let me tell the story properly. One day, while picking up my newspapers from the driveway of our home, I noticed a crew from a tree trimming company working at a house up the street from us. This piqued my interest because, at that time, we needed to have a couple of tall trees trimmed on our property. I was curious as to how such a servicing operation purveyed its trade. So, I decided to walk up the street and watch them for a little bit — and maybe get a business card for a later call and an estimate.

It was informative for me to observe the work crew and to visualize how this process might be carried out on our property. I was so engrossed in what the men were doing that I was startled at a tap on my shoulder — oblivious to the fact that someone had walked up behind me. When I turned to see who it was and what they wanted, a woman asked me how much "we" — in the tree trimming firm — charged for "our" services. Yes, I was dressed very casually. But, since I was standing only three houses from my own home, and since we had lived in this neighborhood for more than two years at that time, I was more than a little surprised that anyone would mistake me for one of the visiting laborers.

The woman's intentions were benign. She might have been shocked if I had told her that her presumption was a racist inference. Yet, her perceptions were based upon a misguided image of a Black person in this suburban neighborhood: that he must be a workman. When incidents like this occur, my reactions vary. If it happens on what I might call a bad day, I'm likely to react strongly to the person who would so crudely stereotype me. Like other persons of color, I've fortunately developed a thickness of skin that causes my good days to outnumber my bad days. This is also a coping mechanism: one that minimizes my personal level of stress. Were I to react strongly and adversely each and every time one of these incidents occurs, I could grow crazy. I might experience a veritable descent into a state of "Black Rage:" the agitated state that is the title and expertly explicated subject of a landmark and still timely 1960's book written by two Black psychiatrists, Dr. Price Cobbs and Dr. William Grier.

For me, reacting strongly (or harshly) would not amount to anything physically violent. My naturally peaceable nature precludes such action. Alternatively, I have been known to have a sharp tongue — specifically when I'm offended. As I've grown older, I've tried to curb that impulse and to restrict the number of bad days that might move me to such strong and even harsh responses. This time, I was caught on a good day. So, I smiled and told the inquiring woman: "I'm your neighbor." She blushed with much embarrassment as she realized that her presumption of my occupation and identity was a lot more than just a "faux pas." She apologized profusely, I accepted and now our two households regularly greet each other warmly and — I believe — genuinely. Alas, realtor redlining and neighborhood resistance and misconception (through passive perceptions or purposeful actions) are elements of America's racial divide. Who could feel welcome under such circumstances? Lorraine Hansberry's classic play, A Raisin in the Sun, powerfully and poignantly spoke to this issue in the 1950s. Sadly, the matter has not disappeared from the landscape of the United States.

Many Americans still have a strong preference not to live in an ethnically or culturally mixed neighborhood. The quest for residential homogeneity is strong. Many real estate agents will say that they are simply following the wishes of those who are already in a particular neighborhood. But, "steering" is a foul practice nonetheless as is stereotyping. And, those who make their neighbors feel unwelcome — with benign intentions or not — are a part of the overall problem.

At another level, the legislative branch of government

can have its own impact on not just where we live but on how we live. Congressional redistricting is a powerful way to marginalize and minimize the votes cast by the underprivileged in this country. Political parties know well that they can direct the destiny of the electorate by drawing voting lines in their favor. This practice was long used in the Old South and elsewhere to disenfranchise people of lesser status (usually Blacks) — to ensure that they would stay mired in their powerlessness and lack of influence. Ostensibly, such moves are touted as bringing a better level of fairness and equity to the voting process. Of course, just the opposite is actually the case.

"Conservative" (right-wing) columnists such as George Will (the William F. Buckley for another generation), Armstrong Williams (a politically conservative and very vocal Black man) and others regularly and pointedly espouse all sorts of seemingly practical reasons as to why race relations in America are just fine. Usually, these writers are quite articulate. (No such prerequisite exists for right-wing talk radio.) Their profundity and veracity are unquestioned by their massive audiences. But, a reasonably close reading of what they write and say shows an unabashed agenda to either move the reader or to keep the reader to the far right of the political spectrum. These columnists purport to be the intelligentsia of "conservative" thought. To an extent, they are. But, in the broader scheme of American political thought, they are cultivators of extremist thinking — seeking to bring as many along with them as possible. Their effectiveness is beyond question. But, for the less lofty of mind, there is the more base appeal. Talk radio leads this charge.

Talk radio is where the would-be Archie Bunkers (From the *All in the Family* TV show of yesteryear) speak and the masses listen. Bunker was the iconic character created by Norman Lear and his company as the quintessential bigot on television, in the 1970s and 80s.

Talk radio has become a bastion of divisive, blue-collar thought. One would hardly point to this arena as a unifying force in American race relations. The perpetuation of the racial divide thrives in this venue. Rush Limbaugh has reigned here for some time. He and a number of others take much pleasure in vilifying people of color and acting (in a not so subtle way) as if they — the radio commentators — are the designated protectors of the "white race." They gain huge popularity points for bashing Blacks, in particular, and other so-called minorities, in general. As concerned as I am regarding the talk show hosts, I'm even more worried about the mentality of the vast number of listeners.

The thinking of the talk radio listeners and the readers of ultra-conservative thought are quite worrisome. Their seeming lack of concern for the Black/White divide is very troubling. Clearly, this country has other divides as well: cultural, religious etc. Ask most anyone for a list of major world problems and the Arab-Israeli conflict would probably make at least the top ten. But, particularly in a post-9/11 era, the differences between these two cultures are magnified here on the home front. Arab Americans suffer from racial profiling — previously reserved for Blacks — as paranoid people (not just in law enforcement) — seek to preempt acts of terrorism on our home soil. In the meantime, anti-Jewish (commonly referred to as anti-Semitic) activity is steadily on the rise.

During the civil rights era, Jews and Blacks frequently were arm-in-arm against the pervasive racism that was heavily institutionalized in America at the time. Still, it was necessary to follow that period with a frank examination of the seeming breakdown between these two groups of people. Courageously, Rabbi Michael Lerner and Dr. Cornel West did so eloquently and expertly in their landmark book BLACKS AND JEWS. Their skillful probing of that inter-cultural situation has stood the test of time.

It is sad, at the very least, that there are so many societal, structural elements devoted — outright or otherwise — to the continuing existence and growth of the Black/White racial divide. These perpetuators do not wish to see a resolution of racial conflict. For them, things would be so much better if the offending races would simply "stay in their place." America can never realize its true potential as long as these elements hold such powerful sway.

Combating the racial divide in America is certainly no mean feat. But, effectively addressing this chasm can begin by a much greater level of awareness on the part of many more U.S. citizens. A more honest look in the mirror would be helpful. We should acknowledge the need for so many of us to grow in our perceptions of one another and in how we treat one another. We need to move away from apologist thinking and activity where we seek to excuse our supposedly benign actions. One must recognize that these actions are actually malignant: fostering a continuing and cancerous growth of misunderstanding and insensitivity in this country. Would that we would soon recognize the need and the benefit of growing closer and more aware of what we have in common, and not simply focus on our differences. Perhaps if we could and would move farther down this road, the dissipation of America's racial divide would become a reality.

Thankfully, there are many who do seek more harmony between the races. May the desires of their hearts be manifest in actions that stimulate this result. May the racial divide soon become a matter of history.

CHAPTER 5

STRUCTURAL ELEMENTS OF THE DIVIDE

Marlin Foxworth, Ph.D.

THE BLACK/WHITE DIVIDE in America has continued in mutations of its original manifestation as slavery since its inception in 1619. That reality is not simply social happenstance. The synergy of the multiple elements in the structure of that *Divide* keeps it in place as an internationally recognized facet of American Society. It keeps it functioning as though it were a time capsule filled with an acceptable social-relations mechanism and lofted into each succeeding generation's collective thinking space for *inevitable social realities*. It keeps it employed as a chief business officer charged with the task of Enronizing the data for determining both who gets what returns on investments in hope and how to convince those defrauded of it that they weren't. The surge of American Society through history over those centuries has included the parallel updating of the structural elements of the *Divide* necessary for it to blend well with the increasing complexities of contemporary social anatomy. The *Divide*, in its modifications, remains. So do its consequences.

Can *Our* American Society become the Democracy with the equality and staying power that so many on the upside of the *Divide* erroneously claim it already has? We'll see. If it is to happen, there must be an appraisal of the structural elements of the *Divide*, its persistence, virulent manifestations and the social damage it continues to wreak on American Society as a whole. That appraisal must include a constructive analysis of the social juxtaposition of the demeaning and destructive effects on the downside of the *Divide* with the denial about contributing to the *Divide* from its upside. That appraisal and analysis have to be done by humans from both sides of the *Divide* who recognize that the creation of an *Equal Us* will be a first in America and who gladly would welcome it being manifested in *Our* varied cultural ways. From that collective pursuit by a *Would-Be-Equal-Us* must come committed action to ply the *Divide* up from the earth and process it to oblivion in a way that would preclude it being recycled. While anticipating that social entombment of the *Divide*, there must be prescriptive, transformative action by the *Would-bes* that will effect the social changes needed to make an actual and sustainable *Equal-Us.*

Language and the Divide

Language frequently falls beneath the radar screen of efforts at social change. Not only language content but also language practices strongly buttress the *Divide*. Language, obviously, is used not only to delineate thought about that for which there is agreed perspective. It is used to shape perspective and initiate action and inaction related to it. *Spin* is an element of language that has colossal significance on both major and minor league social and political playing fields in America. *Spin* often successfully blurs the distinctions between characterization and reality. It serves to subordinate actual meaning

— and sometimes truth — to intended outcome. It does so not just in the context of announced *political* activity, e.g., electioneering, but also in the unwitting polity of common parlance. It is *only* dominant social power that can subordinate meaning and truth in a way that shapes and sustains a social structure with unequal distribution of its benefits in this *land of equal opportunity.*

Spin also has a subliminal variation as an almost unconscious social perspective launching pad in the *Dominant American* psyche. *Spin* shapes language that functions in kinship with racist subordination and it shields such language from public analysis. For example, it is a common and perennial dominant cultural practice to categorize those of it according to their roles, e.g., doctor, teacher, minister, etc. It is the location of the role in America's pyramidical social structure, largely determined by income amount and capital enhancing practice, rather than just the fact of humanness, that implies the social merit of the individual. Although there are various exceptions, just as long enduring is a dominant cultural practice of grouping those who are not of it in subsets of those roles. It was on a popular daily news program, on network television, for example, that one of the two very popular hosts referred to a well-known novelist as a "Black author." The reference was made with a respectful tone of voice. The host extolled the author's productive literary history. There was nothing said about her that was negative. The unwitting message however, aside from presumably good intentions on the part of the newscaster, was that this author lacked whatever was needed to be characterized simply as an *author.*

Would either Ernest Hemingway or John Steinbeck be called a "White author?" Was this daily T.V broadcast journalist a "White newscaster?" When one is referenced as a "Black surgeon," rather than a "surgeon," is that a function of the individual's contributions to the

well-being of patients being insufficient to qualify her/
him simply as a "surgeon?" If Ruby Dee is labeled as
a *Black Actress,* Ossie Davis, her deceased husband, a
Black Actor and what they were together is classified as
a *Black Couple,* then why is there no insistence in *Dominant America* that its social labeling practice tag Laura
Bush as a *White First Lady,* George W. Bush as a *White
President* and what they are together as a *White Couple*
living in the *White House?*

On the other hand, one does not hear allusion to
individuals who are African American and play in the
National Basketball Association as "*Black* Basketball
Players." Nor is there frequent reference to "*Black* Prisoners" in America's penitentiary systems. Reference to
"*Black* Entertainers" is almost never on the stage of public dialogue. (That is so even while entrepreneurs who
are African American acted on the need to create Black
Entertainment Television (BET) and the Black Family Channel (BFC).) The dominant culture and its news
media seem to sense, as contrasted to consciously and
objectively appraising, people who are African American
as being sufficiently ensconced in professional athletics,
prisons and show business to preclude the need for the
color qualifier in those social spheres. What, though, of
being a "Black lawyer" or a "Black senator" or "Black corporate executive" or a "Black entrepreneur" or a "Black
... or ... or ... or ... ?"

Labeling vs Self-Identification

Why does that imposed qualifier remain an addendum to categorization in so many other social roles filled
by *Us citizens* who are African American? Why is it that
the task of ending the imposition of the qualifier by *Dominant America* is analogous to a psychological civil war,
one going on longer than any physical one fought to date
by America? Why is it that many in *Dominant America,*

upon seeing or hearing those questions, would ask, "If getting rid of that 'racial' qualifier is so important, why do African Americans insist on being called "African" Americans?" That kind of question gets tendered as representation of the pretentious value that all citizens in America are just "Americans" and that such a self-attributed cultural characterization is rejection of or disinterest in participating in that "reality." Missing in that *Just-Americans* summary classification is a grasp of the distinction between choosing a self-identification conceived of prideful association with an amalgamation of one's ancestry, culture, family, history, spirituality and kindred community and being labeled by a dominant culture that has yet to accept you and yours as being of equal importance with their own in the formulation, evolution and preservation of America? You do not hear those of *Dominant America* refer to themselves as *White Americans* or *European Americans.* Until the talk-of-equality is transformed into equality, self-identification and resistance to labeling by others are means for confronting the inequality and maintaining connectedness with those constructively spirited by the same experience. Cultural self-identity as a gem in a national collection of such jewels would not preclude the thriving of equality even after the *Divide* is laid to rest in America's graveyard for overcome, historically destructive practices.

Misperceiving Diversity, the Erroneous Concept of Race and the Perpetuation of *Its-Just-The-Way-It-Is-Itis*

Race, obviously a requisite concept for racism, is a primary example of the function of language in shaping social conclusions. Historically, the utility of the concept of *race* has derived from what is read into and assumed about combinations of hair texture and skin pigment and the social stratification that correlates with or results from those interpretations and/or assumptions. A

Race is a category of humans having been so designated out of the conviction that visual discernments, primarily of skin pigmentation and/or hair texture, construct the identifying bedrock element and symbol of inalterable and irreversible separation of humankind into groups. Only slightly less blunt in that conceptualizing is the belief that each of those groups has some particular social characteristics which are inalterably and irreversibly affixed to it and which are not manifested in individuals not of the group.

For example, some conversations in dominant culture communities about the murder rates in some communities that are African American will spark the summary statement: "You know how they are." Likewise in the same communities, conversations about students who are African American having less good indicators of academic success than students who are of the dominant culture tweak theme and variation of the statement: "That's just the way it is."

Those summary appraisals invariably imply the negative consequences to be the inextricable responsibility of the *race* experiencing them. Those appraisals also stave off even the remotest consideration of *It's-Just-The-Way-It-Is-Itis* contributing to racist social negatives being locked into American Society. Maintaining a concept that there are *races* other than the *Human Race* accrues to the benefit only of those with the socio-economic power to maintain the functional use of that notion: those advantaged most materially by the resulting stratification; those who also deny having even the remotest intention for the stratification to exist or continue; those who, over generation after generation, have done nothing of any consequence to end it — despite having the collective power to do so. It is the power of social dominance that propels and prolongs the socially stratifying functionality of the belief that there are *Races*. The human impact of such socially structured disconnection would be so irrespective of the non-dominant culture(s) on which it was hammered by whatever dominant culture in whatever society. People can and do move away from the slam of the hammer, even above the arc of its downward swing. Citizens who are African America do it all the time. Although rising above the consequences of not being of the *dominant culture* is a constant, commonplace achievement for people of color in the United States, the consequences present themselves daily. The form of those consequences may alter, transforming, for example, from the vicious physical violence of the 60s to the destructive virulence of today. Even when the rising-above is expansive and prolonged, it is so without guarantee of continuance. Even Ward Connerly, the former University of California member of the Board of Regents who led the successful destructive attack on affirmative action, can be pulled over for "driving while black." (*CRACKING THE CORPORATE CODE — THE REVEALING SUCCESS STORIES OF 32 AFRICAN-AMERICAN EXECUTIVES*, by Price Cobbs, M.D., and Judith L. Turnock displays in detail manifestations of the *Rising Above* in Corporate America. Cobbs is also coauthor with William Grier, M.D., of *Black Rage*, a profoundly insightful and historically well-known book about America's racism.) Maya Angelou, in her poem "Still I Rise," so succinctly delineates both the historic soul of the *Rising Above* that social bludgeoning and the spirit, insightfulness and courage in African American culture applied daily to do it:

STILL I RISE

You may write me down in history
With your bitter, twisted lies,
You may trod me in the very dirt
But still, like dust, I'll rise.

Does my sassiness upset you?
Why are you beset with gloom?
'Cause I walk like I've got oil wells
Pumping in my living room.

Just like moons and like suns,
With the certainty of tides,
Just like hopes springing high,
Still I rise.

Did you want to see me broken?
Bowed head and lowered eyes?
Shoulders falling down like teardrops,
Weakened by my soulful cries.

Does my haughtiness offend you?
Don't you take it awful hard
'Cause I laugh like I've got gold mines
Diggin' in my own back yard.

You may shoot me with your words,
You may cut me with your eyes,
You may kill me with your hatefulness,
But still, like air, I'll rise.

Does my sexiness upset you?
Does it come as a surprise
That I dance like I've got diamonds
At the meeting of my thighs?

Out of the huts of history's shame
I rise
Up from a past that's rooted in pain
I rise
I'm a black ocean, leaping and wide,
Welling and swelling I bear in the tide.

Leaving behind nights of terror and fear
I rise
Into a daybreak that's wondrously clear
I rise
Bringing the gifts that my ancestors gave,
I am the dream and the hope of the slave.
I rise
I rise
I rise.

However, that continuing need for the exercise of that social, spiritual and intellectual agility raises a question: why should it have to be done?

The concept that there are *races* produces a syllogism that has strong currency in our society that influences the societal operations, including those of public agencies, e.g., public schools, and the "equal" service that ostensibly they are to render. If my *race* and your *race* are different and if our views of our society are each tied to our respective *races*, then each of us is absolved of the responsibility of seeing the world through each other's eyes because we cannot. That syllogistic bestowal to the subsistence of the *Divide* so often has the dominant *"I"* asking why *they* complain so much instead of getting *their* act together like *we* do. The other *"I"* so often does not see how *they* can claim good intentions while creating, contributing to or consistently tolerating the societal practices that damage *Us*. Limited to no experience with the other side of the *Divide* fashions the first perspective. Daily experience with the other side of the *Divide* fashions the second.

If we can't see the world as someone in another *race* does then we are left with what many public figures, e.g., Presidents Clinton and Bush (41), have pushed for: *racial tolerance*. *Racial tolerance* works if it does not presage the dominant culture giving up something it has in order for *them* to find dignity, meaning and *equality*. In education, for example, ethnic or women's studies programs or courses are tolerable unless and until one or a combination of the following occurs: 1) their existence reduces resources available for curricula and pedagogy consistent with perspectives of the dominant culture; 2) there is a push to make them required courses. There are colleges and universities of the dominant culture that have ethnic and/or women's studies. As a rule they are not required, however, except for people majoring in them. Dominant culture academic institutional interest in intensifying such academic focus is, itself, a "minority."

There is a *socially acceptable* and *politically correct* tendency in American Society today to *celebrate diversity*. Genuine sincerity in doing so is plentiful, particularly in public schools. Despite the goodness in it, that celebratory consciousness also unwittingly contributes to the *Divide*. *Diversity* tends to be defined in schools and other social circles as the sum of the inevitable differences in our varied skin pigmentations, hair textures, languages, cultures and races. Given that such variance is perceived as inevitable, this definition leads to the belief that we can never be one people, united in our multiple cultures, and the goal of social relations becomes nothing more than peaceful coexistence.

When human beings, irrespective of culture, *race*, or socio-economic-status, use the term *human race*, all of us mean "all of us." When the word *human* is excised from the term, when *race* is left by itself, none using the term mean "all of us." We all mean only *Us* and *Them*. Born in part from that conceptualizing is the long-standing *Us-And-Themness* of American Society. Sally Satel, however, in her article "Medicine's Race Problem," noted at the dawn of the 21st Century that research has " ... laid to rest the idea that *race* is a biological category." Quoting an article in the New York Times, she wrote, "'Researchers have ... unanimously declared there is only one race — the human race.'" Satel also states, "Much heralded was the finding that 99.9 percent of the human genome is the same in everyone regardless of race." "The Greatest Journey," an article by James Shreeve in the March, 2006 Issue of the National Geographic, reconfirms that race other than the *Human Race* is a *social, not* a *scientific* construct. "Perhaps the most wonderful of the stories hidden in our genes," the article notes in it's last paragraph, "is that, when unraveled, the tangled knot of our global genetic diversity today leads us all back to a recent yesterday, together in Africa."

There are exceptions in the use of the term *race.* Some who use it do so as a descriptor of prevailing social group categorizations with the conviction that the separateness among them is a function of social structure and the hegemony of a dominant culture, rather than an ineluctable biological consequence. Despite the appreciable absence on both sides of the *Divide* of consciousness about *race* being a social not scientific concept, using the term, then, brings to common parlance at least some realization of ongoing socio-cultural separateness in America. Independent of the less frequently intended use of *race* as a descriptor of current social reality, however, its predominant function as depiction of the inevitability of group separateness prevails, consistently bearing heavy social weight as both a choreographer and sustainer of the *Black/White Divide.*

Racism, then, is social action or inaction, including indifference, emanating from the belief that humanity is divided into human groups with inalterable physiological differences, corresponding variance in social perspective and related group action and reaction that justify socio-cultural group ranking and variously manifested, perpetual socio-cultural group separation. *Racism* is a social tool for justifying and maintaining a dominant group position in a social system structured of *dominance* and *subordination*. It includes but is not identical with *prejudice* or *bigotry*.

Distinguishing *Racism* from *Bigotry* or *Prejudice*

Racism contains a dominant culture capacity to create socio-cultural group consequences for those not of its rank. Individuals not of the dominant culture can exercise *bigotry* or *prejudice* against individuals of the dominant or other groups but such is radically different from being able to shape and sustain group status for them throughout America. That incapacity is not a function of cultural weakness but rather the consequence of a social system structured of *dominance* and *subordination*. No matter what prejudicial perception some people in any African American communities have of those in America who are of the dominant culture, such cannot keep low the employment and formal education rates, keep high the imprisonment rates or bludgeon the hope of people in communities of the dominant culture. Summarily proclaiming, for example, that "White people can't dance," or otherwise negatively appraising Americans who are of the dominant culture, would have no impact on the social and material benefits for Dominant America regardless of the number of citizens who are African Americans who would do so, the variety of social venues in which it was done and its frequency.

Should it have been from Europe that slaves were brought to America in the early 17th century and should they have been brought to the same social system but one created and run by people descended most recently from Africa, certainly there could come from some in the *dominant culture* an assessment that disproportionately high rates of imprisonment, poverty, dropping out of school and correspondingly low success rates in K-12 education and college enrollment for citizens who are *White* were and amalgamated consequence of "You know how they are" and "That's just the way it is."

Racism must be understood as effect, independent, even, of intentions to the contrary. Yes, there are still many who intend it. Yes, there is still the Ku Klux Klan and like organizations. Yes, the Strom Thurmonds of America and his ilk can still be praised publicly, elected to public office and supported and endorsed by many also in it. More contemporary, widespread damage is done over time, though, by the *racism* that comes from not understanding or taking no notice of the nature of *dominance* and *subordination* in American Society and the manifestations of it in the shaping and perpetuating of the *Black/White Divide.* It needs to be seen through the experiential prism of those of *Us* on the *downside* of the *Divide.* How, for analogy, should we assess the perception of a man that women should stop complaining about labor pains when they give birth? How should we consider and respond to such a perception in light of the rational conclusion that no male pregnancies are likely in the foreseeable future and, consequently, direct, personal, physical experiences with the birthing process for men are non-existent?

Social Structure, Dominance and Subordination, Assimilation — Minorities and the Non-Melting Pot

In any society to date where there are two or more cultures one of them is dominant and the other(s), consequently, subordinate. The manifestations of both *dominance* and *subordination* may vary from society to society but a critical reality remains, irrespective of the country in which they exist and of the proffering of good intentions to the contrary: the dominant culture runs the society. The dominant culture is the one that sets the rules for social operations, including inter-group interactions.

It establishes and enforces the canons for acceptable citizenship — including laws and their enforcement praxis — participation in higher education, etc. It sets the regimen and etiquette for assimilation into its ranks and the boundaries of *tolerance* for those whose social ascent — even soaring — is accomplished without assimilation. (Dr. King and Malcolm X are classic but, by far, not the only examples of doing so.) Whatever its strengths, values, mores and constructive history and irrespective of its collective courage, staying power and focused intelligence, a *subordinate culture* does not play that role in a dominant-subordinate relationship. That is so despite the individual *Rising Above* that takes place constantly. Indeed, non-dominant cultures, though, can and do set the regimen for social praxis within their own social and community boundaries.

Conceptualizing individuals as *minorities* functions as solid foundational footing for the *Divide.* Throughout America's history, its laws and prevailing societal practices have been justified by a major tenet of democracy, i.e., the majority rules. A *Majority* in that democratic context is defined by the agreement of more than 50% of a population participating in a legal decision making process on accepting or rejecting a candidate for public office or a proposed social plan, program, practice or law brought before society for decision. Being a *minority,* then, means not being of like mind with and deciding differently than the majority of citizens engaged in the process on the decision made. Being categorized as either *majority* or *minority* in that process can change from issue to issue simply by equating concurrence of an individual's position with more than or less than 50% of the fellow citizens participating in the established decision-making process on candidates, issues and/or considerations brought before them.

However, the term *minority* in this *democracy* also

means being of a *race* different than that of the dominant culture. Unlike in the popular lexicon of democracy, though, this *minority* characterization does not get removed even on those occasions when one so designated is in agreement with more than 50% of those engaged in the process with the decision made. Nor does it get removed even when the *dominant* populace is numbered less than 50% of the total population, as has been the case, for example, in California since 1999. Nor does the California *dominant culture* itself get referred to as *minority* consequent to it being less than 50% of the total population. (The August 30, 2000 article, "Census: Whites not the majority — State shift in numbers a symbolic milestone," by Tom Verdin, of the Associated Press, in *The Daily Review*, Hayward, California, delineates the reality.)

Yet, reference to *minorities* persists. The absence of numbers constituting a *majority* renders the definition of *minority* as a socio-cultural categorization of people who are, in various ways, subject to the control of the dominant culture and its system for distribution of material and social benefits. The persistence of non-numerical typecasting and related talk of *minorities* by those in the dominant culture has its social consequences, including a reduction in the inclusive prospects for this democracy.

Many of its dominant culture claim America is a *Melting Pot*, a country in which socio-cultural distinctions have been blurred to oblivion. How is it possible to claim that the melting away of such distinctions has occurred while still maintaining there are *races* and that all the humans of them are possessed of sufficient substantive differences to merit *tolerance* of variance by socio-cultural groups in access to the benefits of America's social structure, a denial of *equality* itself? How is it possible to claim that the melting away of such distinctions has occurred while still maintaining *assimilation* as a desirable and/ or needed and available practice for *some* of *Us*? Why, too, is it that the *assimilation* in this supposed *Melting Pot* is never under consideration for those of *Us* who are of the dominant culture? If *assimilation* is proffered in the *dominant culture* as desirable and/or needed — but not for itself — what does that say about the veracity of a social lexicon that includes *assimilation* and *Melting Pot?* Does it not mean, at best, that the societal invitation to *equality* has been written but not yet put in the nation's mailboxes?

Culture, Caste, Equality and Equity

Death and taxes have long been characterized in America as an inevitable duo. *Culture* necessitates the expansion of inevitabilities to a trio. Consideration of *culture* in America, though, is usually shallow, blurred or simplistic. Most often it is a fleeting reflection on language, the arts and food, and/or stereotypical summary conclusions about *their* characteristics, behaviors, etc., e.g., *they're* like that, or *they* think that way, or *they* act that way. The reality is that *no one* is born without being born into a primary culture. Each culture has its methodologies: there are no exceptions. Culture is insufficiently understood in American Society, in general, as a set of human experiences, varied in detail and nuance, none more or less human than another, which act as filters through which we see our prospects for meaning and respectful social treatment and from which we conclude the appropriateness for group affiliation.

America's disapproval for societies around the world that are organized by a *caste* system is variously intense and hypocritical. They are seen and appraised as unfair and undemocratic. A *caste* is a classification of citizens locked historically by the power of a *dominant culture* into a location in a society's hierarchy. It was the late John Ogbu, Ph.D., an Anthropologist at the University of California, Berkeley, who made it so very clear that *sub-*

ordinate or caste-like social categories exist in America for people whose primary ancestral tie is with human cultural groups that became part of the American social structure by virtue of conquest, colonialism or slavery. Given the substantial history of all three domineering practices in American history, it is hardly a surprise that the socio-cultural categories continuing to face the most prolonged fight for *equality* and over the need for *equity* to get there are Native Americans, Latinos — particularly of Mexican ancestry — and African Americans. The refusal to address the historical, contemporary and intense negative consequences of those demeaning and destructive practices does much to keep the *Divide* from being appropriately confronted.

Equality is claimed by both major American political parties as a chronicled and authentic historical descriptor of American Society, one differentiating it in varying degrees of fact and self-appraisal from most countries around the globe. *Equality* is sameness in human worth and in the corresponding human treatment, including institutionalized systems, governmental, legal and social, for enacting it. *Equality* is the absence of fixed categories of *them*. It does not call for pretense that each of us has identically the same individual characteristics, like saying, for example, that each of us is possessed of the same height, weight and talents. It does depend, though, on the inalterable conviction that human worth is based on the fact of humanness, not on the appraisal, via a sliding scale of value, of an individual's alignment or characterization with a socio-cultural-economic group.

America has an economic structure with a wide span of human assessments for determining the distribution of material worth. The process for that distribution is variously conscious and open or sub-rosa and unacknowledged. It is one thing for the structure of an economic system to assign widely varying material income values along a spectrum of complexities and consequences of income producing roles. It is another for that disproportionateness to be played out by gender and/or socio-culture group. It is of profound importance to the maintenance of the *Divide* that being on the downside of the distribution of material gain is seen only as an indication that the poor have not done what is necessary to have greater income. There is on the upside of the *Divide* no history of addressing the inevitable inequalities in America's social and economic system — another example of the power of *It's-Just-The-Way-It-Is-Itis.*

Equality is the absence of *inequity.* *Equity* is the social balance needed to address the absence of *equality* resulting from the chronic disparity in the distribution of benefits in a society. *Equity* is touted in much of Dominant American as rendering undue privilege, e.g., Affirmative Action, and, subsequently, as the antithesis of equality. *Equity* is widely accepted in that dominant social venue in much the same way that using the "F Word" would be accepted at a nursery school picnic. There is a clear distinction between one choosing not to reap the benefits of a social structure, on one hand, and, on the other hand, not securing the benefits as a consequence of the unequal inclusion in that structure of the socio-cultural-economic category of humans with which an individual is identified. It is one thing, for example, to get a bad grade in a social studies class when the lesson is about the history of the culture and social system that fashions your categorical primacy and *dominance* and is presented by the cultural methods of it. It is another to get a bad grade because of the lesson having very little, if anything, to do with the history and methods of the culture with which you identify and with its history of *subordination.* Given the social necessity for succeeding in the system as it is currently structured, neither bad grade automatically obviates all individual responsibility for it. Yet, even subliminal messages about being less worthy than others can make it easier for any human being to be less than ecstatic about pursuing the lesson. It is one thing to pursue success in a school fashioned by a social structure valuing those from whom you come and another to pursue success in school to preclude intensifying the consequences of already being less valued, of being continuously relegated to second-classness. *Equity* is the process by which systemic blockages are removed to make sure success and failure are both systematized and institutionalized equal opportunities for every one of *Us*.

Conservative, Liberal and Radical Perspectives of the *Divide* and Social Change

Both *conservatives* and *liberals* weigh in on addressing the *Black/White Divide*, on helping *minorities* address *their* problems and issues. Sincerity ripples through the efforts. The consequences often keep bad from becoming worse or worse worst — for some. Yet, despite the sincerity and the sporadic, usually short-lived, variously effected, decent consequences, the scales of social justice used are too often the same in effect, even when not intended, as those provided during election time by a company called "Spin Doctor Manufacturing." The weighing in for *conservatives* with respect to the continuing *Black/White Divide* usually proves symptomatic of severe social justice anorexia. *Liberals* also often lack the needed supply of building materials to construct a sufficiently strong social immune system that would bolster a cure for the *Divide* or, at least, fashion an unrelenting, collaborative drive for the cure with the populations suffering its consequences most.

Conservative and *liberal* perceptions of the *Divide* and what should be done about it vie for preeminence in public dialogue. That is particularly so during election time, when and where it is anticipated that the outcome may be influenced notably by voters who are people of color. *Conservative* in American Society, its politics and social structure means what the term implies: it is the striving to conserve, to keep in place a social structure including its mechanisms for distribution of its material and other social benefits. *Conservative* in America also means keeping in place the system by which those benefits accrue disproportionately to the dominant social stratum. People of that rank justify the conserving of it via an invitation to those not of it to join it. Given the invitation, then, citizens who do not become part of the social category are seen through the prism of its ranks as rejecting an honest invitation and being singularly responsible for not doing so and for the ensuing consequences. There is in conservative circles no admission that the social structure conserved inevitably contributes to the *separateness* and *inequality conservatives* claim to deplore. Citizens called "minorities" who become exceptions, particularly with respect to attaining high material benefit, are touted in *Conservative America* as indicators of the legitimacy of the system and of the righteousness of conserving it.

Thankfully, despite its failings, there is clearly merit in a positive appraisal of American Society. Indeed, there would be serious, even fatal, governmental response to writing this kind of book in many other countries in the world. (The prospects for negative governmental response, however, seem to be surfacing under America's current administration. There is an inkling of the McCarthy Era.) The "American Way" is seen as the best way in conservative circles. Substantive opposition to it, even if not to all or most of it, is seen in those circles as opposing the best and, consequently, being wrong. Historically consistent, disparately low reception of the benefits of this "best" socio-economic system by those of *Us* called "minorities" is usually seen in conservative circles as the function of flawed people and *their* choices and behavior precluding the available gain. Given that view, the *Black/White Divide* is seen as germinating from the unwillingness or inability of the people on the *downside* of it to take advantage of the assistance offered *compassionately* by those in Dominant America to join it in reaping America's benefits.

Like *conservative, liberal* is a social perspective that justifies the primacy of the "American Way." Unlike *conservative, liberal* acknowledges imperfections as the inevitable consequence of being human and, therefore, of social structures, including the "American Way." A *liberal* approach is to pick from what is seen as an available number of options for addressing the consequences of those social structure imperfections in the "American Way" and, without changing the structure, apply the selected option(s) to diminish the intensity of the consequences. That is done, though, in a Western Medicine sort of way: a prescription is provided that is intended to end some ailments, reduce or obliterate the symptom(s) of some serious infirmities locked into the recipients and, hopefully, reduce or slow negative consequences, even if the ailment persists and its complex causes go insufficiently researched and, therefore, unsatisfactorily addressed. A plethora of programmatic societal elixirs have defined *liberal* history in America.

The laws enacted for civil rights since the movement creating them have been constructive. Yet the pestilence of *racism* remains in the body of America's social structure, outweighing the effect of those laws. The election time politics professing strong interest in finding and enacting a permanent cure for what has proven to be a plague of *inequality* in America almost always fade away when the voting booths are closed. Voting often means trying to select the individual for office who offers the best sounding societal analgesics. The *racist* disease of the *Divide* persists. Usually, though, social sedatives, not cures, are what get produced for addressing the *Divide*. It is one thing to lessen symptoms, consequently helping people feel less pain while experiencing a debilitating or deadly disease. It is another to help people get through the disease, ending it in them, individually. It is yet another to end the disease, to remove it from the face of the earth and preclude its return.

The sedating effect of those social elixirs is always as fugitive as a pickpocket who leaps on a motorcycle and powers away from the scene of the crime. The pain quickly pounds back, worsened by the theft of social currency, even if it couldn't buy most of what was needed. So, the *Black/White Divide* perseveres. The most profoundly negative consequences of it remain for those of *Us* who are African American, a socio-cultural category that, despite its history and presence of intellect, spirit and courage, is synonymous in varying degrees of reality and possibility in America with the *downside* of the *Divide*. Those negative consequences are economic, educational, governmental, legal, medical and political. They are social and personal in multiple other ways as well.

Most leaders from the *upside* of the *Divide* whose political wallets are packed with the currency needed to secure major social change, who led historically and lead now while and where the negative social consequences persevere, claim not having made nor having tolerated any contributions to those consequences. But the consequences are! They persist, stay, continue, don't go away! After nearly 400 years of that persistence, the conclusion needs be drawn that nothing presently extant in American social structure has been sufficient to make the difference needed. *Radical* change is a *must* if the *Divide* and its momentous, noxious repercussions are to end. However, the categorizing of *radical* in the posts of dominant social power as contrary — if not contradictory — to the "American Way" has rendered ineffectual the intermittent efforts at effecting such change. *Conserving* or *liberalizing* a social structure that produces and maintains the *Black/White Divide* cannot be justified. Social structures, like human bodies, do not malfunction only when the spirits in them intend it. *Radical* social change is alteration in societal framework based on the reality that social structure has its own consequences, independent, even, of wide spread intentions to the contrary. To change a social structure is to change some social inevitabilities. Although *radical social change* can mean total replacement, it can also mean replacing faulty components of a systemic structure that historically and unceasingly damages those of a sociocultural category that did not create the structure, are not equally included in it and have had insufficient power to date, within its current boundaries and through its prevailing rules of operation, to change it. *Radical change* can do in a social system what heart bypass surgery or hip-replacement surgery or a kidney transplant does to a body. The body still functions after the surgery is successfully concluded but, with no loss of service to any other parts of the body, it now serves what it should have but had not and could not before. The Civil Rights Movement produced some but nowhere near enough change. The Movement was put on American History's Sociology Library shelf. That absence of collective action, contributes to the persistence of what humans in the soul of the Movement had fought so courageously to change.

Yet, because of dominant culture valuation of it as being oppositional to *its* social system, *radical change* suffers from a plague of absence in our country. This absence is based on what appears to be a wide spread conclusion among those who would either keep America's social system as it is or programmatically adjust it for its imperfections that such change is inalterably antithetical to America's core values, one of them being, of course, *equality.* That appraisal of *radical change* contributes greatly to the sustenance of the *Black/White Divide* and to the *inequality* of which it is structured.

The Violence of Indifference

The less than satisfactory pursuit of *equality* and the dearth of needed *equity* to find and keep it are sustained by the dominant, persistent inattention to them. The inattention is fashioned by *indifference. Indifference* is the powerful presence of absence. The absence in *indifference* becomes part of everything it condones. It deducts useful, even necessary, energy and focus from the social dynamism and magnetism imperative for transforming what is into what should be. Research is not required to identify the perennial *second-classness* for those of *Us* on the *downside* of the *Divide.* Nor is research necessary to clearly uncover the *violent* consequences of the creation and maintenance of the *Divide.* To say nothing, do nothing, write nothing, challenge nothing about it is *endorsement of it in effect.* Endorsement of it is — independent of any proffered intentions to the contrary — *violent.* Violence often begets varied forms of itself in response.

Violence is a lamentable reality in America, as it is in any society throughout the world. It is common in Dominant America to attribute an inclination to engage in *violence* to communities that are African American, while not necessarily to all individuals considered African American. *Violence,* though, does not play out in only one culture and it is not only physical. It is also a process of a societal structure by which the state of well-being for an individual or a socio-economic-cultural group of humans is lessened or removed without justification. A social system in which *second-classness* for socio-cultural categories of citizens is perennially sustained is a *violent* society. The insistence in Dominant America that the existence of a *second-class* is a function of a collection of insufficiencies ensconced in the people of whom it is comprised, a *minority*, is analogous to silent endorsement of social, psychological and spiritual beatings. Effecting and continuing the social bludgeoning of a socio-cultural category of humans through a supposedly unintended action, *indifference* or the absence of *equality* in a social system does not mean the resulting human damage will be reversed by that absence of destructive intention. No, the existence of this psychological, social and spiritual *violence* would not excuse physical *violence* in reaction to it. However, if the systemic social message I receive is that neither I nor the people with whom I am identified, by myself and/or throughout the social structure and its history, are valued as much as those of the dominant culture and that becoming part of that *dominance* is needed to have the best life possible, yet unceasingly impracticable, then ending the life of one among *us* and ending my own are sometimes seen as not out of the question. Rather than such being labeled *"Black-On-Black Violence,"* it might be better understood for what it is: disvalue plummeted on the disvalued. "Black" or "Race" has nothing to do with it.

Furthermore, literally or figuratively, if you are not of my community and you drive by me, a person of color, after seeing me injured and lying in the street, you have not enhanced the prospects for a caring relationship between us — even if you weren't breaking the speed limit. Such behavior does not necessarily make you a person of evil intention. Your *indifference*, though, functions well to define *Our* relationship. It also shapes my perception — and that of others in the neighborhood that witnessed the incident and many comparable ones — of the prospects of that relationship ever having its negative elements removed.

The Historic Substitution of *Good Intentions* for Results

Good intentions are the continuous shield for institutionalized inattention to the structural and persistent nature of the *Divide*. The following is analogous to the consequences for the *Divide* of that substitution of intentions for results. Imagine two adults talking outside a high school classroom during a break in a presentation they were making to students about getting a job. Shortly after the discussion begins, one of the adults sees something unusual behind a bush next to the building where they are standing. Asking the colleague to hold on for a minute, s/he looks more directly behind the bush and, with shock, finds that a handgun had been tossed there. Immediately upon picking up the gun, it is discovered that it is loaded. The two engage immediately in a conversation about reporting the find. Concern about the prospects for *violence* on campus leaps instantly to the surface of the dialogue. The one holding the gun is unfamiliar with firearms and is lightly fingering the gun to see how it feels. Yes, s/he lightly touches the trigger to see what it feels like, too. Yes, the gun goes off. However, since s/he did not intend to shoot the other person, that person cannot have a bullet in her/him or be bleeding or be in pain or be crying or be on the ground ... or be dead! Really ... ?!?

The substitution of *good intentions* in Dominant America for its inattention to the *Divide* and the *violent* results it drops on the *downside* of it largely go unacknowledged. Yet, the intended *violent* and destructive behaviors in some poor communities that are populated by humans who are African Americans are assessed by many in Dominant America as an elemental justification for the *Divide*. "Why," it is asked essentially, "would anyone in their right mind not want to be separated from people who behave like that?" Indeed, the murders and drug dealing in some such communities function neither as the heart of neighborliness nor as an invitation to consider it. However, given that the *Black/White Divide* existed before the *violence* in communities that are poor and African American began and that the forced creation of segregated communities was a profound manifestation of Dominant America's *violence* to begin with, using that *violence* in some communities that are African American as justification for the *Divide* is not only hypocritical but an additional facet of *violence* itself.

While there is not the remotest excuse for the *violence* in any communities that are African American, there are reasons for it. Is not America in full swing now from being a country with an economic system to becoming an economic system with a country? Is not the upper class growing, the middle class shrinking and poverty growing? Is not *Our* country moving from being the *United States* to being the *United E$tate$?* Where in that expansion of wealth and the national and international hegemony of America's wealthy is there any, let alone intense, concentration on addressing both the inevitability of poverty in our socio-economic structure and on the disproportionate poverty in communities of color, generally, and in communities that are African American in particular? It is about the buck. We talk about the *equality* of life in America but act in a way steadily widening the gap between words and truth. Where is that *equality,* for example, in a social system in which more money rather than the fact of life produces access to top quality health care? Where is that *equality* in a social system where people on either side of the *Divide* know and have come to accept as inevitable that one side of the *Divide* experiences its highest manifestations of "downs" and lowest "ups?" Does not anger and the willingness to risk and even end life, including one's own, get triggered today around the world and in *Our* cities in response to the arrogance of that powerful system, the disproportionate distribution of the benefits it creates and the *indifference* of most who run the system to the abiding human damage it does?

Inequality and Hybrid Economic Enterprises

Those experiences, in aggregate, often equate with lesser individual and community interest for participation in the system that recognizably produces fewer benefits and from less to no hope for *us*. Not being able to afford the car you want doesn't mean you no longer crave driving it and having those you love riding in it — anytime you want. Just because *equal* inclusion of you and yours is historically and currently lacking in a system of material production that works so well for others doesn't mean you lack the capacity to fashion a system for material benefit that is adjusted to the contextual realities of your life. Given that the only economic system that is demonstrated in America is the one possessed of that *unequal* inclusion, the principles of its operation are what are learned. Again, the elements of competition are often adjusted to the circumstantial phenomena of the communities in which the hybrid system is born. Just as is the case with America intensifying its willingness to kill others around the world for their resistance to its hegemonic pursuits, a comparable willingness is often enacted in some *hybrid* economic systems in some non-dominant communities. Whatever arguments may be proffered for the two systems being abjectly unalike in purpose and morality get lost at the grave sites of the individuals destroyed by either of them.

The reality of versions of America's economic system being sewn into the fabric of some communities that are Black and riddled with poverty is made clear by Reverend Doctor J. Alfred Smith, Sr., in his book, ON THE JERICHO ROAD. He noted the threats he faced as a consequence of actively opposing drug trafficking in the area of Oakland, California, where he has been Pastor of Allen Temple Baptist Church for decades. After he and members of the congregation had walked the streets in the community to both oppose drug dealing and to attract people to a spiritual means for rising above that method of livelihood and profit making, his office manager, Marie Johnson, was called by the head of a local drug cartel and told to pass on his threatening message to the pastor. "He said," she explained to Pastor Smith, "'you tell that preacher to stay off East 14th Street. Tell him to leave East 14th Street to us. His place is down here at the church'. Pastor Smith, he said that he and those hoodlums are going to run up in here next Sunday, drag you out of the pulpit and beat you down in front of the entire congregation. What are you going to do, Pastor?"

The details of what the Reverend Doctor Smith did are summarized so well in the reality that this threatening "leader" relinquished his profit making drug enterprise and became a custodian of the church and a very loyal member of its congregation. The Reverend Doctor Smith also makes the point about adapting an economic structure and system to the realities of the *downside* of the *Divide*. He recalls that this drug C.E.O. " ... was serious about his intentions for me. For people in his profession, the homicide of a man of God would be a simple business decision. Drug dealers are capitalists, and evangelists affect the bottom line."

In further explanation of that perspective, he writes, "Look at it like this: Mary has a $500-a-day drug habit. Mary becomes a believer. She gets help for her problem and becomes a productive, tax-paying citizen. What happens to the man who was supplying her with the drugs? Answer: he is out $2,500 a week. What happens if he loses three or four such customers?"

"Ultimately," the Reverend Doctor Smith concludes, "the drug lord doesn't care if the addict prays, fasts or stands on his head as long as the drug lord can pay for his gold car rims. However, the preacher or anyone else who tampers with his ill-gotten gains will quickly find him — or herself in trouble." Although there are undoubtedly scores of exceptions in America's economic system, what do we do with a system that has built into it the *tolerance* of those *who don't care if those not satisfactorily included in it pray, fast or stand on their heads as long as the company lords can pay for their Rolls Royces?* Indeed, what do we do with a system that professes a *compassionate tolerance* of *them* when the more profound and unspoken *tolerance* is of a system that subordinates, reduces hope for and perpetuates the *second-classness* of *them?*

Religious Contributions to the Divide

The Reverend Doctor Smith saw destructive contributions made by clergy to the lives of humans living in communities that were Black. One day, many years ago in Kansas City, Missouri, where he was born and raised, he experienced going to a church of the dominant culture for the opportunity to hear a well-known youth minister preach. He was the only human who was African American in attendance. Not long after the service began a man who was of the dominant culture slipped him a note. It said, "If you want me to arrange for you to have your own youth crusade rally please let me know." Pastor Smith noted in that message that, "My white brother was trying to wrap his bigotry in a cloak of civility, but what he was really saying was something like this: 'Nigger, don't you know that we don't even want to pray next to you and your kind. You are not welcome at gatherings such as this.'"

Pastor Smith recalls of the event that, "The organizers had been very ethnocentric in their choice of music. Although they had run an ad that said 'Everyone Is Welcome,' they chose a speaker from their culture who was prepared to speak to it alone ... I thought to myself, *What if that preacher had looked out at the lone black-eyed pea in the bowl of white rice and asked, 'Where are the rest of our black brethren?' What if he had addressed the issue of Jim Crow? Surely those Christians would have listened to one of their own.* Instead, he reinforced their evil with a silence on the matter that stank to heaven like rotted fish. By his silence the preacher was telling these people that as long as they didn't cuss, smoke or dip snuff, they could righteously belong to a society that mistreated people based on the color of their skin. He should have been ashamed of himself. I would have been.

"Wasn't there any Christian who had the courage to finally use that pulpit to denounce racism and segregation? Wasn't there a preacher anywhere who would call the powers that be into question in the name of Jesus Christ?"

All these years later, Pastor Smith observed that, "Relatively few pastors have ever read an African American history book or studied urban sociology. When racist policies displace inner-city Christians, prominent ministers skirt the issue completely, or even worse, they throw out some utterly asinine remark like 'There'll be room for everybody in heaven.'" The *violence* of *indifference* in this form gets shielded by the pretext of religious spirituality. Strange succor for the *Divide!*

The *Divide* continues. It will keep on keeping on unless and until *We*, through our multiple cultural iterations, successfully collectivize and enact an effort to replace it with an inseparable *Us*, one structured of conviction that our inalterable sameness as humans and our varied and multiple cultural methods for demonstrating it are not only not contradictory but are the foundation elements of needed and justified *hope*. That collective effort absolutely must be based in an ongoing analysis of the elements of the *Black/White Divide*. That effort must become very quickly an intensely focused effort to remove the *Divide*, in all of its elements, from the soul of *Our* nation.

Will WE?

So, how will *We* ...

Grasp the reality that *societal structure* has its own consequences;

Understand that the fundamental trigger of *racism* is the misconception that there are races other than the singular *Human Race* and that the existence of races is a scientific rather than social construct;

Rid ourselves of any concept of *race* other than the *Human Race;*

Understand racism as effect regardless of intention;

Distinguish between racism and prejudice or bigotry;

Identify the role of *prejudice* or *bigotry* and its difference from racism in the downside of the *Divide* in any summary negative appraisal of "Whites";

Make sure that the fact of racism and its destructive results in communities of people of color, generally, and communities that are African American, specifically, are understood as being ensconced in *social dominance* and not in being of the "White Race;"

Become passionately intolerant of compassionate *tolerance* as an acceptable social substitute for a *United Us* structured of all of *Our* cultures;

Understand *diversity* as alterable variance in human method and style rather than inalterable human difference;

Respond constructively to the fact of religiosity not always precluding racist and spiritually damaging practices of those affixed to it;

Understand that *Us* can be all inclusive and can successfully challenge the assumption that its opposite, *Them,* must exist.

Decide to face the realities of *dominance* and *subordination* in America and establish a unity and process to end that structure;

Face the necessity of ending the fear of and opposition to *equity* and recognize it as a requisite for equality;

Decide what we will accept as evidence that sustainable *equality* has been achieved;

Make sure that *minority* only means being with less than 50% of fellow citizens on any social issue under consideration through a legal and ethical process for doing so;

Be self-critical and socially critical of any systemic, individual or collective manifestations of *violence*, including *indifference*, and structure an ongoing means for ending it and reducing its prospects for reoccurrence to zero;

Structure public and private institutions with *integration* and relinquish forever the spinning substitution of *unsegregation* or *desegregation* for it;

Become crystal clear that integration does not require *assimilation* or the relinquishing of one's primary culture;

Develop in all social venues a means for making *good intentions* and *good results* inseparable;

Make sure the structural elements of the *Divide*, their history and presence, become content for education about what must be overcome in America's social structure and that the education occurs not only in both public and private educational institutions but also in public and private institutions serving society in general;

Collectively decide what must be conserved, liberalized or *radicalized* in American social structure if equality is to be real — then do it!

The values upon which the United States of America is built are unsurpassed for the conceptualizing of the worth of each human. America's social practices, however, don't yet match that conceptualizing. The elements of the *Divide* need to be removed in a relentless, unified, social remodeling job. It was Michael Lerner, Rabbi of Beyt Tikkun in San Francisco, Founder and Editor of *Tikkun Magazine* and author of several books, including JEWS AND BLACKS, written with Cornel West, Professor of Religion at Princeton University, who provided a critically useful perspective for making such change. I had introduced him to Pastor J. Alfred Smith and, at the pastor's invitation, Rabbi Lerner was talking one Sunday, shortly after the September 11th atrocities, to the Allen Temple Baptist Church congregation. He was describing how people were regularly threatening his life because of his support for the creation of a Palestinian State. Friends were telling him that, because he is a Rabbi, his advocacy for Palestinian statehood was *unrealistic*. It was then that Rabbi Lerner said, "Being *realistic* means that what is has to be. So," he concluded, "with respect to peace in the Middle East, maybe it's time to stop being *realistic*." So too with ending the *Black/White Divide*. It will never occur unless we are passionately willing to overcome the criticism that doing so is *unrealistic*, that the *Divide* is "just the way it is." It is only through a collective choice to be *unrealistic* that we can end what divides *Us*, in any of our cultural manifestations, before the *Divide* ends *US*. Will *WE* make the decision to do what is necessary to create the first genuine *US* since America began? Yes, the politics in America since the beginning of the 21st Century increasingly decrease hope. Still ... will *WE* rise?

CHAPTER 6

BLACK RAGE REVISITED

Ralph Gordon

DURING THE COURSE OF HISTORY, some years are more memorable than others: 1066 (the Norman Conquest), 1492 (Christopher Columbus' arrival in the Americas), 1941 (the bombing of Pearl Harbor and the entry of the U.S. into World War II) — and now 2001 (the tragic terrorist attacks on U.S. soil). The year 1968 is also etched into many of our memories as one of particular note. Since it was so tumultuous, 1968 was especially memorable, not only for America but for the world as well. Two very famous men were assassinated in this country in 1968: the Rev. Dr. Martin Luther King Jr. (fighter for human rights) and Senator Robert F. Kennedy (presidential candidate). Protesting students were significantly threatening in their attempts to overthrow the government of France. The former Soviet Union (Remember the U.S.S.R.?) invaded the then nation of Czechoslovakia. This was not only an invasion: it was a governmental overthrow and an enduring occupation. In Southeast

Asia, the United States suffered horrific losses as the Tet Offensive of the enemy (the Viet Cong) brought the Vietnam War directly into the face of the American military machine and into living rooms via television sets across the land. And, in the wake of the assassination of Dr. King, cities all over the United States experienced massive civil unrest and burned with the fires of disturbance, dissent and disruption.

In the midst of all of these global and national occurrences, a landmark book was written and first published: BLACK RAGE. This powerful work was written by two psychiatrists: Dr. Price M. Cobbs and Dr. William H. Grier. Their wise words of analysis and warning still hit home today — in another millennium that is plagued by many of the same racial problems that existed long ago. Although it was entitled BLACK RAGE, the book was written at a time when the term "Negro" had not yet faded from the screen of our lexicon. (As a matter of fact, the word "colored" wasn't far gone either.) Over forty years later, the timelessness and timeliness of the Cobbs and Grier work is in abundant evidence. This is a most unfortunate truth because one would have hoped that things would have improved much more by now. Considering the resources of this nation, racial matters should have improved substantially. But, it takes more than resources. Real change and improvement requires a concerted will and effort. The deficit of a willingness to bridge the Black/White divide in this country persists today.

The two psychiatrists employed their clinical backgrounds (including the use of case studies) to hold up a prism and take a carefully close look at the American psyche, in general, and at that of Black Americans, in particular. Their perspectives are both psychiatric and sociological. The writing in BLACK RAGE addresses matters of inter-racial conflict, intra-racial skin complexion, gender, family, health, education and vocations. What Cobbs and Grier saw in 1968 was not very pleasant. Their masterwork was a veritable portrait of pathology. These two authors and physicians uncovered a plethora of issues surrounding the matter of race in America. While writing this book (our book), Marlin and I reviewed a number of sources of information. Unquestionably, BLACK RAGE sits at the top of our list of influential material. Its sheer honesty, detailed analysis and keen insights provided us with further impetus for what we had to say. The informed perspectives of those authors — Cobbs and Grier — inspired us anew, as we moved forward in our quest for a dialogue of substance and significance on what we see as the most pressing issue facing our nation: the Black/White racial divide.

Neither one of us — Marlin nor I — is a psychiatrist or psychologist. We did not bring a clinical perspective to this task. Yet, as members of this society who think deeply about what we observe and who do not blink when we see it, we are acutely aware of the way skin pigmentation is used to determine how people are treated in this country. We see it as far more constructive to confront and to discuss this matter than to ignore it. As stated earlier, these processes and more moved us to write this book. It has been said that, for a writer, "experience is capital," a virtual mother lode to be mined. That has been quite true for us as we write what is at once an attempt to be objective yet an admittedly subjective volume. The lifetime experiences of each of us shape who we are, what we think, what we say and what we write.

Our individual backgrounds are distinctly apart: with Marlin from public education administration and myself from the world of high technology sales — him from Los Angeles and me from Philadelphia. Yet, as each of us has faced the Black/White divide, we are able to tap into a deep vein of experiences as quasi-Diogenes men, in search of honesty about this thing called "race." As did the psychiatric authors back in 1968, Marlin and I have used our perspectives and backgrounds to look closely and carefully at where our society has come to and where it appears to be heading.

BLACK RAGE deals directly with the existence of the stereotypical "angry Black man" — the historical and prototypical big fear of this nation. It is ridiculous for this country to be so fearful and so contemptuous of Black men. The damning and damaging fire is fueled on a daily basis. Black men are categorized stereotypically and singled out for harsher treatment in so many ways. Even in the hallowed halls of corporate America, where the Black woman is not particularly seen as a threat, the Black man's existence is usually an anomaly. In day-to-day life, things are even tougher. It is disingenuous to treat a person so badly and then not expect either an angry or otherwise disturbing reaction on the part of the recipient. As the Drs. Cobbs and Grier noted, the Black man in America holds a special place of anxiety in this country's collective consciousness. This is a perspective that dates back to the days of slavery, when the Black "buck" was deemed dangerous and a threat to the White female, in particular, and to the slaveholding society, in general. Today's prevalence of interracial marriages and relationships notwithstanding, these societal beliefs still simmer not far beneath the surface — energizing the Black/ White divide with a barely subliminal charge.

Cobbs and Grier did not limit their analyses to issues of Black male anger. The ire of women of color is amply detailed as well. And, the depths of other emotions are plumbed too: anxiety, hate, frustration etc. All of these feelings persist today for people of color. I can relate to this. Many times when I face clear-cut behaviors of racism and/or prejudice, I am perplexed as to why and how such maladies could persist in these supposedly modern times. Like others, I wonder what it will take to remove

the last vestiges of anachronistic and antagonistic perspectives. I wonder when we will be freed from the fear
that one more person will automatically underestimate
people of color based on their skin color. Like my forefa-
thers and foremothers, I wonder: "How long?"

I wish that my examples of stupid treatment were
limited to some backwoods person who obviously has
not had the opportunity to mature in his or her personal growth. But, these damning things happen in circles
where people are supposed to be relatively enlightened.
When attending a function, primarily populated by
Whites, a person of color is invariably asked: "How do
you know John" (the person in charge or for whom the
event is being held). The presumed answer is that you
must have worked with the person. Surely, you couldn't
actually be real friends or (God forbid!) relatives.

Another venue for these affronts occurs in the work-
place — a place where the specter of so-called affirmative
action seems to always loom. In other words, Mr. or Mrs.
Person of Color: "How did you get your job anyway?" Or,
if you're living in an area that is not dominated by "your
own kind:" "How did you find this place?" Or: "What do
you do for a living?" The inane queries themselves are
enough to cause rage to bubble to the top.

On a daily basis, those of a darker hue receive a
plethora of reminders that many in the U.S. regard them
as inferior. Sometimes it is via condescension or patroni-
zation. A number of Whites will express surprise when
a Black person speaks with sharp pronunciation, elo-
cution and eloquence. Or, when an American of African
descent accomplishes much, he or she might be labeled
as "a credit to his or her race." This insulting and con-
descending categorization is enough to prompt a reaction of rage. Racial minorities who do not cause those
in the majority to feel discomfort and/or apprehension
inspire thoughts of: "Why can't they all be like him or

her?" These perverted measuring sticks are burdensome, to say the least. They are irritating, when you consider them further. And, at worst, they can be incendiary factors. The pot of rage can readily move beyond simmering and boil over. Again I say: the wonder is that more Black people are not downright enraged in this country.

Even with all of this, Americans of African descent have no monopoly on the franchise of racial marginalization and victimization. Arab Americans, like Blacks, have learned what it's like to be damningly profiled by a nation jittery from terrorist attacks. Latinos continue in their struggles for respect and for an escape from jaundiced and stereotypical views of marginalism. Asian Americans can claim a list of discriminatory issues as well. Black Americans, perennially at the bottom of the societal totem pole, suffer from all of these ailments and more.

Grier and Cobbs' masterwork, BLACK RAGE, looked back at slavery, for some of the root causes of behavioral dysfunction in modern times. The relevance of such comparisons continues. Although the big house of the plantation has vanished from the American tableau, the presence of the so-called "house Negro" persists. These apologists for right-wing politics would have one to believe that they are thinking independently and wisely. Yet, the covers need not be peeled back far to see the puppeteer's financial strings, leading these folks in their performances in public forums. Condoleeza Rice (presidential cohort), Ward Connerly (affirmative action foe), Shelby Steele (college professor and writer), Armstrong Williams (journalist), Clarence Thomas (Supreme Court justice) and others epitomize this sad situation via their backgrounds of connection to specific interests.

Many observers — both Black and White — have marveled at how Dr. Condoleeza Rice could remain so dutifully dedicated to a presidential administration (in her roles as National Security Advisor and then Secretary

of State) that clearly shows disdain for the rights of minorities. In the meantime, a Ward Connerly persistently
puts more energy into fighting against helpful measures
for people of color than anything else. In his curious posture, all is well, the playing field is level, life is good etc.
Writers and commentators like Shelby Steele and Armstrong Williams bring intellectualism and harshness to
arguments that do great harm to their own brothers and
sisters of color. Yes, the "house Negro" has moved from
being merely a mainly benign and pitiable character. Today, he or she is an instrument of those who would deep-
en the Black/White divide by: 1) holding up these stolid
role models as symbols of racial progress while 2) using
these "house people" to perpetuate policies that not only
keep the chasm in place but widen it. Perhaps we need
the psychiatrists, Grier and Cobbs, to do psychoanalyses
on these present-day pathological folks. A diagnosis of
deep self-hatred would seem to be the probable result.

It is as if the plantation has simply morphed into a
modernized structure — replete with all of the vestiges of
the 19th century: a master (who sees himself as benevolent), house attendants (who think that they are favored
and perhaps better than their in-the-field counterparts),
overseers (whose job it is to keep the field folks in line)
and the field folks themselves (those who have not and
may not ever make it into the "big house"). This contemporary edifice yields the same results: a people divided
with conflicting perspectives on the reality of their existence. It is a malaise to be addressed and healed. It is a
divide to be bridged. It is a challenge and a goal for the
writers of this book: revisiting this massive and deleterious matter and chronicling the rage and its results of
this age.

Today, the root causes for black rage are many: continued prejudice, discrimination and racism; media depictions which make minorities marginal, simple or even

invisible; slick "conservative" appropriations of humanist terminology (for example, Ward Connerly's American Civil Rights Institute) etc. Rather than simply being enraged, we have chosen to be engaged — via the power of the written word and ensuing action. It is our prayer that four decades from now, the same murky waters will not have to be navigated by another generation of attentive authors.

CHAPTER 7

BLACK RAGE ... STILL

Marlin Foxworth, Ph.D.

WITH HIS MOUTH CLOSED, the glare in his eyes spoke articulately and succinctly for him instead. The clench in both fists uttered backup for the message. The refracted light from the all white backdrop glared a bit in a still way on his black hair and brown skin. How he stood alone, sleeves rolled up in clear purpose, said even more about his intention to face what was on both sides of him, not on his side, in front of him, not of him, in back of him but not backing him. "Come on!" his focused presence was saying. "Step to me with all your mess! I'm ready for it."

This Black Man is the figure on the cover of BLACK RAGE, the analytical and profoundly insightful book, written by Price Cobbs, M.D. and William Grier, M.D., and published first in 1968. "Two psychiatrists," begins the statement about the book on its cover, "tell it like it is — the desperation, the conflicts and the anger of the black man's life in America today!" The Black Man on that cover, though, stands across America today, still in a White backdrop, the light from it still refracting all around him. He still has to say, "Bring it to me. I'm ready for it." With only a little editorial tweaking and updating, Drs. Cobbs and Grier could have their book published as a contemporary delineation and challenge of today's Black/White Divide. The "conflicts and anger" in "the black man's life in America" about which Cobbs and Grier wrote then are not only so now but apply variously to the lives of women and families that are African American. The racism in the social structure and practices, both denied yet sustained in America, make it so ... and keep it so.

Quit Complaining and Get Your Act Together

There is a long-standing attitude locked into America's dominant culture that everything anyone needs to know about being an African American has been provided. There are, after all, Black Studies courses and departments at colleges and universities, Black Entertainment Television, t.v. series and movies about African Americans, with African American stars and some with exclusively African American casts and/or African American directors and producers. Both television and print media regularly present information about what's happening in — and sometimes to — the lives and communities of people who are African Americans. The Civil Rights Movement achieved a great deal of what it set out to, e.g., civil rights laws, including voting rights, have been passed and there is no longer formal and legalized segregation. One month of every year is designated for Black History and that's not done for any other race. We're in good shape. There is no substantive discrimination against Black people. Sure, there are exceptions but that's the point: they're exceptions, no longer the rule. People who haven't made it just need to take advantage of the opportunities to do so. Our accomplishments over the years in accepting a diverse population just need to be tweaked. Equality is a reality, one needing only refinements. If you haven't made it in America, you need to get your act together. So let's get on with it and quit the complaining.

Having such a perspective is much like confidently describing life on Mars when neither you nor anyone with whom you associate has been there. The conflict for equality in America remains. Cobbs and Grier noted 40 years ago that, "The unique quality of this conflict arises from the strength of the call for equality. All Americans feel committed to the principle of 'all men, created equal,' but it does not occupy a central position in their view of their place in America. It is a case of 'All men are born equal, but white men are more equal than anyone else.'"

Mistaken Assumption That Equality Has Been Achieved

There is an erroneous conclusion in America today that its equality, having been achieved long ago, is in good shape, needing only diminutive mending. That mistaken conclusion encapsulates knowing of the Civil Rights Movement but cannot be drawn if one were a part of it. Of that ever-present absence of sufficient knowledge, Cobbs and Grier observed:

"Americans characteristically are unwilling to think about the past. We are a future-oriented nation, and facing backward is an impediment to progress. Although these attitudes may propel us to the moon, they are deficient when human conflict needs resolution. They bring white Americans to an impasse when they claim to 'understand' black people. After all, the thoughts begin, the Negro is also an American and if he is different it is only a matter of degree. Cliches are brought forth and there is a lengthy recitation of the names of famous Negroes. Long association has bred feelings of familiarity which masquerade as knowledge. But there remain puzzles about black people; all is not understood, something is missing."

Does not that minimal familiarity, masquerading as knowledge, manifest itself variously in the 21st century? Obviously, there is no doubt that those of the dominant culture recognize Dr. King. His "I Have A Dream" speech is given replay time on television every year during Black History Month and in April in remembrance of his assassination. Indeed, it is probably played on television more than any speech by any person of the dominant culture recorded in America's history. Absent from that twice-a-year public recognition of Dr. King is any detailed dissection of the social circumstances in communities that are African American that sparked his melding of spirituality, social analysis and vision, prescriptions for change and corresponding activism. Even more tellingly absent is a nationally needed appraisal of the contemporary manifestation of the debilitating social circumstances in such communities. Just as absent is any examination and functionally preventive response to what motivates the James Earl Rays in our society to conclude that open, constructive challenges to social structure merits ending the life possessed of the perspective motivating the challenge. Why is it we have not yet identified the social elements perpetuating the ignorance required to accept violence as an appropriate vehicle for driving away values different from one's own?

Functional knowledge about the basics of operation in Dominant America is a survival requisite for a person who is African American. There are exceptions to that need, e.g., attending a church with a congregation that is African American. However, all of those exceptions in aggregate don't obviate the need to know what Americans of the dominant culture want and expect in a social system that is structured by and for them. Education, employment, law, speech patterns and politics are but a few classic illustrations. Yet, unless one were to choose to live or work in a community that is African American, survival as an American who is of the dominant culture requires no knowledge about African American experience, history, culture, or social issues. The absence of need for that knowledge does not preclude getting it. Certainly there are those in the dominant culture who want and pursue it. However, too often when the knowledge is gotten at all in Dominant America it is without needed elaboration. The significance of the experience, history, culture and issues by which any perception of Dominant America has been shaped in communities that are African American is of little to no consequence in Dominant America because how it might be seen through a socio-cultural-experiential prism that is African American necessitates neither thoughtful consideration nor change. The anomaly in that general indifference resides in the range of concern from moderate discomfort to fear in Dominant America about violent rebellions, called "riots," occurring again in urban communities that are African American, like they have periodically over the last 40 plus years. What if the violence is not contained within the geographic boundaries of the community(ies) that are African American within which the "riot" occurs? What if it spills over into *our* community?

Women Who Are African American And The Experience of the *Divide*

Women who are African American experience the downside of the *Divide* in theme, content and variation of what men experience. That is always so, independent of socio-economic status. Included in that experience is an appraisal and test of womanhood that is rarely noted for its symbolic gravity. Anyone in a setting with a large number of people who are African American cannot but notice that the majority of women in the room have straightened their hair. So doing appears to be merely a matter of style. Indeed, that variance in hairstyles would appear to most in Dominant America as comparable with that for its women. It is hardly a concern of intellectual discourse that women, like men, try to be as attractive as they can.

Cobbs and Grier, though, through the prism of the therapeutic service they have provided, observed the oft unobserved about life for a woman who is Black in America. They found that, "One aspect of the black woman's life which attracts little attention from outsiders has to do with her hair. From the time of her birth, the little girl must submit to efforts aimed at changing the appearance of her hair. When she is a babe in arms her hair is brushed and stroked, but in short order the gentle brushing gives way to more vigorous brushing and ultimately combing." Pain results from the "vigorous brushing" needed to transform the "kinky" hair into something more attuned to the standard of beauty set for women by the dominant culture. The significance resides in an accompanying negative self-appraisal. In response to the pain, Cobbs and Grier explained, "Surely the deadly logic of children would try to explain this phenomenon in some such fashion: 'If such pain is administered with such regularity by one who purports to love me, then the end result must be extremely important.' And yet, however she might search, the child will never find a reason weighty enough to justify the pain to which she must submit."

There are exceptions today, in both fact and degree, to experiencing that negative self-appraisal. Straightening hair today can derive from a genuine liking of a style. It also can be done to forestall another day's reminder that one does not and will not meet yet one more of the dominant culture's standards. Or, in theme and variation, it can come from both. Whenever that straightening comes from a negative self-appraisal, though, by itself or in tandem with any other motivation(s), it functions like a psychic hot comb. There are burns, sometimes scars. Cobbs and Grier observed that, "Long, straight hair and a fair skin have seemed to be the requirements for escaping the misery of being a black woman." That misery is not derived from any honest and objective appraisal of the fact of *blackness*. When it comes, it is from the inescapable environment in which what you are can never meet the standard of acceptability of those who have the power to set it. "In this country," Cobbs and Grier found, "the standard is the blond, blue-eyed, white-skinned girl with regular features."

Cobbs and Grier zero in even more acutely on the color bludgeon of culture dominance that helps sustain the *Black/White Divide*. "The girl who is black," they wrote, "has no option in the matter of how much she will change herself. Her blackness is the antithesis of a creamy white skin, her lips are thick, her hair is kinky and short. She is, in fact, the antithesis of American beauty. However beautiful she might be in a different setting with different standards, in this country, she is ugly." There is still access to the use of that bludgeon for all born into the dominant culture. Although it is not used by everyone who could, when it is used it effects a pummeling that both specifies and generalizes. "You, in particular," it says, "not only do not match what we know is best to see and those from whom you come are not and cannot be what is best."

Here now, in the face of that raised bludgeon, comes a regular manifestation of subtle courage, another demand to "Come on! Step to me with all your mess! I'm ready for it." So say the sisters standing together, the one with the dreadlocks, the other with cornrows, another with a natural, the other with her hair straightened only when she feels like it but never because she feels she must. This all while the dominant cultural ignorance about and indifference to the systemic nature of the burns continue.

From Plantation to Ghetto:
Cultural Hegemony And Fear Of Change

There are exceptions to that indifference in Dominant America. Some people who are of its ranks, learned and not, of religious faith and not, in positions of social and governmental significance and not, well off and not, recognize and deplore racism and the dominant cultural indifference sustaining it. Some actively oppose it. However, it persists! Undeniably, something is missing! It will remain until even those for whom racism is almost never on the radar screen come to see it as damaging them as well. It will remain until opposition to it from inside Dominant America's boundaries matches the intensity of the opposition to it from outside them. It will remain until that collaborative opposition to its sustenance by the dominant culture functions with the kind of sociopolitical alacrity that can flip a front-runner to an also-ran in an election campaign ... and keep her/him from ever running again. It will remain until we collectively get that racism in this country is a major variable in keeping it from being the model of social equality it claims to be but is not. Until then and at best, racism remains an irritant in the dominant culture. That is so more for it being spoken of, sometimes provocatively, again and again by those in other socio-cultural-economic strata than for its substantive significance for the collective experience of Dominant America. The never-ending fact of racism, often penned with historic whiteout, is a descriptor of what should have been changed but wasn't and of what may yet transform rage to a rational collective rebellion in various forms.

What Cobbs and Grier noted in the following about the handling of history in the *Black/White Divide* is here now, just as it was then.

"History is forgotten. There is little record of the first Africans brought to this country. They were stripped of everything. A calculated cruelty was begun, designed to crush their spirit. After they were settled in the white man's land, the malice continued. When slavery ended and large-scale physical abuse was discontinued, it was supplanted by different but equally damaging abuse. The cruelty continued unabated in thoughts, feelings, intimidation and occasional lynching. Black people were consigned to a place outside the human family and the whip of the plantation was replaced by the boundaries of the ghetto."

Cobbs and Grier assessed that, "The worst slum and the best slum are very close together compared with the distance separating the world of black men and the world of whites." The conclusion that "we're in good shape" gets slammed into the historical trash bin of social perception by the simple fact that there are still ghettos. They have expanded. Their significance lies in large part in the important distinction between choosing to live in a location filled with people of one's primary culture and having to do so, generation after generation, because of the tie between racism and the disproportionately high poverty fixed in communities that are African American. Cobbs and Grier described a related trend that continues today. "There is a dread," they pointed out, "that Negroes will impoverish the country by proliferating on welfare rolls. Recently there has been a fear that they will gain political control of the cities now that whites are fleeing to the suburbs. No one can doubt that the white American is afraid." Something is missing.

Ending that fear can come only from ending the socio-political-economic circumstances and structure that create ghettos and, therefore, ending ghettos. Ending ghettos, though, cannot come from a continuing dominant cultural perception that their existence is a function of residents in them not making the decisions necessary to enable them to move out, on and up. There is also an element of that perception that the durability of ghettos is symptomatic of their inevitability. The presumptive assurance that ghettos will continue shapes the classic and enduring conclusion that it is impractical, let alone wasteful, even un-American, to focus public fiscal and human resources on structuring a social system without them. Consistent with that judgment is the willingness to focus private resources — a "compassionate" rendering of them — on assisting individuals with the willingness and commitment to leave the ghettos to do so.

Given the history of the abject uselessness of such "compassionate" assistance to identifying, admitting and stopping systemic contributions to creating and sustaining ghettos, ending them can come only from active social recognition, all the more in the dominant culture, that placing the practical before the idealistic is antithetical to progress. Ending the existence of ghettos should not be a function of required assimilation. It should be the result of a successful political, cultural, spiritual and economic commitment to political, cultural, spiritual and economic equality, to the equity needed to achieve it and to the right and power to choose and build communities structured of that equality. Thus, ending the existence of ghettos must be understood for the threat it would provide to the cultural integrity and hegemony of the dominant culture.

Ghettos continue as powerful remnants of the destructive spirit that first dragged humans who were Africans over the Middle Passage to the colonies. Cobbs and Grier simply identified a significant variable in the continuity of that spirit, in its virile generationalizing of the *Black/White Divide*, when they wrote, "For white America to understand the life of the black man, it must recognize that so much time has passed and so little has

changed." Any contemporary denial that such is the case
is necessarily based on missing the reality that racism
has transformed — although certainly not entirely —
from a function of conscious intent to the effect of indifference without readily discernible methods. An effect of
that effect is negation of any consciousness of its nexus
with racism. Consequently, such denial concludes that
one cannot be a contributor to and need not attempt to
resolve a problem that does not exist.

In terms of perennial second-classness, however, something as simple as a five minute drive-through in any
ghetto today will make it abundantly clear that over the
time that has passed since Cobbs and Grier wrote BLACK
RAGE so little has changed about so little having changed.
In 1968, they almost prophetically described the contemporary otherness in the ghetto. "The viciousness of
life in America for black men," they explained, "makes
them remove themselves even further. If I establish first
that I am a stranger in your land, I will at least avoid
the shock of being attacked in my own home by kinfolk.
We are strangers and I dwell for a while in your world —
therefore, whatever you do to me cannot truly come as a
surprise."

Any present-day denial of the continuity of that viciousness must derive from the perception that "viciousness" is manifested only in physical violence that is
intended. If, then, one did not directly enact the violence,
one cannot be held responsible for it. Given that lynch-
ings have almost stopped entirely and that racist physical assaults by police on people who are African American
have subsided, viciousness so defined certainly cannot
be compared today with its forbearers in the 60s. If, on
the other hand, violence is defined as a systemic social
function producing both the removal of socio-cultural
categories of human beings from a state of well being
and the tolerance of that removal by human beings not

likewise impacted, the viciousness and its intensity continue. That systemic removal from a state of well-being is structured by never-ending, disproportionate, systemic negative consequences for people who are African American. Poverty resides disproportionately in the ghetto. The system of K-12 public education continuously produces lower indicators of academic achievement, corresponding disproportionately low enrollment in higher education and disproportionately high suspension, expulsion and dropout rates for people who are African American. Disproportionately high imprisonment and length of prison sentences are a long standing reality for people who are African American. These and multiple other comparable results, even absent propelling intention, are vicious. Anger, even rage? How could it not be?

Need For Radical Change But Tolerance For Only Conservative And Liberal Responses

That viciousness is exacerbated by the reality that the only responses ever applied or tolerated by the dominant culture to these systemic results are conservative or liberal when it is radical change that is needed. The viciousness of the social environment is magnified when many of those benefiting most from the system, i.e., citizens of the dominant culture, characterize the disproportionate downside data to be the result of people the numbers represent not yet having taken advantage of a good system. To conserve that system, the benefactors of it variously employ the related power to admonish those they see as not taking advantage of the system to do so. There is no admission of systemic flaw in the process. It says, in effect, "We have to work to make the system function positively for ourselves. You should do no less." The magnification of viciousness is comparably enhanced when others of the dominant culture see only various and sundry forms of programmatic tweaking as the needed and, therefore, acceptable solution. Such tweaking has been liberally endorsed for the assistance it has provided individuals for generations despite the reality that the social conditions seen as prompting the tweaking have remained fixed in our social structure and system for each year of those same generations. They have not, cannot and will not be tweaked away in a social system structured of the elements to which the tweaking is continually applied while never ending the social realities for which it ostensibly is done.

A push for radical change is taken in conservative and liberal circles as irreversible commitment to totally replacing the present social system with one structured from the perspective of the left — as such, a threat. However, social structures, like human bodies, do not malfunction only when the spirits in them intend it. Conserving a social structure preserves its consequences. Tweaking the social structure in ways that never create and lock into the system the ostensibly intended equality functions as a guarantee that the rage that has been will be. Without needed radical change, we'll keep getting what we've kept getting. What rage then, in what form(s), with what consequences, with what reactions from those experiencing it and those not?"

The 'No Longer Officially Enslaved' And Language

Cobbs and Grier identified an elemental, historical facet of American social structure when they wrote, "The black man was brought to this country forcibly and was completely cut off from his past. He was robbed of language and culture. He was forbidden to be an African and never allowed to be an American." The upset in the late 90s over the effort in the Oakland Unified School District to accept what it called Ebonics as acceptable language is an exemplar of the staying power of the triggers of Black Rage. The criticism from both communities of the dominant culture and those that are African American of Superintendent Carolyn Getridge and the board of education for their support of Ebonics generally took two forms. The first, more African American than Dominant American, was that the process for addressing the issue was more a tactic than a strategy and, consequently, should have been thought through more carefully before it was launched. The second, more Dominant American than African American, was that Ebonics was nothing more than bastardized English and, consequently, should not have been given the slightest attention as a legitimate educational consideration.

The negative appraisal of Ebonics as mutilated English and unjustifiable focus for a school district begs the question about what constitutes a language. If a language is a human system of sound that has meaning, rules for its use, a span of tolerable exceptions to their application, with requirements for which cultural groups are to use it, including its dialects, as defined and set in place by the dominant culture in a social system, then the objection to Ebonics could be rendered without objection. If, on the other hand, language is all of the above with the exception that it be defined and set in place by any culture or subculture for its own use, not as required by the dominant culture, then the objection to the effort at recognizing Ebonics needs to be seen for its acceptance of and/or contribution to the cultural preeminence of Dominant America.

After what was called "emancipation," it was necessary for survival that the humans who had been enslaved be able to speak to each other, particularly against oppression in a society modified from slavery to segregation, without incurring the wrath of the former slave owners and other segregationists in the dominant culture. Although not called "Ebonics" by them, Cobbs and Grier, address the development of a patois among ex-slaves after the technical end of slavery. They noted that such language provided a " ... circumlocution so necessary to the beleaguered blacks it became a more refined art." They considered the following about the utility of such patois up to the late 1960s:

"If we are willing to agree that the primary adaptive purpose of the patois during slavery is no longer functional — that is, conspiracies and escapes are no longer discussed in words of double meaning — and if also it is clear that the patois now brands its user with a great many negative attributes, and if further we appreciate the ease with which a more generally acceptable manner of speech can be acquired, we must then look for other explanations for the continuation of the patois in general usage among blacks. Explanations are likely to be found in the unconscious usages to which such speech is put.

"In this sense one important unconscious use of the patois rests on the Negro's perception, and, in fact, his white confrere's perception as well, that the true status of the races in the United States at this time is that Negroes are regarded as slaves who are no longer officially enslaved. In this light the same attitudes exist on the part of the white majority toward the black minority and the hostility and aggression which the white potentially feels toward the black must be dealt with by Negroes who seek to live in this country. The patois, then, may continue to serve the purpose it served originally during the period of enslavement."

Cobbs and Grier point out " ... the patois continues to serve an adaptive function even though the circumstances to which adaptation must be made are less clear-cut and the nature of the adaptation itself may be unconscious." "Still," they find, "driven to this verbal depreciation, the black man puts the patois again to his own uses. The 'jive' language and the 'hip' language, while presented in a way that whites look upon simply as a quaint ethnic peculiarity, is used as a secret language to communicate the hostility of blacks for whites, and great delight is taken by blacks when whites are confounded by the language." Does not such language, triggered by comparable social, exclusionary circumstances, with purposes beyond hostility, including prideful self-definition, exist today?

Fruitful discussions about a focus on Ebonics might have been ongoing had the objection derived from concern that needed time and energy not be lost from concentration on developing proficiency with America's dominant language, rather than from having concluded, without discussion, that Ebonics was illegitimate. That appraisal of Ebonics as "illegitimate" denied both some historic and contemporaneous institutional concentration on the primary culture of a student who is African American and might use the dialect. Rather than being "robbed of language and culture," s/he was denied institutional focus on them. Rather than being "...forbidden to be an African and never allowed to be an American," s/he was indirectly told that being a human who is African American who speaks Ebonics, even if using Standard (read "dominant") English in school and a variety of other social venues, lacked requisite significance for institutional concentration. Being simply an American, then, would be expected, despite the reality that there has been no mechanism throughout America's history that would inalterably and equally produce that result for people not of its dominant rank. Ironically, the prospects for students of the dominant culture to learn something more about the diversity so often talked about in public schools were also denied them in the process.

Assumptions, Conscious And Unconscious Messages, Education And The *Divide*

"Children," noted psychiatrists Cobbs and Grier, "are responsive to the expectations of their environment. They read clearly both the conscious and the unconscious message." The contradiction between the assertion of many in the dominant cultural today that skin color is no longer significant and the reality of skin color as a prevailing assumptive social prompt remains a forceful buoy of the *Black/White Divide* in America. Children who are African American today learn quickly that the fact of skin color is an inalterable component, often more so than the fact of humanness, in dominant cultural assessments of their mights, coulds, can'ts, won'ts, watch-out-fors or don't-sweat-its.

The historical and present connection between dominant cultural assessments in public education of students who are African American and the capacity of students to read the corresponding messages are cemented into the ongoing disaggregated data on the indicators of academic achievement showing students who are of the dominant culture consistently above students who are African American. Cobbs and Grier found that, "One of the keystones in white America's justification of its exploitation of black people is the assumption that black men are stupid." There are exceptions to making such an assumption among teachers who are of the dominant culture. However, whatever the number of them, it has been insufficient to demand, achieve and institutionalize in public education the end to the more subtle contemporary manifestations of that assumptive bigotry. Administrators in schools with students who are African American will experience little to no initiative or supportive insistence on the part of most teachers to address the issue in any way other than through participation in Black History Month activities, almost all of which are superficial, official noblesse oblige and require no analysis of the realities of life as a student and citizen who is African American. Teachers who are willing to address the issue are just as likely to experience the absence of initiative and supportive insistence from the ranks of administrators. Cobbs and Grier described realities then that are here now for students who are African American: "For him the long process of education is something akin to the trial of a long-distance runner who is occasionally peppered with buckshot; he may complete the race but it will take something out of him." The historic, collective courage to stay in the race begs wonderment about what could happen in American public schools and society if both the present-day social and instructional equivalents of buckshot and the weapons to fire them were excised from and forbidden to return to the arena of public education.

Then and now are melded so clearly in Cobbs' and Grier's finding that a child who is African American " ... finds himself in a world when even his own parents can barely see beyond the color of his skin. It is as if he yells and waves his arms but no one notices him; everyone sees only his dark cloak. The process of learning, a uniquely personal event under any circumstances, becomes for this child a lonely task, in which his triumphs pass unnoticed and any idle act may bring down a rain of admonition to do better, along with poorly concealed contempt."

There is today in public education no institutionalized functional effort to address the reality that students who are African American represent a percentage of the suspensions and dropouts from school that is consistently higher than the percentage of total enrollment for the same socio-cultural category of students. The converse is so often also true with respect to data on the positives. For example, it is not unusual when disaggregating school district data to find our students who are African American to be consistently on the downside when it comes to things like grades, enrollment in Gifted and Talented Education (G.A.T.E.) courses, college enrollment, etc. The imbalance is often more the case for males than for females. At the same time, the imbalance for students who are female and African American is so very often found to be closer to that of males who are African American than is the case for either gender in any other socio-cultural group.

Heating the Rage and Prolonging the *Divide*

Cobbs and Grier rendered timeless assessments of circumstances in African American life that heat the rage and prolong the *Black/White Divide*. They wrote: "Today black boys are admonished not to be a 'bad nigger.' No description need be offered; every black child knows what is meant. They are angry and hostile. They strike fear into everyone with their uncompromising rejection of restraint or inhibition. They may seem at one moment meek and compromised — and in the next a terrifying killer. Because of his experience in this country, every black man harbors a potential bad nigger inside him. He must ignore this inner man. The bad nigger is bad because he has been required to renounce his manhood to save his life. The more one approaches the American ideal of respectability, the more this hostility must be repressed. The bad nigger is a defiant nigger, a reminder of what manhood could be."

Though the requirement " ... to renounce his manhood to save his life" persists today in many communities that are African American, the converse has increased and is being displayed steadily in African American urban communities. Through the killing of men who are African American by men who are African American, the requirement is sometimes to renounce his life to save his manhood. The man on the cover of today's Black Rage, living in the ghetto, not seeing any prospect for constructive change, confronted by himself, literally, and himself in the iterations of others, cursed and called "nigger" by those he curses and calls "nigger" is saying *still*, "Come on! Step to me with all your mess! I'm ready for it." And step to him he does.

For many, particularly young men, the ghetto has become a freeway with no readily detectable off ramp. There are intended destinations but they are always around the curve. Often your life is risked by someone in the lane next to you who swings over in front of you without signaling you that s/he was coming. Often your life is risked by someone in the lane behind you, riding your tail so close s/he would have to crash into you if you touched your brakes even for a second. Often manhood in the ghetto calls for responding to the risks by reciprocating them. Knowing that one's life does not match the criteria for significance in what you see and hear about life outside of the ghetto — where the big time scrilla and the fancy cribs are — does not mean that the crest of manhood cannot be reached as defined within the ghetto's boundaries. Sometimes that definition includes the willingness to risk the ending of one's life or that of another's in confronting confrontation. It's better to get got than to get stepped to. Life goes then. Manhood does not.

"Black men," observed Cobbs and Grier, "fight one another, do violence to property, do hurtful things to themselves while nursing growing hatred for the system which oppresses and humiliates them. Their manhood is tested daily. As one patient expressed it: 'The black man in this country fights the main event in Madison Square Garden every day.'"

Those elements of life in the hood did not become so deeply rooted there because of the annual, perennial, generational selection of them by residents. They were not picked from a wide and attractive range of monetary, educational, political, employment and housing options in a social structure shaped of equality. The ghetto was not fashioned via the enactment of a strategy for community building carefully thought out by people who wanted to reside there. The ghetto was not shaped by inalterable intellectual ineptitude and commitment to social malfeasance being locked into the essence of being African American. Those elements of life in the hood are the consequence of America's social structure, the dodging political acumen of the powerful in its dominant element and the ignorance and indifference there about the daily realities faced by those who are not of it. The lack of caring as personified in the absence of collective action needed to constructively alter America's social structure reproduces itself in the humans from both ends of the spectrum. The reciprocating effect of that lack and absence dwells in theme and variation of a sense that I can ill afford to care that you don't care. That sense has two gross manifestations: 1) The fact that you don't care cannot be allowed to impede my continuing to receive the benefits of this social system as it is structured today; 2) The fact that you don't care cannot be allowed to impede my continuing to survive in this social system as it is structured today.

The sustenance of the *Black/White Divide* by the dominant culture does not obviate responsibility for it in communities that are African American, even in the ghetto. It does take, however, greater courage to survive in a social system structured, in part, with blockages to the advancement of one's self, family and primary culture, than it does to tweak a system structured for the advancement of one's self, family and primary culture. "He lives in a large city," Cobbs and Grier wrote of the black man in the ghetto, "but he shares his insight with every black child in this country. He must devise individual ways to meet group problems. He must find compensations, whether healthy or unhealthy. There must be a tremendous expenditure of psychic energy to cushion the shock of learning that he is denied what other men around him have. When he states his desire to attack a white man, he consciously acknowledges his wish to attack those who keep him powerless."

In a distinction they observed between Black and White power, Cobbs and Grier noted that, "Whereas the white man regards his manhood as an ordained right, the black man is engaged in a never-ending battle for its possession." That distinction in the nature of power in America is, itself, as powerfully descriptive today of the context in which the struggle for equality continues as it was then. The dominant cultural insistence that humans who are African Americans take total responsibility for the perpetuation of negative conditions in poor African American communities is, in part, a denial of the historical progression of racism. It has bumped its way from slavery to legalized segregation, to contemporary, extra-legal segregation. It has strolled from the exclusion of African American historical contributions and cultural methods in the goals, focus and operation of this country's social institutions to superficial acknowledgement of them — usually just during February each year.

Some sense, however, is to be derived from that insistence. It resides, though, not in its justification but rather in the need to take on the task in an environment where self-preservation is the best — if not the only — assurance of any preservation. Equity, in the context of needed social justice, is still only a word in an American dictionary. Equality is a sine-qua-non in the lexicon of Dominant America's self-appraisal and national and international political advertising. However, absent either of those concepts being pistons that actively, successfully drive the engine of needed social change in America, it makes sense for people on the downside of the *Black/White Divide* to learn how to adapt to that social system. Rising above it does not end it; it does keep it from ending you.

If this is to be a nation filled with a variety of cultures, including those invited and those having gotten here without choosing to do so, steeped in the truth of equality rather than cloaked in the pretense of it, given to the provision of various social, institutional and governmental manifestations of equity in justified response to historical and contemporary abuse of some of Us by some of Us and to the institutionalized consequences, We must address the applicability today of an observation Cobbs and Grier made in the 60s:

"The white man tried to justify the lot of the slave in many ways. One explanation made the slave a simple child who needed the protective guardianship of a benevolent parent. For many whites this distortion has persisted to the present. A modern version holds that black people are little different from other citizens save for a paucity of education and money. The observer is left with the comfortable feeling that blacks are stunted in growth, have profligate ways, and are uninterested in learning. This attitude obscures the multitude of wrongs and the ruthless oppression of blacks, from slavery to now."

That social camouflaging, described so well by Cobbs and Grier, persists. We are not through with either Black Rage or the *Black/White Divide*. Those of Us on the upside of the *Divide*, where there remains the power to keep it in place, will have to be willing to own up to the contemporary versions of that separateness and to Our sustaining indifference to it. Then We must be willing absolutely to walk across the *Divide* and work in daily collaboration with those of Us on the other side until what We must have as a nation together is made real, until there is no *Divide* across which any of Us must ever walk again. What Cobbs and Grier posed as critical to the solution in the 60s begs our attention now: "When all the repressive forces fail and aggression erupts, it is vital that we ask the right questions. The issue is not what caused the riots of the past few years — it doesn't require the perceptiveness of a genius to know. Rather, we must ask: What held this aggression in check for so long and what is the nature of this breached barrier."

The risk of social eruptions is nurtured by the inattention in Dominant America to the real structural elements of the *Black/White Divide*. Absent answers to questions about why and how it continues and the actions to end and replace it with an Equal Us, one structured of all Our cultural iterations, *We* await the next Rodney King and a comparable social explosion over unaddressed issues and the prevailing indifference in Dominant America to facing them.

Black Rage ... still. It will continue until a new rage engulfs a majority of Us in America, irrespective of individual culture and its history, over why WE continue to let this happen to US.

CHAPTER 8

WHO ARE THE REAL ROLE MODELS FOR OUR CHILDREN

Ralph Gordon

IN TODAY'S INNER CITIES, many of our children look up to various kinds of people for inspiration, motivation and for leadership. The role model category is heavily populated with rappers, athletes, and other entertainers. These children also look to neighborhood persons of dubious prominence (often via ill-gotten gains). Yes, these are the real role models for far too many of our children today.

It is a sad commentary that so many of the role models are not chosen from within the family of the child or from positive, close adult acquaintances. It is as if the child must reach out to some unattainable figure for someone to look up to. Often the characteristics of those individuals are hardly targets for really good growth on the part of the child.

Looking up to athletes has almost always been a part of the American psyche for growing up. Kids naturally have high regard for the stars in their chosen sports. Yet, it is one thing to have high esteem for star athletes. It is quite another to model one's behaviors after sports figures and to target one's aspirations in the directions of these icons. A clear example of such misguided ambition is the place of admiration that professional basketball holds in so many underprivileged neighborhoods. Far too many boys in the "hood" (and no small number of girls, thanks perhaps to the growth of the WNBA) seem to think that dribbling and shooting a basketball will be a guaranteed ticket to fame and fortune — with not a great need to really learn how to do much of anything else.

First of all, the chances of even being chosen to play for pay — in any sport — are miniscule. The odds may not be as long as they are for winning big in the lottery. However, a skilled gambler would hardly place this kind of bet. Pity the poor kids who think that they are likely to do well along this unlikely route to being successful and making big bucks.

America encourages this fantasy by pulling more and more lower-income children out of schools earlier and earlier, primarily to populate the ranks of the National Basketball Association (NBA). The washout rate for draftees in any sport is high and the NBA is no exception. When a draftee does not perform up to par, as is the case more often than not, the big money of that professional sport can disappear quickly. The effects of this fall from grace and wealth can be devastating. This is true because the premature professional athlete has usually not been prepared to do anything else other than to play ball. He probably hasn't done that well academically in high school — further limiting his chances to advance. All the while that the aspiring "b'ball" athlete is focusing on the dream, he should acquire as much schooling as possible. But, the NBA engine runs powerfully and inexorably, in conjunction with the shoe sponsors. Education is hardly a priority for these procurers and backers. Therefore, this plucking of youth (mainly from inner city school systems) continues. To maximize the success of these efforts, the role model athletes are plastered in front of millions of gullible young eyes, especially in depressed and distressed neighborhoods across the land.

A fairly close look at many of the role model athletes shows individuals who might seem to be ready for professional sports but who come up short in a number of other areas of life. The off-the-playing-field mishaps of so many jocks are testaments to this fact. The message remains that these role models can still make it big — in spite of their run-ins with the law and/or their boorish personal behaviors.

All of this goes against the grain of what was detailed in Richard Wright's classic novel, NATIVE SON. There, we saw the protagonist, Bigger Thomas, as one who had not had the experience of going outside of his own inner city community. While accompanying his mother to her job in the outside world, Bigger inadvertently commits a heinous crime and suffers a harsh fate, mainly because he was ill equipped to deal effectively with the new and different environment into which he had been placed. So it often is with the instant millionaires who skip so many maturational steps en route to stardom and wealth. And, we wonder why these nouveau riche players run into so much trouble.

Another cluster of role models for our youth — particularly those who are economically disadvantaged — is made up of rappers. When more affluent kids look up to rappers, they typically follow a path of adopting the apparel and affecting the mannerisms of the hip hop culture. But, the upper income children don't abandon their studies in exchange for the borrowed cultural clothing and styles. Academic achievement is not usually a casualty in these situations. The parroting behavior can simply represent a phase in the growing up process. The hip hop wannabe hardly aspires to being a rapper as a career goal. For those who are much lower on the economic scale, however, things are dramatically different. Absent sufficient motivation for reaching other career goals, the hip hop celebrity stands on a pedestal of seeming reality and attainment for the underprivileged youth. With that goal firmly in place, the need for any academic excellence is regarded as unnecessary and even distracting.

Regardless of the economic standing of the aspirant, in a consideration of the rapper (as with the professional athlete), the model can fall far short of a high aim. A number of rappers have a misogynous message of degradation when talking about women of color — the very women whom the youth need to respect and honor. No women should be associated with terms denoting female dogs or prostitutes — especially those who are demeaned in so many other societal ways. Many of our young people learn the lingo of veritable verbal abuse early — and then believe that it is not only acceptable but normal and preferable. What a standard this is for our young people. Even when the message of the rapper is not damning and damaging, one should question the efficacy of this entertainer model as a goal for our children. A musical culture that promotes belligerent posturing is hardly the best inspiration for young people. And, it cannot be ignored as a causative factor for the frequently resulting violence at rap concerts and even in the everyday lives of many of the performers.

The culture of rappers has yet another claim to fame. Here, we see younger and younger folks being brought into the spotlight. It now seems to be commonly acceptable that the youngest of our kids can embark on a rapping career as soon as they wish. Shouldn't children learn how to speak and communicate effectively and properly before rapping fluidly? And besides, what are the chances of the average person making it in life as an entertainer anyway? The odds can't be much better than the situation with professional basketball.

All of this role model focus on athletes and rappers feeds right into the stereotypes that are set for youngsters of color in particular, and for many minority adults as well. Provincial and racist American notions are quite comfortable with Black males in the roles of sports figures and entertainers. A tall African American male must be a basketball player, right? A young, Black rapper is now a fixture on the public stage — even giving birth to a growing number of cool, White rappers.

Some national polls have shown that most young people in the U.S. regard either their parents or their teachers as their role models. It would be interesting to see these poll results broken down demographically. The count would certainly be different for economically disadvantaged youth — many of whom lack the presence of at least one of their birth parents in their lives. For those children where neither the school nor the home is the primary source of inspiration, the seemingly traditional paradigm is turned upside down. This is especially true for those who either live mainly in the streets or have a virtual existence that is seated in the fantasy world of athletes and other entertainment figures. To apply conventional testing and polling results to such a population is to act as if all American children emanate from a fictional nuclear family on Main Street.

Unfortunately, the real role models for a vast number of our children are drawn from a pool that is hardly nourishing for their growth: professional athletes, rappers and other entertainers. The paths of these emblematic figures lead so many of our kids into the fantasyland of wholly unrealistic aspirations, neglected education, abusive behaviors and a failure to attain a vast array of crucial life skills. Parents, educators, mentors, spiritual leaders and others must move to counteract the misguided images that so many young people possess today. Positive and constructive role models must effectively be put forth. They must step forward. Children need to see that the odds in life are much more favorable for them when realistic and wholly attainable careers and goals are sought after. And, no matter what the aspiration, a sound education should always be obtained and ready for use. Kids should aim high but at targets that are not based on a mere pipe dream of rarely reached stardom. We should let our youth know that it is better to be a rising star and then a shining one in the real world than it is to be a shooting star for just a moment in the unreal world.

It is tough to turn a tide. The powerful influence of idealistic role models is strong. But, the job can be done — one life at a time — by the presence and actions of real role models for our children.

CHAPTER 9

ROLE MODELS

Marlin Foxworth, Ph.D

OFTEN USED WORDS and phrases in the American political and social lexicon easily become clichés. "Role Model" is a case in point. Decades ago the term wasn't even used. There was just social consciousness about humans who regularly manifested behavior steeped in constructive human values. There were those special people, in any generation, who rose above conflict and, when demeaned, even attacked, would not react in kind. Those were people inalterably convinced of the universal value of human life, people not locked into prejudicially employing culture, ethnicity, gender, socioeconomic status and what is called "race" as tools to assess the worth of another.

Back then role model wasn't a position for which you applied. An individual became one without being conscious that it was happening. S/he did what shined bright light on the dictionary of human meaning and, by so doing, attracted others to the prospects of behaving the same way. Talk and action for such models were inextricably tied and language and phraseology were not elements of verbal and written deviousness. What was said or written was the product of a valued merger of belief and commitment to others.

Obviously contemporary television has profoundly influenced what behavior our young people see as meriting imitation. Pursuit of profit is the foundation of what is produced on commercial television, despite whatever other constructive intentions there may be in the process. Comments are made throughout the field of K-12 education about the negative influence of television on young people. What is usually missed in the analysis and appraisal of that influence, however, is the likelihood that commercials are more momentous than the programs funded by them in structuring the vision of young people about the preeminence of material possession in the hierarchy of American values. In doing so, those commercials are also a profound impetus for a young person's search for the methods needed to get the things desired. The older of the young often model for the youngest how to do it. Sometimes following what is modeled produces loss, including loss of life in communities long riveted with poverty. In communities where there is middle to high levels of material wealth, what is shown as desirable can, simply, be purchased most often. In those neighborhoods the loss to constructive human value deriving from readily satisfied attachment to the material and to related privilege is much more difficult to discern and address. Police don't roam the streets looking for it.

Today in America the pursuit of material possessions and of the behavior needed to do so very clearly overpowers the pursuit of universal human meaning in the structuring of models for our young people to imitate. The success of such models sends many kids scurrying for the means to secure what they are skillfully shown is best to possess. Poverty does not preclude a young person's interest in pursuing that possession. If the legal fiscal means to acquire what has been shown as enviable to possess aren't readily available in a community it doesn't mean the desire for such possessions goes away. Within the parameters of a community, then, models can be found for securing, extra-legally or illegally, what has been identified as both desirable to own and to be known for owning.

The use of extra-legal or illegal means for securing what has been demonstrated as desirable to possess is often attributed to poor communities of color. The attribution language is often part of racist palaver, usually denied as such. For example: "Why is there so much crime in the Black community?" The inference from such talk is that there is something inherent in being African American that produces inordinately high crime rates. It is almost always the case that those in the businesses given to attracting the young to material possessions do absolutely nothing to address the growing inequities in the economic structure and practices that proffer the attraction. The point made by most businesses and corporations is simple: to make money and enhance profit, the product has to be made attractive. To make it attractive, it needs to be modeled. To demonstrate the absence of prejudicial perspectives, people of color are sometimes used to model the product. If someone is attracted to it but can't afford it, that's on them. If poor communities of color can afford the product least, that's on them. Disclaimers like the following are used to address those realities: "We don't want that but there is nothing we can do about it."

Young people can certainly learn of the acceptability of silence when it is modeled for them daily. In government, churches and education, as well as in the corporate world, far more modeling is done via the absence of purposeful action than because of it. Too often those who have climbed over racist social inhibitors to positions of social responsibility, in roles with large public recognition, do more to sustain the position and the material/social benefits it provides them than they do to address altering the system over which they had to climb. The message from such lost prospective role models is consistently apparent, although almost never frankly spoken: "I had to go through hell to get here and I'm not going to let anything mess that up!" For sure, the models of silent inaction scream a message to our children that the intense work needed to end poverty, racism, sexism and violence cannot be done or is not worth pursuing. The wordless stillness also lets our children know that if the means for securing what is desirable materially are not readily available, they are on their own to figure out how to do it. Many do ... many do not ... regardless of the cultural prisms through which the utility of material gain may be seen.

The bigotry, silent or outspoken, does not preclude intelligence and inventiveness on the part of humans against whom the prejudice is wrought. Such is so irrespective of the culture or ethnicity of the humans in any environment on the receiving end of the historic and seemingly intractable demeaning in America's social system. A small number learn to seek material benefits like those of the system from which they have been excluded by creating or becoming part of a system-modeled-after-the-system, one also with material gain as its primary, if not exclusive, goal and with comparable means for opposing and/or ending competition. Drug trafficking organizations and individuals are classic examples of that reality at its worst.

Our young cannot help but hear and see the television news the adults in the household access daily. Given the ongoing broadcasting of the increasing and intensifying hostility to the United States from outside its borders, a question needs to be raised about both the utility of our country's current processes for securing and maintaining constructive relationships among us throughout the world and about the point at which those practices are distilled to a model from which our young conclude how it should be done. While there is not the remotest excuse for the bitter, cruel, destructive, hate filled bastardizing of religion by Osama Bin Laden, he and his are by no means singularly representative of the perception in so many cultures around the globe that America — within its boundaries and internationally — is arrogant.

There is an insufficiency of funding, non-material contributions and media coverage comparable to that America contributes to war being applied to that task of gaining or creating and keeping productive international relationships, particularly in countries with populations of color. Such diminishes the prospective impact of the good our country has done as an element in the development of our children. Without conscious, intense consideration of the negativity of such modeling, we cannot be sure if we are unwittingly and subliminally teaching our children to butt in and kick butt rather than concluding we sometimes may disagree with those of us of other cultures but can handle it constructively.

Setting aside the proffered democratic good intentions for the wars America has waged on other countries since World War II, the argument can be made that security for its economic system and material preeminence has been factored into the killing it has done in the process. It is also not an accident that those Americans killed while protecting democracy in America's wars today are not the children of the 1% of the United States population that possesses 80% of its wealth and controls the mechanisms for keeping it that way. Not being graduated from or even attending high school and/

or college does not preclude the capacity of an individual to grasp the essential elements of an economic system modeled each and every day for her/him in the media, particularly on television and radio. Nor does it preclude the development of the capacity to engineer and enact a system within America's borders, which employs international trade and is based on that model — even if doing so also produces the deaths of urban combatants and innocents. The increased representation in news media of the corruption and resulting material benefit for some people at high levels in America's corporations should not be overlooked for its contributions to the structure of some highly visible role models. The utility of such models for shaping behavior is sometimes enhanced by the human experience of being excluded from or insufficiently included in the preeminent socio-economic system. Those replicating the material corruption modeled are numerically diminutive in communities of color. Despite that, the media focus on them is so very much greater than that given to those in the same communities who ethically, morally and legally rise above, generation after generation, the socially structured demeaning visited on them.

So very, very many more humans learn to manage the struggle with systemic bigotry and its denial through a psychological, spiritual rise above them. Neighbors, storekeepers, parents, other relatives, religious and spiritual leaders, teachers and more model that rising above. However, there never is skillfully structured advertising for that modeling in corporate media. There would be cost but not material profit in doing so. Nor is there any apparent nexus between the constructive and even courageous behavior demonstrated and accumulation of the material that is at the top of the list of America's values. The absence of connectedness between the behavior and material benefit reduces the prospective utility of such

behavior being a successful model in a society so strongly driven by the pursuit of material gain.

A society cannot create a good voice. However, it can
be found and the person possessed of it can be taught
how to sing. Yet, s/he who would seek to be a role model
cannot be. A role model is not a position to fill but is a
human who attracts others to the constructive human
values s/he communicates about and employs as the
underpinning of action. The task, then, is not to create
role models but to find them where they exist and shine
the light on them via any media we have available for
the task. (Although National Public Radio and Television,
radio and television stations and programs with a non-
dominant cultural base and a multitude of periodicals do
well in the communication of values and behavior needed
for social reform, they are insufficient by themselves to
move the majority of America's population to the needed
change.) If there isn't enough energy available for shining such light, we need to create new social batteries for
the project. How do we find in our young people — and
for them — those with the knowledge in their souls that
there is only Us, there is not a Them, and the voice to
sing of it in a way that gladdens the ears and expands
the thoughtfulness of an ever increasing number who listen? As we keep finding them, how do we individually,
collectively, privately and publicly encourage and praise
them for what they model — even for those of us who are
older? Will we find the courage, insight and socio-cultural-economic-political energy and means to let our young
internalize and enact the values needed to overcome the
socio-cultural-economic *Divide* Dominant America says
it doesn't want but maintains?

CHAPTER 10

STEREOTYPES FROM BOTH SIDES OF THE RACIAL DIVIDE

Ralph Gordon

THE BLACK/WHITE racial divide is an American reality. It needs a number of things to maintain it and to perpetuate it. Some of these things are structural. Others are behavioral, based on a variety of ingrained and very often misguided perceptions. The stereotyping of certain ethnic groups falls into the latter category of behavioral structures.

When it comes to perceptions about one another, humans can be incredibly presumptuous and lazy in their decision-making processes. Rather than taking the time and exerting the effort to really get to know what someone else is all about, stereotyping offers what appears to be an attractive and effortless alternative. To conserve physical and cerebral energy, people fall back on their preconceived notions of other ethnic groups. Whites do it and Blacks do it too. However, the fact that both sides of the racial divide engage in this practice is of no comfort because stereotyping does absolutely nothing to bring

the races closer together. It only serves to move us farther apart, by contributing significantly to the Black/
White racial divide in America.

Stereotypes allow people to simplify their perceptions
of others. The inclination is to over-simplify those who
are supposedly "different" from ourselves. Many people
will wrongly pigeonhole those who appear to be different.
To validate their misperceptions, the "stereotype-er" will
keep the "stereotype-ee" in a box of pre-programmed notions. When one typecasts a member of a different group
(racial or otherwise), one need not bother to think much
about what the other individual is really like. The observer can simply follow the pre-set formula and notion for
what the other person is "supposed to be." In this lethar-
gic mode of thinking, use of the familiar (though flawed)
concept breeds not only further contempt but comfort as
well: contempt for the seemingly affirmed and validated
image and also satisfaction and comfort with the apparent validation of the firmly held perception.

All of this can cause much harm. The damaging habit
of stereotyping enables people to look at others — who
are ethnically different from themselves — as being almost faceless and nameless. It relieves a person of the responsibility for getting to know what others are really like
— or to know what others really need or want. Again, it is
a practice that is mired in lethargy. Imagine how it must
feel to be the recipient of such treatment. You are not a
person or even a number. You are just one of "them." A
particularly pejorative reference of stereotyping is to say:
"you people." Imagine what this must do for a person's
self-esteem, or lack thereof. The harm that is done can
even result in a backlash from those who are typecast.
Or, at a minimum, it can cause the recipient to engage in
"reverse stereotyping," if you will.

As a relatively tall Black man (I'm over 6 feet), I've gotten used to people — Whites and Asians especially — ask-

ing me if I'm a basketball player. In a retail establishment, I almost expect someone to ask me if I work there. Is it because I simply look like the hired help? Not really. On more than one occasion, while wearing a bright orange rugby shirt and visiting one of my favorite hardware and home supply stores (Home Depot), I've been asked to provide service. Silly me. Perhaps I thought that the designer logo on my fairly expensive shirt would exempt me from such an indignity. Not so. I'm wearing the orange hue of the aprons that Home Depot employees wear. The colors of the garments match. Oh yes, and, there's one more thing: my skin color. So, I must be an employee, right?

Poor me. I thought that I had fixed the problem by not wearing that orange rugby shirt to Home Depot any more. But, one day I wore it to a car wash establishment. The bright young attendant thought that I was one of the workers because of that shirt. Have I missed something? Are there certain colors of the spectrum that will doom this Black man to identification as one who works in a retail establishment instead of one who spends money there? Go figure. My numerous stories regarding this type of treatment (or mistreatment) can easily be matched by so many other people of color — particularly Black men. But, African Americans are not the only ones in this leaky boat.

In today's post-9/11 world, Arab Americans have been rudely and crudely brought into a world of victimization that has heretofore been virtually monopolized by Blacks: the world of being stigmatized and marginalized by racial profiling. The fear of terrorism returning to our shores has elevated the emotions of some to the point of hysteria. Paranoia about Arabs is at an all-time high. All are lumped into a hateful pot, their protests notwithstanding. Still, many Arabs may be able to get by and "pass" as members of the dominant White culture in America. This trick of pigmentation is one that is readily available to many. Very, very few Blacks have that option today. African Americans are too frequently mired in the throes of racial categorization by far too many in American society.

As I said at the outset, the practice of stereotyping is a key element in the perpetuation of the Black/White divide in our society: practiced by people on both sides of the color line. With Whites in far greater control in America, it can be safely argued that their stereotypical perceptions of Blacks are far more frequent, damaging and damning than the converse condition. The United States' historical practice of racism has created a number of canned images for people of color, continuing into the 21st century.

Historically, the media have taken lead roles in establishing and maintaining stereotypes. Key examples include print advertising as well as television and film. In the old days, "Mammy" and "Sambo" images were commonplace. They were the acceptable norm. Not so long ago, television and movies presented us with a wide array of derogatory images of Blacks. Even today, the TV networks take much comfort in showing Blacks as almost always comic, token in their representation and preferably invisible. The invisibility is particularly perplexing and ridiculous when a show is set in an urban setting.

The argument is that commercial viability must be the criterion — as if honest portrayals of people of color won't find and maintain an audience. The blockbuster results of *Roots* — the birthplace of the mini-series — should have laid waste to this misconception. But, minimizing displays of the diversity that really is America is the supposedly safe route chosen by those in charge of television and film. Perhaps we might refer to this as stereotyping by exclusion. Or, since the perception of Blacks falls mainly in the sports and entertainment fields, perhaps it is really stereotyping by marginalization.

Black men are the most frequent victims of this situation. The notion that Black males primarily make fine athletes and entertainers yet reigns as an ingrained concept among many. Then, within the sports categorization, more racism is practiced. Arguments still rage — though more quietly these days — about the requisite intelligence of Black men to quarterback football squads, to coach athletic teams etc. Clearly, talk of Black men focuses most often in the arenas of sports and show business. I wish that I knew this only vicariously.

Wealth would be no problem for me if I had a sizable piece of currency for each time I have been asked if I were a basketball player. Is it just because I'm over six feet tall? Not really. Since I'm less than 6'4" tall, I would hardly qualify to be a guard (ball handler) on most teams — even though this is typically the smallest position available in the NBA (National Basketball Association).

Once, while I was sitting in a first class airplane seat, attired in a business suit with my computer on my lap, I was asked by a White woman if I was a basketball player. When I replied that I was a computer software salesman, the inquisitor had no further interest. Only a Black athlete would have been worthy of her attention, I guess. That's all right since I didn't feel like handing out autographs anyway! I must honestly report that one part of me is slightly flattered to even have the suggestion that I could be an athlete in my steadily advancing middle age. But, the reality of this situation is the fact that I am deeply insulted by those who think that this somewhat tall Black man cannot be anything other than one who earns a living through sports. It's as if the minds of so many people can only fit a tall Black man into one box: basketball. However, my airplane encounters have rendered one other occupation that I've been asked about: flight attendant! Wow. How sad and stupid.

In the structural elements chapter, I tell the story of

how one of my neighbors thought that I was part of a work crew. How disturbing to be mistaken for a faceless laborer just a couple of houses away from your own residence. A look at this situation may shed some light on how easily many Black men are victimized by the DWB — "driving while Black" — syndrome. Law enforcement officials and staffers will tell you ad nauseam and ad infinitum how it is necessary to stop and detain those who resemble wanted suspects. But, this practice has been so wrongly handled that many Americans are now aware of its discriminatory prevalence and ramifications.

Citing the instances of these insults is particularly illuminating when applied to a college-educated Black professional. It highlights the fact that neither getting an education nor reaching a certain level of vocational attainment is a preventative against being adversely pigeon holed due to one's skin color. Here is another case in point.

A few years ago, when I went to pick up a Silicon Valley customer for a lunch meeting and the receptionist casually referred to me as his "driver," the depths of my outrage cannot be described. Being a limo driver or a chauffeur is an honorable profession. My grandfather was a chauffeur, most likely because of the limited career opportunity alternatives during his lifetime. Two generations later, however, must I be reminded that nothing much has changed? Am I to believe that the perceptions of people will impose the same limitations upon me? Must I, as the recipient of such boorish behavior, not be deeply disappointed by these presumptive insults? Similarly, when I'm wearing an orange designer polo shirt in a Home Depot store and other patrons still think that I'm a floor employee, should I not be offended?

The flip side of the racial stereotype is problematic also. When noting exceptions to the stereotypical model, jaded observers have been heard to say — as they express their surprise — she (he) is "a credit to the race." This is supposed to be a compliment for the person of color. Instead, it is a component of a racial underestimation of certain people. It is as if the person who happens not to fit into the mold of misconception is setting some new standard that most of the rest of "those people" could never hope to attain. Icons regularly achieve such status, usually in areas where society is real comfortable with its famous people of color: the entertainment or sports worlds. Oprah Winfrey, Michael Jordan and Tiger Woods are prime examples.

Learned Blacks know better than to buy into such nonsense — even when the general populace seems to be headed down this wrong road. Years ago, when the *Bill Cosby Show* was a television staple, many Americans balked in disbelief at the fact that Cosby's character was a physician and that his wife was a lawyer. Their middle class lifestyle, in a New York City brownstone home, was deemed to be unrealistically plush. From my viewpoint, the Cosby household's living quarters and lifestyle were actually toned down, to avoid just that kind of impression. In reality, a successful doctor and attorney couple could easily have afforded to live in much more luxurious surroundings. Furthermore, the Cosby clan was not the anomaly that so many might have thought it to be. I, and many of my friends, knew then and know now a number of Blacks who are least as materially successful as the then TV Cosby family.

Perhaps if more Whites took a stroll across the divide in this country, they too would have the chance to meet and to know more of the Black middle class, a segment of the population that has existed in one form or another for more than a century.

Just because Blacks have been on the receiving end of this problem is no excuse for the recipients to dish it out as well. Still, it sometimes happens.

Spike Lee, the noted Black film director, brilliantly

illustrated this point in his film, *Do the Right Thing*. The movie featured a racist White man who greatly admired Michael Jordan — claiming that the basketball phenomenon was not really Black. Here, we see the search for comforting images and perspectives. Lee has been hailed as one of the best-known filmmakers in America. With movies like *Malcolm X, Do the Right Thing,* and *Jungle Fever,* he has cut a wide swath across the cinematic landscape. Yet, one criticism of his films is that he creates simplistic, one-dimensional White characters. It is unfortunate that this highly talented moviemaker would provide fodder for this type of accusation. His later work, such as *The 25th Hour,* has sought in part to undo this impression. But, the damage remains.

There are many Blacks who will tell you that Whites have no rhythm. Is that universally the case or even predominantly so? I still remember my sister asking a White coworker, whom I brought by her home (unannounced) for dinner, if he ate fried chicken. She and I now laugh at her supposition that certain foods were exclusive to the "brothers and sisters." When my friend fell asleep right after eating, my sister chuckled at how this White man appeared to fit into another stereotype that seemed reserved for Blacks!

It's confession time. I have been guilty of committing the crime of stereotyping too. Imagine my surprise when a White businessman hit me with a Richard Pryor line — in a men's bathroom — about the water being cold. Those who are familiar with this gem from the rich repository of Mr. Pryor's storytelling know the response: "Yeh, and it's deep too." I could barely utter the requisite reply to one whom I never suspected would have such perfectly appropriated and timed humor. That's an example of the lighter side of stereotyping.

When Blacks oversimplify their views and perspectives on Whites, a number of problems can develop. A whole segment of insightful and honestly sympathetic and empathetic Whites are excluded from view when a Black person takes the posture that all White Americans are automatically and reflexively racist. Despite the pervasiveness of this sickness in the nation, it is folly to paint all of a white hue with a dastardly brush. One would ignore history by not acknowledging the large number of Whites who have valiantly fought in the struggle for freedom and equality. It's not necessary to go all the way back to a John Brown (a White fighter for freedom of slaves) or even to a Viola Liuzzo (a White martyr in the civil rights movement) to find stellar examples. The sympathetic voices who have partnered with Blacks, and continue to do so, are legion. Stereotyping all Whites as racists is a slap in the face to these colleagues in the never-ending struggle against injustice.

When considering White-created stereotypes of Blacks, one need not focus on the output of a single movie director or other artistic talent. The images are rampant and pervasive — as they have been throughout the years. If a reminder is required, an observer need only tune in to one of the modern minstrel shows on either the UPN or the WB20 TV networks. In these universes, all Blacks are funny or wily or in possession of some other pre-conceived (by stereotyping Whites) notion. The White viewer can take comfort in these reaffirming images. The pervasive buffoonery may strike some as a reincarnation of the worst Stepin' Fetchit days of old.

Meanwhile, the major television networks present a different yet no less damning picture. Here, we might as well say that Blacks are stereotyped by exclusion, as we note the dearth of African American characters on the major television networks. The sheer invisibility is palpable. Long ago, the great dramatist Douglas Turner Ward created a symbolic and emblematic play: *Day of Absence.* Its title came to represent a consideration of

STEREOTYPES FROM BOTH SIDES

how this country would function if all Blacks simply did not come out of their homes for a day. Well, network TV seems to have answered that question by relegating the vast minority (is that a contradiction?) population in this country to a nearly invisible status. People of color show up less and less frequently in the so-called mainstream shows, even when the programs are set in locales where it would be difficult to not bump into a person of color while just walking down the street.

Not so long ago, there was a TV cop and buddy show called *Starsky and Hutch*. In addition to its action stars, it featured their loyal confidante: a Black character called Huggy Bear. His slinky, sleepy-eyed appearances were so reminiscent of the Stepin' Fetchit character as to seem to be a channeling experience. Imagine my feelings of insult and disdain when a White co-worker told me that I reminded him of Huggy Bear and that he meant me no disrespect. Perhaps I should have told him that he reminded me of Ronald MacDonald.

How refreshing it would be if more and more people would cease to take the seemingly easy route and stop relying on the faulty formulae of stereotypes to look at and assess individuals in terms of how each one presents himself or herself. Borrowing from the old saying, it would be so refreshing to accept people based on the content of their character and not categorize them simply on the basis of the color of their skin. Let's ban all stereotyping as we move toward an elimination of the Black/White divide.

CHAPTER 11

THE BLUDGEON OF STEREOTYPES

Marlin Foxworth, Ph.D

PERCEPTIONS OF GENDER, socio-economic status and that social fabrication called "race" are each strong cellular, muscular and skeletal components of American social anatomy and of its body politic. The locked-in-place nature of stereotypes, despite the moderately nuanced alterations in them that sometimes come over time, continues to lend powerful energy to social issues that live among us — generation after generation. Nowhere is that more telling than in the *Black/White Divide.* The continuance of those stereotypes of what is referred to as "minorities" is contingent upon whether they help strengthen and perpetuate the hegemony of those of the dominant culture and its access to social largesse, e.g., wealth and power. The continuance of those stereotypes in the dominant culture for those not of it contributes to the process of subordinating those not of it to it. It also serves as one of a multitude of energizers for humans subjected to that subordinating effort to oppose it. A *Divide* indeed!

The culture of each of us is often the discerning prism through which others are seen and stereotyped. It is the location of one's primary culture, however, in a social structure that determines the consequences of the stereotyping done. Yes, some who are African American may perceive, for example, that people who are *White* can't dance. In America's dominance/subordination social structure, however, such stereotyping will have no significant impact on Americans in that dominant social category.

On the other hand, in a *Newsweek* piece, early in 2003, the author, a member of the editorial staff and not African American, used spiking the football in the end zone after a touchdown is scored as an analogy for political idiocy. There was no lingering on the reference. It was made succinctly and the writer moved on. Should a reader tarry with the statement for no more than a few seconds, though, a rational question about it should be raised. To what culture in American society would spiking the ball most likely be attributed? Despite the fact that some scholars indicate there are about 50 African American Cultures, did not the author imply African American culture, generally, was a source of idiocy? Such an implication speaks clearly about ignorance of the influence of culture on values inherent in sport. Thomas Kochman, in his book, BLACK AND WHITE STYLES IN CONFLICT, points out that things like spiking the ball "... violated the white norm that one should be charitable to the opponent one has just defeated." The points for a touchdown don't increase when the ball is spiked in the end zone. However, Kochman also makes it clear that demonstrating gladness about successful performance in an athletic contest is a legitimate element of sport that can be found in African American Culture. Spiking the ball and comparable displays following triumphant athletic performance are manifestations of that legitimacy. Doing so is no more idiocy than not doing so! Doing so, however, is often stereotypically seen from the dominant America loft as another negative manifestation of the way *they* are. That, simply, contributes to the *Divide.*

Picture this exaggerated scene on a high school campus. Two males who are high school students and African American are standing outside a campus building and talking after school. Not far from them is another student who is male and of the dominant culture. The school day has just ended and he is waiting for a friend to pick him up and take him home. A female student who is of the dominant culture walks by and one of the males who is African American comments loudly about the attractiveness of her anatomy and, with only a modicum of subtlety, suggests that they ought to get together privately. The young lady chastises him for his comments and walks on in a huff. The male of the dominant culture wonders why those *Black guys* always like our girls.

Change the scene slightly. The same two males who are African American are having the same conversation in the same place. The male of the dominant culture is still standing in the same place. This time, though, it is a female who is African American who walks by. The same male makes the same comment about her attractive anatomy and renders the suggestion that they get together. This time, though, the young lady turns to the young man making the comments and says, "You don't look half bad your own self. I like that shirt you're wearing. Why don't you give me a call?" Then, with her phone number hurriedly called out, she walks on. Her response tweaks the interest of the dominant culture male in her and he wonders why Black girls are more interested in and available for sex.

"In white culture," notes Kochman, "women who admit a general sexual interest in men fall in the 'less respectable' category and are therefore seen as sexually available."

In contrast, he notes, "In black culture, it would be wrong to infer female sexual availability simply from the expression of sexual interest or sexual assertiveness, since the culture presumes that all women have general sexual interest in men and are sexually assertive. Black women are not viewed as more or less 'respectable' on the basis of these criteria. It would also be wrong to infer sexual availability simply because an approaching male hopes for it."

Consider the following exaggerated example in pursuit of the point. That female who is of the dominant culture may be on her way around to the back of the gym for a liaison with the backfield of the football team. She doesn't verbalize an interest in sex and, therefore, is not likely to be seen as "loose" by those of her own culture who are unaware of her sexual promiscuity. The female who is African American may be on her way to church and, by asking for a phone call, may be only asking to get to know the young man. By implying interest in sex she may be only recognizing that since there are billions of people in the world everybody who lives long enough to reach puberty is interested in sex. Assessing her response as blatant sexual interest becomes a dominant cultural filter through which she is seen as "loose" — even when she is nothing of the kind.

These stereotypes become blockages to appraisals of who each woman, each a human of the feminine gender, is and what the values of each are in a sexual context. From that derives an assumptive appraisal of each social category of *them* and how they behave. Another case of how we keep from knowing *us*. Again, though, the dominant cultural perspective and corresponding stereotyping will produce the negative appraisal for the young lady who is African American and have the most jaundiced social consequences.

Public school district data show that students who are African American are disproportionately enrolled in

Special Education, have disproportionately high suspension, expulsion, and dropout rates and the converse for college enrollment. Those data, when disaggregated by culture/ethnic group, speak of and help perpetuate the stereotyping of students who are African American as less capable academically. Consequently, school data are used, in effect, to characterize students who are African American, particularly males, more often as problems than scholars. Such is so despite the reality that there is nothing inherent in being African America that would preclude being just as proportionately spread across the academic achievement spectrum as any other socio-cultural category of students. Those stereotyped as the less capable academically — and often their parents too — are seen characteristically in the academic venues structured by and for the dominant culture as the source of the problem. The institutional structure of schools that allows the gaps in the data on academic achievement to persist is not seen as the source of the problem that it is. Another historical stereotype hammering down!

Even though there are exceptions, the stereotype of students who are African American as less good than students who are of Dominant America and Asian cultures is a mainstay of public education. The negative stereotype is sustained, in large part, by a variety of protective devices. Those devices falter, however, in face of both statistical reality and the absence of concerted individual and collective efforts to alter the practices that produce the numbers. "I want all my students to succeed," many teachers and administrators will say, despite the fact that the statistical disparities have existed every single day of their careers. Those self-proclaimed good intentions are further contradicted by both the absence of constructive action as a logical projection of the intentions and by the acceptance of those disparities as inevitable. More premium stereotypical fuel for the *Divide.*

There are still those in America's dominant culture who appraise the verbal interaction style of many in African American communities, particularly those considered poor, as rude. Kochman notes, "Whites want social interaction to operate at an emotionally subdued level. To realize this goal, they first establish the rule that expressive behavior shall be subdued, which develops sensibilities capable of tolerating only relatively subdued outputs." The training of teachers in colleges and universities is almost always and exclusively done with values of the dominant culture. Given that training as a prism, most often teachers, irrespective of their own primary culture, see the insistent interaction style sometimes used by students who are African American as aberrant. Consequently, using a perfectly legitimate interaction method in class can end up as an occasion for disciplinary action. There is nothing wrong with teaching students how to use different methods. There is something wrong with the use of a legitimate method other than that of the dominant culture as a trigger for a stereotyping appraisal: "You know how they act!" Perennially disproportionate school disciplinary statistics are tied to the continuous sustenance of the use of stereotypes and their pernicious consequences. Discipline of students is indeed necessary. However, on the occasions when it is a function of misperception and related stereotypes, it is destructive. Such stereotypes become structural elements of school praxis and, as such, serve to perpetuate lower indicators of academic success for students who are African American.

Kochman provides an insight to how the misperception of the influence of culture on style results in the stereotypic appraisal by the *White* (dominant) culture of the *Black* (non-dominant) culture. Kochman writes, "... the consequences of different cultural patterns, perspectives, and values affect not only the quality of black and white social interaction but (perhaps even more critically from the black standpoint) black social and economic success. These are, after all, contexts in which white standards alone usually determine what constitutes good performance and, consequently, where accommodation to black performance styles has been absent or at best negligible. They are also the contexts in which the white rule of 'shape up or ship out' is most strictly followed."

Definitely to prosper and even to survive, some facility with America's dominant culture, its values and methods is needed in communities that are African American. Dominant America is not faced with the same requirements with respect to culture and values in communities that are African American. Stereotypes of African Americans serve as ammunition for justifying the continuance of destructive social conditions and contemporized segregation. Weapons of mass destruction indeed! Stereotypes of Dominant America held in communities that are African American, however, have no significance on either the survival or prosperity of that social stratum.

If an airplane pilot sees a steep mountain as an airport and elects to land there, phenomenal destruction will result — inevitably. Will WE understand soon enough that the continuing stereotyping of those of US who are African American can only function to perpetuate the inequalities we have not yet overcome? Or will Our journey as a country find US trying to land on that steep slope?

CHAPTER 12

LANGUAGE AS A FACTOR

Ralph Gordon

LANGUAGE IS A KEY component of a society. America is certainly no exception. It is a tool that we use on a daily basis. It shapes how we view and treat one another. It can even be a weapon wielded by those with ill intent. Frequently, this tool is comprised of a set of terms for the propagation of a particular group of concepts. With all of these things going for it, language is a critical factor in the perpetuation of the Black/White divide. The racial divide in America requires a lot of help to stay in place. It is not an automatic or natural outgrowth of human existence. It requires a lot of help to maintain its existence. That help can be structural or linguistic. The racial divide owes its survival to a number of societal elements and practices — not the least of which is how we communicate with one another. The perpetuation of the Black/White divide is facilitated by the use and misuse of language in America. The English language has long been a co-conspirator in the maintenance of racial separation and discrimination in the United States of America.

A number of ostensibly benign terms have been quietly malignant in our everyday speech, especially when a person has not yet reached a level of sufficient awareness of those who may be perceived as different. Consider this memory from my childhood. I recall that when crayons were of a beige hue they were dubbed "flesh colored." More significantly, bandages bore this same labeling. Imagine the impact that this has had on generations of children — like me, with my dark brown skin — whose skin color did not match the manufacturer's indication. If your skin is not "flesh colored" then you must be an aberration, right? Or, perhaps your flesh is not actually "normal." This situation exemplifies how the seeds for problematic self-esteem are sown via language that is purposefully misused. The language used in the labeling of crayons and bandages was easily a causative factor for many of the pejorative self-images perpetuated by the racial divide.

Some will say that this was just an innocent oversight. Could that be the case for something that was institutionally communicated for decades and decades? Or, might we draw a more logical conclusion that Black skin wasn't meant to be categorized as "flesh" along side of that of the dominant race in America? Perhaps this is a part of a broader attempt at dehumanization of those of color who are regarded as inferior, at worst, or unimportant, at the least. It was tacitly assumed that certain labels — such as "flesh colored" — were harmless and a given in the American vernacular. This was hardly the case.

Even worse have been the associations with the term "black." Dictionaries and thesauruses have long listed numerous negative denotations and connotations when the word "black" is used. "Black Friday," "Black Death," "black lie" and other terms carry a decidedly negative image. The bad guys in the cowboy movies and TV shows of my childhood always wore black hats. Even today, the cliché remains that "blondes have more fun" — not those black-haired brunettes.

On the contrary, the word "white" is linguistically blessed with all kinds of good indications. A "white lie" is a lesser prevarication, so to speak. "White as snow" connotes purity in the American lexicon. And, of course, "good guys" always wear white hats and ride white horses, don't they? With all of this, one can understand why so many people have been reluctant to refer to themselves as "black." The subsequent trend has been to call oneself African American. This move may be satisfying in terms of language. But, it is hardly a racial classification.

At this writing, the terms "African American" and "Black" have become virtually interchangeable in everyday usage. Yet, the term "African American" is essentially one of heritage. It pays tribute to the understood origin of most Black people in America: West Africa. This terminology follows the pattern of other immigrants to our nation: Mexican Americans, Italian Americans, and others. However, unlike the other prefaces, Africa is a continent and not a country. So, using its name in this way is a tacit acknowledgement that most Black Americans — still in a pre-Roots condition of genealogical uncertainty — cannot determine which African nation they have come from.

There is another problem of significance with trying to make the terms "African American" and "Black" synonymous. Consider this. A White person, becoming a United States citizen after emigrating from a nation in Africa, actually has a greater claim to being an African American than does a Black person whose family has been in the U.S.A. for decades or even centuries. Hence, the application of the term "African American" to Blacks only is more likely a misapplication of language that unintentionally helps to perpetuate the racial divide. Properly used, the term "African American" would be based on the direct country of origin of a person and not on the skin color of that person.

Prior to being called "Black" or "African American," people of color were generally referred to as "Negro." This Portuguese (and Spanish) word means "black" and was popularized during the heyday of slavery. The term stuck for over three hundred years thereafter. What a vestige. In a country that has never promoted the use of either the Portuguese or Spanish language, this reference for so many of its citizens — though widely accepted and used for centuries — became seen by many (especially in the militant times of the 1960s) as historically heinous.

The term "Negro" was also tied to the so-called three races of humankind: Caucasoid (white), Mongoloid (Asian) and Negroid (black). The Caucasus Mountains were supposedly the place of origin for the Caucasian race. Mongolia was the extrapolated source for the so-called Mongoloids. Yet, pray tell, where is "Negroland?"

Today, we are much more enlightened as we realize that the races of humankind cannot be so easily categorized. In America, there is a sizable and growing push for multiculturalism. Also, there is an increasing recognition of a large segment of people who defy simplistic racial categorizations and see themselves as multiracial. These are major factors in the move away from the concept of a triad of "oids" to segment humankind. I pray that this confounding and erroneous language labeling will stay in the dumpsters where it has been justifiably thrown.

Some times, words are selectively deployed. Another malignant label is the term "riot." This word for a violent uprising seems only to be applied by the media to events that involve people of color or those who are incarcerated (usually inmates of color). Whereas, with White participants, an uprising does not go through a purposeful metamorphosis and then become tagged with the "riot" label. When White youth tear up a town like Fort Lauderdale, during a college spring break, the word riot seems never to creep into a description. Yet, it rears its ugly head even when Blacks are putting up a mild protest that may have gotten out of hand. Whether used as a noun or as a verb, the term "riot" conjures up a lot of selectively targeted ugliness. Sometimes it seems that the term might more aptly be applied to the law enforcement officers who are supposed to maintain the peace — but, no matter. The pejorative application of the label persists.

The misuse of language is not confined to bad labeling. Sometimes the words are not changed at all: they are simply appropriated and then misused. Case in point: Major elements of the language of the civil rights movement have been shrewdly taken over by anti-affirmative action forces. One group, long led by Ward Connerly, calls itself the "American Civil Rights Institute" despite the fact that its work is diametrically opposed to the goals and objectives of the human rights movement. These folks disingenuously prop themselves up as the true interpreters of Dr. Martin Luther King Jr.'s dream for racial harmony and equality as well as for the goals and objectives of the drive for civil rights as a whole. This twisting of terms and concepts has been successful with the electorate in a number of states, as numerous pieces of regressive legislation have been passed in concert with the linguistic misdirection.

Sometimes, the linguistic damage is self-inflicted. Case in point: Ebonics. It was painful to watch so many well meaning and even well educated people touting an American way of mis-speaking as a bona fide export from the African continent. Africans were standing up and speaking out against this erroneously applied notion. For a time, it seemed as though this apologist movement would succeed. Blessedly, common sense and historical accuracy prevailed. Yes, there are challenges to getting children from certain economic and cultural strata to use proper English. But, it would be damning to simply write the whole situation off and validate poor language by ascribing it to a made-up school of linguistic tradition — from any continent.

Language can be used for good or for bad. It can be employed to educate and enlighten. Or, it can be used to subvert noble goals and to deceive. It can shape perceptions, mold minds and set the stage for policies. Through its use of euphemisms, language can seemingly soften harsh blows. People who are laid off from their jobs are considered to be "reductions in force" or a part of "downsizing" initiatives. Soldiers who are inadvertently killed by their own troops are said to be victims of "friendly fire." Innocent people who are caught in war time crossfire are considered to be "collateral damage." A president can deceitfully lead his country into a deadly, misguided, costly conflagration with an unclear purpose by labeling it a 'war on terror.'

Language also targets certain terms and then demonizes them. The "conservatives" and right wing forces have moved many in this country to think that the word "liberal" is something akin to being a communist. The mere mention of a "quota" is enough to get the cackles up for any "non-liberal." The late Senator Joseph McCarthy must be frolicking in his grave. Affirmative action, a policy that was set up to correct the abuses of racism and discrimination, has been turned into a whipping boy by well-heeled campaigns across the nation. Those who have been discriminated against for generations are no longer seen as the victims. Whites who lose their inherently racial advantage are now said to be the biggest potential losers. Oh yes, the word "colorblind" plays into this as we misuse language to pretend that skin color no longer matters in this country. And, God forbid that we use what has become an awful word: "preferences." Interestingly, the word "preferences" is rarely applied to those who gain privilege by virtue of their non-black skin color, family heritage or other connection. President George W. Bush gained entrance to Yale University, riding on the coattails of his alumnus dad. Keen "conservatives" could never conceive of the appropriate label for Mr. Bush, the younger: an affirmative action beneficiary.

The failure to eliminate certain words constitutes a severe problem. The "n" word, as it is known in polite circles, has seen a revival and a move to an almost benign term in its own right. It is most unfortunate to see a derogatory, pejorative and epithetic term move to such a seeming level of respectability. Much of this proliferate use can be ascribed to the very people who have been historically maligned by this term — Americans of African descent. Another self-inflicted wound results from the misogynist use of the labeling of a Black woman as either a "bitch" or a "ho" (whore). Such sexist denigration is at once damning and damaging. This colloquial abuse of females is part and parcel of the objectification of women, in general, and of Black women, in particular. It is perpetuated by an entertainment segment, notably some rappers. But, it is tolerated by those who don't want to offend the rappers who claim to be "keepin' it real."

The use and abuse of language is a prominent factor in the perpetuation of the Black/White racial divide. We need more citizens to recognize these abuses and to forcefully and effectively stand up against them. Perhaps then, the racial divide can be truly bridged as more of us speak with a universal language of brotherly and sisterly love and appreciation — no matter what our skin color may be.

CHAPTER 13

EDUCATION AND THE DIVIDE

Marlin Foxworth, Ph.D.

IN 1994 the Hayward Unified School District (HUSD), just outside Oakland, California, had approximately 20,000 students from kindergarten to the 12th grade. Our student body represented 88 cultures and 40 languages about which we were aware. Our students who were African American and Latino comprised together over 50% of the student population (69.61% in 2008) and also were represented by the least good data on academic achievement. Those gaps in the data for students who were African American and Latino had long been representative of both our school district and of school districts throughout the state and country. That reality was and still is perennial in public schools, a systemic result of *It's-Just-The-Way-It-Is* philosophizing in the profession. That way of seeing or refusing to see those gaps in the accomplishments of the education system was strongly supported by the powerful social stanchions of silence and inaction. It was the case in this district, as in myriad others, that many, from all of our cultures, who led, taught and otherwise worked in the system, wished those gaps would end. However, there was a constant shortage of professional colleagues genuinely committed to the radical changes needed to do so. For those committed insufficiently, or not at all, the paychecks came just the same, on the same pay scale, on the same day of the month.

Our board of education had one member who was Latino. The rest were of the dominant culture. The proportionate absence of People of Color on the board, even in a district with Students of Color as the majority, fit the norm. The board itself, though, was unusual. It didn't fit the norm. There was among the board members a collective, though individually varied, grasp of the reality that those gaps in the indicators of student achievement were a systemic problem and could not be attributed justifiably to the socio-cultural categories of students persistently on the down side of the gap. Something had to get done about the issue. The board members knew it and were open to a recommendation for prescriptive action.

Steps Toward Creating US

In December of 1994, my ninth month on the job as district superintendent, I planned to recommend that the board adopt two programs for our students. One, the Puente Project, had been a long established and successful program for providing mentors for students who are Latino and, by so doing, enhancing their academic success and preparation for college. The other, Student Achievement and Learning Teams (S.A.L.T.), had been established in the San Diego Unified School District and contributed phenomenally to the enhancement of academic achievement for students who are male and African American, for whom there were the least good achievement data ... as in Hayward.

The prospects for angry reaction to the two recommendations popped to the surface early in my planning discussions with involved administrators and staff about the presentation on the two programs to be made at the board meeting. We asked community members and leaders, particularly those who were African American and Latino, to attend the board meeting. They did, in large numbers. We anticipated no opposition to the recommended programs would be coming from the communities they represented. We expected some reaction in various forms to the recommendations by people who were from the dominant culture. Some might be strongly supportive of the recommendations to launch the two programs. We reckoned there would be some who would come to vehemently oppose the approval of the programs but who, when opening the door and seeing the boardroom filled with People of Color, would either turn around and leave or say nothing during the meeting. We also anticipated there would be others who would open the door to the boardroom, sit down and wait for an opportunity to speak, either for or against the recommendation, and do so when comments from the public were called for by the board. The latter, even if speaking in opposition to the recommendation, would be acceptable because of their forthrightness.

Our anticipation that there would be some active support at the board meeting from our citizens who were of the dominant culture was ill founded. The other behaviors were anticipated correctly. Opposition to the programs did come after the board meeting from a couple of individuals who remained silent while the meeting was in session.

An explanation of the history and value of both programs was preface for the recommendations to the board that both be established in our district. The Puente Project had steadily addressed the reality that in California, part of which was once a northern segment of Mexico, much of which is constructively influenced by Mexican culture, where our students of Mexican and other Latino ancestry are as capable of being on the top academically as any other socio-cultural group, that proportionate share of the top runs short. There was conviction in the project leadership that the education system needed alteration and hope that it would occur in a not too distant tomorrow. There was also in that leadership a realization that students who are Latino and for whose culture(s) the system originally had not been created needed assistance to rise up educationally in the system exactly as it is today ... until it is changed to what it should be. The consequences of not doing so had shown in multiple ways; not the least of which were dropping out of school or not going on to college or under-employment or some violent street activity in barrios, disproportionate imprisonment and even early death.

Felix Galaviz and Patricia McGrath were both on the professional staff at Chabot College in Hayward when they founded Puente in 1981. Their unified spirit and commitment, along with that of Frank Garcia, a HUSD Board member who also was an administrator of the Puente Program working out of the President's Office at the University of California were powerfully focused on the advancement of students who are Latino. (Garcia was appointed Executive Director of Puente in 2005.) The program currently functions to verifiably enhance the education achievement of students who are Latino in 60 community colleges and 35 high schools in California. They understood that the gap in student achievement data was so despite there being no justification for its existence.

The Student Achievement and Learning Team (S.A.L.T.) program founders clearly recognized the gap in the data on student achievement between students who were male and African American and those who were male and of the dominant culture for its persistence as a structural element of the *Black/White Divide*. As was the case with the heart and leadership of Puente, they knew that hope for change was felt this and every minute but was futuristic in its prospects and that students needed guidance to make it through the system now. The enactment of that vision manifested itself most clearly in the program's accomplishment in the San Diego Unified School District. At the outset of the program only five students who were African American in the districts high schools had a grade point average of 3.0 or above. After a few years of the program there were 500. That change came with no diminution of standards. The program, simply, worked.

Knowing that comparable data inked the same damaging, historic problem for Hayward students who were African American and Latino, the board voted unanimously that night to take on both programs in the district. The meeting ended. Agin Shaheed and Leonard Thompson, two of the founders of the program in San Diego, later provided powerful insights and training for the staff members who were to run the program in our district.

As I walked out of the boardroom toward my office, a teacher, of the dominant culture, who had sat in on the board meeting but had not spoken out, stopped me in the lobby. "Can I ask you something?" she said. I acknowledged that she could. "Isn't this a democracy?" she pried a little caustically. I said that it certainly was, that it had its flaws but that I liked it very much. "And," she went on, "aren't public schools supposed to be for everyone?" I allowed that they were. "Then how," she verbally punched at me, "can you justify having a special program for a special group of kids?'"

My response came in something less than a second. "You know, you're right. We shouldn't have a special program for a special group of kids. So, I'm going to go back to the board and ask them to rescind their decision. But — to be consistent — I'm going to ask them to get rid of Special Education and the Gifted and Talented Education Programs. And how do we justify having only 12 kids on a high school basketball team? How many kids do you know who play soccer ... speaking of a 'special program for a special group of kids?'"

Admonishing me to shut up, she waived her hand at me in disgust and walked away. I was approached again before I left the lobby. This time it was by a parent, of the dominant culture, who also had said nothing at the board meeting. She questioned me the same way and, when given the same kind of reply, also waived me off in disgust, turned and walked away. The programs went into motion, though, fashioning constant success for the students in them. Opposition, usually in the virile form of indifference and applied more to the S.A.L.T than Puente, was part of the district environment from the moment the board approved the programs. Despite the opposition to S.A.L.T., it became a symbol in the district and the African American Community for academic achievement and hope. It also made it clear for many that the gaps by cultural groups in the data on academic success were a systemic issue not the result of academic ineptitude of non-dominant cultures as so many not of them so wrongly had perceived.

We hired three advocates, dedicated men who were African Americans, one each for the elementary school, middle school and high school with the highest population of students who were African Americans. Those advocates also worked strategically with other schools throughout the district. In a year or so a couple of them left and the work of those who replaced them was as intensely and productively focused on the needs of our students. The work for these advocates wasn't just a job: it was a way of life, a commitment of themselves to the lives of our students and their families.

Support . . . And Not

Support for the program was solid in the African American Community over the years that followed. Although people who were of the dominant culture did not speak out supportively the night the programs were approved, many, including many educators, actively supported the program. One family, of the dominant culture, wanted their daughter in the program and we gladly accepted her. Another, also of the dominant culture, wanted their son in the program and he too was welcomed into it.

The program always faced the contemporary, moderately subtle, just-beneath-the surface forms of opposition that supplanted the more openly vicious but more honest resistance to the civil rights movement in the 50s and 60s. My recommending the program, for example, triggered a perception among some teachers, staff and community members of the dominant culture that I was "too Afro-centric." With the anomaly of one district office employ, that perception was never rendered to me face-to-face. That viewpoint and opposition were never followed by an alternative suggestion for how best to end the continuing gap by socio-cultural-economic group in the indicators of school success. Prior to the establishment of the program, when there was no institutionalized, systemic effort to end the gap in the indicators of achievement while raising productivity for all of our students, when our students who were of the dominant culture were always on the top, there was no charge that I or any of my predecessors had been too "Euro-centric."

There were, though, a number of constructive exceptions to that oppositional indifference. The most profound example came from a collective request from teachers at Tennyson High School to have the program placed also at their school and to have Charles Hill, a Special Education counselor (Now a principal in another district), a man of insight and consistent commitment who is African American, be their advocate. The teachers and administrators who wanted the program at Tennyson and wanted Charles Hill to run it there were varied in culture, including not only African Americans and people of the dominant culture but a variety of other cultures as well. We found the money and did it. Over a few years, Suliaman Ali, Angus Bates, Todd Green, Angelo Luster, Anyika Nkululeko, Andre Robertson and Michael Roosevelt, dedicated, intelligent, caring men who are African American and, like Charles Hill, so glad that they are, worked along with him to make the program succeed at the schools where they were assigned. It did! It did without pre-selecting students for the program who were previously only on the top of the academic success list. Our students came into the S.A.L.T. Program from all over the academic success map, from its bottom to its top. Within about a year after the start of the program, at the suggestion of Anyika Nykululeko, we changed its name to "Adewole," a Yoruba term that means, essentially, your future is here at home with the people who love you.

After Adewole was in existence for a few years, the collective grade point average for the 300 students in it was 2.6. The average G.P.A. for the whole district was 2.56. Shortly after this data was made available throughout the district, I was asked on a couple of occasions by teachers of the dominant culture if I was saying that African American students had a higher grade point average than that for the whole district. I responded by saying that I wasn't telling them that: the data was. Then, because of irritation with my response demonstrated by one of the teachers, I asked, "Did you ask me that question when White kids' grade point average was higher?" I had not checked the G.P.A. for our students of the dominant culture at the time simply because there was no indication in our data that they had been left out or kept down. I simply used the question to make a point about the tone, anger, unjustified shock and prejudice in the teacher's haughty inquisition. The teacher clearly understood the statement and, rather than engaging in constructive discussion about it, got up and left. The point was made. The prospect for working with that teacher, at least for the moment, also walked out the door.

Education and a Social/Political Forest Fire

Less than a year later, when the intention of the Million Man March was announced in 1995, it was clear that the issues sparking it were ignited by a perennially simmering and periodically flaming social/political forest fire. Any one or a combination of things provided that clarity: direct experience, conversations — including just passing ones — even minimum knowledge of the history of the Civil Rights Movement and of the declining support in the dominant culture for confronting the contemporary manifestations of the social conditions that propelled the movement, data about gaps in success in public schools and the economy, prison statistics, regular multimedia news reports, etc.

It was just as clear, in the school district as well as in society generally, that most who do not live in an impacted area, had no relatives or friends there and found no need to drive through or visit it didn't feel the heat of the simmering. Were it to burst into flames, they could read about it in the newspaper or see it on television but could not be burned and scared by the fire or experience the worry about the prospects of having to inhale its suffocating vapors and, maybe, die because of it. Most would not have their children frightened or harmed by it. Most would not think much about how to put it out or engage in a process for replenishing the environment vitiated by it. Most could read the names of those who died in the blaze but would not know their faces or attend their funerals.

Most would not have heard their cries nor have seen the tears of those who love them or knew them or lived near them, people who could have died also but did not.

Most would see the fire for one of those awful things that just happen. Most would not know the environmental complexities contributing to the fire and would live in conviction that handling it was the responsibility of fire fighters, not of themselves. Most, knowing they neither lit the fire nor had any intention to do so, would accept no responsibility for it nor sense any need to lend a hand in refinancing and rebuilding what was lost because of it. Most would not know the unpublicized heroes who acted to save others from the debilitating consequences of the fire or who might have worked diligently to eradicate the cause(s) of the simmering and who might have ended up among the injured or dead for having done so.

Most would want to be clear about what had to be done so that what was ignited over *there* in that forest could be kept from ignition over *here* in this neighborhood. Most would accept the invisible protective barrier securing them from the heat and flames over *there* without having built it themselves and without knowing it is fabricated of the kind of social bricks in the Berlin Wall or in the one some would build between Israel and Palestine. Most ... not all. There is a societal *Some*, however, people who do not live in that forest, yet are inalterably dedicated to both collapsing the *Divide* between it and the neighborhoods of which they are a part and to replacing it with the magnetizing and nurturing elements of a multicultural *Us*. There are also those in that collection of *Some* who may not be as thoroughly committed yet to participating in the structuring of that *Us*, who are eager to enhance their own understanding about social divisions and the consequences of them and who are open to more intense participation in the creation of that *Us* once their increasing experience with related issues makes it clear that it is right to do.

There were many employed by the Hayward Unified School District who grew up in that forest and many who made up both elements of that societal *Some*. Collectively they acknowledged the significance of the march for academia and accepted the opportunity provided them to discuss it and to fashion a curriculum about it. In varying degrees they understood that education is not just something that emanates from a curriculum guidebook or from established textbooks. It is not just a process for passing on to those in a class the capacity to answer questions repeatedly asked of and answered by those schooled for years — even generations — before them. Together, they understood that education imparts the capacity to ask insightful and probing questions about matters impacting the quality of life for all humans, not just for those with the power to shape social systems and reap the major benefits from doing so.

Together they asked, in theme and variation, if a million citizens marched on the nation's capital, that being approximately four times the size of the march led by Dr. King 32 years before, what did that portend? If it is to be only men doing so, why is that? If it is only men who are African American doing so, why is that? Given that the March was to take place during a school day, how should we surround our students with people who cared about them and who could pose thoughtful questions for them about the March, what it signified about social realities in our country and what it heralded for our future? How could we make sure that the focus on the March and its propelling issues could be structured in such a way that the process would help prevent violent reaction among our students should a model for such break out in Washington, D.C.?

Kindred Spirits and Threats

A day or two before the March, the *Daily Review*, the area newspaper, put out a story on our district's decision to do a curriculum on it. The headline said that students were to get the day off for the March. That headline was false. We had never considered giving students the day off for the March. What we did was communicate with parents that if they intended to keep a child out of school that day and told us in advance we would provide some independent study material for them, just like we did on any other occasion when parents took a child out of school for a short time and followed our procedure for doing so. The content of that inaccurate headline fused with the intense opposition to the March that was boiling in our community and in surrounding areas. From the date of that edition of the *Daily Review* right up to the time of the March, I had approximately 40 phone calls put through to me by staff from people who wanted to talk to me about the decision to address the March in class. One of the calls was moderately supporting. The rest ranged from demeaning to hateful. District office clerical staff handled a much greater number of calls that derogated or threatened my life.

The day of the March my secretary, Mary Pipkin, came into my office to tell me that Craig Calhoun, Hayward's Police Chief, and Captain Rodger Powers were outside and wanted to see me. I told her to send them in. After I greeted them both, Chief Calhoun said he had a question for me. I told him to go ahead with it. "With respect to this March," he began, "you know you're doing the right thing, don't you?" "Yes, I do," I responded simply. "So do we," the chief replied, "but we've got to get your back." The police department had been hearing also about people threatening to kill me because we were doing the curriculum for the March. It is important to note that both Craig Calhoun and Rodger Powers are people

of the dominant culture gladly given to meeting their professional responsibilities in a community structured of
multiple cultures.

The night of the day of the March we had a regularly
scheduled board meeting. The chief put plain-clothes officers in the boardroom and had a plain car in front of
mine and one behind it when I drove home after the meeting. From then on I always was careful. Next to my office
in the district's four story administrative building was
the one shared by Sue Berg, my administrative assistant,
and Mary Pipkin, the office secretary. Next to their office
was the lobby to the building. When I saw people I didn't
know walk into their office or into the lobby I found myself looking down at their hands to see if there was anything in them. When I left my office and walked through
the building to the outside steps that led down to the
parking lot, I scanned it for seconds from the platform at
the top of the steps to see if anyone I didn't recognize was
loitering in the area. I found myself looking around my
car to see if there was anything unusual near or under it.
I didn't actually panic: I just stayed cautious. Ironically,
right after the March was over the same newspaper that
had triggered so much negative reaction with its inaccurate headline printed a story saying I had been praised
for making a wise decision regarding the March.

The opposition to the actions we took to address the
March stopped about as rapidly as they were triggered.
Over! Done! Not another word, at least any spoken in
public, was uttered. Puente and Adewole continued to
make progress, lessened in possibility by the reality of
continued individual professional indifference, mostly
unwitting, to those gaps by culture in student achievement data. Our efforts expanded — but not enough for
our own satisfaction — the consciousness about the nexus between the social realities that stimulated the March
and the history and continuity of the gaps. Awareness

was embellished — but not enough again — about the need for constructive connections among the cultures of educators, the cultural awareness and proficiency of educators, the cultures of students and their histories and the expectations held for students.

Culture, *Educationese* and Educational Methods

Certain expectations for student behavior come from all teachers. The methods used to teach and appraise student learning, both formally and informally, are intensely valued in any culture. Those methods and expectations are initially and largely formed by three sets of experiences, i.e., constant daily interaction with people of one's primary culture, interaction with teachers while a student and education and training while becoming a teacher. The first two categories of experiences unconsciously effect the development of teacher expectations. The latter is conscious and, given the fact that the vast majority of teachers, irrespective of their individual primary cultures, are educated and trained at and graduated from colleges and universities built on the values and operated with methods and styles of the dominant culture, it easily out weighs the first two for significance as a foundational contribution to expectations held by every single teacher for every single student s/he would teach. Each class and the individual personalities and behaviors in them could tweak those teacher expectations but their foundations almost always remain the same, too often culturally exclusive.

In *Educationese,* a persistent language spoken in public education, "I treat all my kids the same" is a common proclamation among teachers when faced with continuing gaps by socio-cultural-economic group in data on school success. That manifesto is tugged to the surface almost invariably in professional dialogue about such gaps in what is called "achievement data," e.g., standardized test scores, enrollment in advanced placement courses and admissions to universities and four-year colleges. An inference in that *Educationese* proclamation comes grossly in two related elements. First, if I treat all my students the same and most of them do well in meeting our academic standards, then neither I nor the system I represent can be contributors to gaps in the accepted indicators of success among socio-cultural-economic groups of students. Second, if I treat all my kids the same and *they* end up on the short end of the achievement data, even year after year, *they* and/or *their* families and/or *those* of *their* culture have to improve *their* commitment or enhance *their* abilities or get more involved ...or ... or ... or ... some other or(s). I want *them* to be successful and am always available to help. That posturing is constant regardless of the persistent reality that students who are African American or Latino are disproportionately and perennially on the down side of the gap. As within schools where there is more than one culture, the same posing is common in discussions about gaps between schools when they are segregated by socio-cultural-economic status. There is almost never evolving dialogue about the major locus of responsibility for the gaps being institutional and systemic.

The definition of "treating all my kids the same" needs to be assessed for the anatomy of that treatment as well as for the specifics of its enactment. The methods used — or neglected — for teacher-student interaction are profound elements in determining its utility. Culture influences the style of every single teacher-student interaction. If the teacher is of the dominant culture and the student is African American, differences in interaction style are not automatic but common, particularly if parents of the student have limited formal education and the student comes from a poor or working class environment but the teacher does not. The negatives in the interaction consequences for students are exacerbated when the teacher and her/his school administrators and support staff have little or no experience in communities that are African American and have done little or nothing to learn about African American Culture(s), particularly as they relate to methods and views of the dominant culture. Yet, teachers in schools with large African American populations, particularly in communities that are poor and working class, don't have to relate to cultural methods of students who are African American to become tenured. The students who are African American in those schools, however, must adapt to the cultural methods of the teacher to survive in the system.

Institutional acceptance of variance from those dominant cultural practices is manifested in genuine commitment to academic disciplines that are analytical about other cultural methods, values and historic and social perspectives, e.g., African American Studies, Cultural Anthropology, Ethnic Studies. That commitment is in colleges and universities and, with a diminutive number of exceptions, not in K-12 schools. That institutional commitment is to the study of other cultures but not to employing their methods and values for the operation of public education institutions themselves. The values, expectations and methods of the dominant culture that the vast majority of teachers and school administrators are trained to enact are not always in conflict with those of other cultures. However, often they are.

For example, consider when teachers in high school English classes have students read fiction. Fiction, because it is about human interaction, contains emotion. Discussion of emotion, even that emanating from review of literature in a classroom, sometimes begets emotional demonstration. Teachers are trained to have expectations for students regarding the handling of emotion in classroom dialogue. Imagine the following scene. It is an English class in an inner-city high school. Discussion is going on about emotional interaction between two characters in a work of fiction. One student who is African American steps assertively and abruptly into the classroom conversation and renders her perception of the author's intention in shaping the dialogue a particular way. Before she concludes her assessment of that intent, another student who is African American responds, without either raising his hand or waiting for teacher approval to do so.

"Girl," he says a little loudly, "You gotta be kiddin'! The dude who wrote that book didn't mean what you said!" He then proceeds to depict his version of the author's intent in contradistinction to his classmate's view.

She responds as intently to him. He again to her. Point-counterpoint goes on with the energy of a hard pushed intellectual playground swing. The fervor of each is matched by the other. The teacher is a little frustrated but before she/he decides to intervene authoritatively, the young man remains silent for a moment after his classmate adds another analytical piece to her case. Then he says, "You gotta point! Now ... say that again, girl." She does. He nods agreement to her latest statement and slides comfortably back down a little in his student desk. The discussion moves on to other students, the teacher now being more assertive about the need to raise one's hand before participating and about staying calm when doing so.

Culture and Interaction Style

In his book, *BLACK AND WHITE STYLES IN CONFLICT*, Thomas Kochman analyzes cultural differences in several elements of classroom modalities. In addressing classroom discourse, he notes, " ... when blacks and whites engage each other in public debate about an issue, they are divided not only over content — the issue itself — but, more fundamentally, over process: how disagreement on an issue is to be appropriately handled."

Kochman finds, "The modes of behavior that blacks and whites consider appropriate for engaging in public debate on an issue differ in their stance and level of spiritual intensity. The black mode — that of black community people — is high-keyed: animated, interpersonal, and confrontational. The white mode — that of the middle class — is relatively low-keyed: dispassionate, impersonal, and non-challenging. The first is characteristic of involvement: it is heated, loud, and generates affect. The second is characteristic of detachment and is cool, quiet, and without affect."

Kochman so skillfully delineates more distinctions between African American and Dominant American styles in classroom modalities. He notes, "For example, blacks distinguish between argument used to debate a difference of opinion and argument used to ventilate anger and hostility. In the first form of argument — for persuasion — the affect shown is expressive of debaters' relation to their material. Its presence indicates that people are sincere and serious about what they are saying. On the other hand, the affect present in the form of argument that is a ventilation of anger and hostility is more intense; it is more passionate than earnest. It also emphasizes less a positive attitude toward one's material than a negative attitude toward one's opponent.

"Whites, on the other hand," Kochman clarifies, "fail to make these distinctions because argument for them functions only to ventilate anger and hostility. It does not function as a process of persuasion. For persuasion whites use discussion that is devoid of affect and dynamic opposition. Consequently whites feel that people are not engaging in persuasion when affect and dynamic opposition are present."

Kochman does not stereotype when he delineates Black/White cultural distinctions. His description of Black methodologies derives from analysis of the human behavior and styles functioning in communities that are African American in contrast to the behavioral methods and styles in America's dominant culture. His focus on the stylistic conflict between those cultural methods is profoundly useful for analysis of the *Black/White Divide*, generally, and of its destructive hammering in education on students who are African American, specifically. Substance for prescriptions to overcome the debilitating effect of the *Divide* and, even, to end it are ensconced in his description and analysis. Ironically, the students of America's dominant culture and the quality of American society at-large are damaged also in public education institutions by the powerful daily exclusion of non-dominant cultural methods for human interaction, especially those influencing teaching and learning. It is one thing to have academic disciplines and/or departments focused on a variety of cultures. It is another to include those culture practices in a variety of ways, including simply acknowledging their functionality, throughout the institution. Not learning of methods employed by cultures other than one's primary one lessens prospects for constructive relations with humans of other cultures. Such diminishes both the quality of life of all involved and of the prospects for our country to enhance its democracy, within its boundaries and beyond them.

The behavior described above is common. I saw such dialogue as a teacher in my English classes in the '60s, as a principal visiting classrooms in the '70s and '80s, as a school district administrator in various roles visiting schools in the '80s and '90s and doing the same as a district superintendent from the early '90s' well into the 21st Century. Rather than being seen as the perfectly legitimate way at getting at the truth or at an understanding of another's perception that it is, this assertive method of dialogue is often seen as aberrant classroom behavior. When that is the case, students engaging in such a method are correspondingly seen as needing to be disciplined in the classroom and requiring better training at home. It is not just coincidental that there is a relationship between the individual, collective and historic spin off on that perception and the age old disproportionate negatives in the indicators of academic success and in the disproportionate suspensions, expulsions and placements in Special Education in public schools for students who are African Americans.

Another classic example tied tightly to Kochman's analysis of the influence of culture on interaction style came from an experience involving school but not in a classroom. It was around 1989 or 90. I got a call from Judge Wilmont Sweeney, the Presiding Judge of the Juvenile Court of Alameda County. I don't remember how we had met but I know it had something to do with the working relationship between the Juvenile Court and the Oakland Unified School District for which I was a district administrator at the time. Trust and respect arrived early in our interactions. We would speak periodically about what we could do together to help individual young people who had come to his attention in court.

Judge Sweeney called because he had heard that the school district was going to be closing down a school in East Oakland and he wanted to use the facility for a school that would serve and educate young people who would otherwise be sent to a California Youth Authority Detention Center. We met to talk about how we could get the job done. I suggested that we have a public meeting in the community to discuss the issue, that I introduce the topic and that he wait until after the initial response from the public to step into the dialogue. I did so because I anticipated that there would be intense, even angry, initial response to the proposition that young people who had been in trouble with the law be brought into the community, despite that it was for them to be educated. Judge Sweeney, by virtue of the interblending of his intellect, commitment to the young people he served and experience as a man who is African American with the struggles to rise to the top of his profession, understood instantly the prospects for such responses. He and I also anticipated that, at some point in the dialogue with community members, after the initial frustration and anger over the suggestion were sufficiently vented, the tone of the dialogue would change and he, then, would step into the discussion and close the deal. We knew the intelligence, spirit and caring in the community would overcome any fear or discomfort about "troubled youth" being in the neighborhood's school facility every day. We set up the meeting.

At the opening of the meeting I introduced Judge Sweeney and the topic. He sat quietly, part way across the room. The responses came quickly and in the style expected. People from the community raised their voices at me and impassionedly asked things like, "Why do you want to bring these criminals into our community?" Questions and comments kept coming in leitmotif. People were yelling at me and I was feeling great! It wasn't just that things were going as anticipated. It was simply that people were using what I knew to be a perfectly legitimate style for getting at the truth. In an environment that was of the dominant culture it might have been insulting. In this social terrain it was not.

The affect swooped and bounced through the room at mixed speeds until a gentleman, who had spoken intensely before, stood up. He acknowledged, in a much calmer tone, that people in the room had stated their concerns and that maybe there was another point of view they should hear. I commented that he had raised something important and said, "Judge Sweeney's right here. Maybe he'd like to come up and talk about it." He did.

He was persuasive and insightful. The use of that school building for Judge Sweeney's program was accepted that night. Being respectful of the culture of the people speaking and of the culture-based methods used in the process interfused with the intelligence and caring in such neighborhoods, often overlooked by those not of it, and contributed pivotally to that acceptance. The same approach regarding long-standing issues about education in communities that are African American and poor would contribute just as constructively to harmonizing efforts to end the gaps in the indicators of academic success and to altering the system that produces and/or tolerates students who are African American being disproportionately on the downside of those gaps. The approach, by itself, will not achieve that needed systemic and institutional change in education. Indeed, all who are African America don't use the same methods. However, without employing that approach when and where needed, particularly in communities that are African American and poor or working class, the change will not come. The persistence of the *Divide* will be abetted.

There is a conviction among many educational professionals that those particular assertive African American classroom interaction methods are inappropriate. Consistent with that conviction is the opposition to them being used and disciplinary responses when they are, e.g., admonitions to raise one's hand for participation in classroom discourse, being sent to the office for corrective action and, as the data consistently show, disproportionately high rates of suspension. Often there is indifference rather than disciplinary response, i.e., if a student does not play by the rules for discourse, s/he might not get called on to participate in it. It is not the fact of disciplining students who are African American that is at issue. It is the disproportionality of that discipline. It is ignorance or indifference about the influence of culture on the forms of human interaction. At the same time that it is necessary for students to learn how to adapt to dominant cultural methods it also is necessary for the institutions of learning to be constructively inclusive of the methods of non-dominant cultures.

There is a nexus between Kochman's work and a particular element of that done by the late John Ogbu. Dr. Ogbu, an anthropologist at the University of California, Berkeley, had researched and written extensively on education and African Americans. He described three different kinds of "minority" experiences. There are "autonomous" *minorities,* people for whom the discrimination in America dissipated and finally disappeared, e.g., Italians and Irish. There are "immigrant" *minorities,* those whose circumstances in America are best understood in reference to their experiences and diminished sense of hope in the countries from which they emigrated. For example, some might wonder how a family of eight, recently arrived from a particular East Asian country, might tolerate living in a two-bedroom apartment. The point may be that if they were back in their country of origin they might not have a place to live or health care or a job or education or enough food and, worse, might be imprisoned, or tortured, or dead. The living conditions in America are wonderful by contrast.

Ogbu also found "subordinate or caste-like" *minority* experiences to be embedded in American Society. He pointed out that such experiences bonded with a sociocultural origin in America born of colonialism, conquest or slavery. Ogbu's analysis explicates a major distinction between this set of historic, ongoing, collective encounters and those of autonomous and immigrant experiences. The distinction lies in the intractability, from the onset of colonialism, conquest and slavery to the present, of the variously materialized separateness between those experiencing ongoing subordination or caste-like-ness and the dominant culture.

Ogbu also pointed out that a "secondary" cultural difference emanates from that ceaseless subordination. It takes the form of oppositional posturing in light of dominant culture positions. It can be summarized in effect with this: You may be able to diminish and control my future but you can't mess with my day. If you say something is "up," I may say it's "down." If you say something of top quality is to be called "good," I also may think of it the same way but I'm going to call it "bad." Indeed, in the discourse of some African Americans, "bad" is a complimentary term. For example, one of Michael Jackson's most famous albums was called *Bad.* It is common to hear in African American parlance, among the educated and not so educated alike, positive appraisals tendered like the following: "That's a bad tie you have on, man;" or "That's a bad outfit, girl," or "That speech was bad!"

The Erroneous Concept of *Race*
And the Absence of Needed Change

Given the separateness of so many of us who are Native American into what are, in effect, nations within our nation, a consequence of conquest is so very apparent. Considering the historic and contemporized impact of colonialism and slavery, it is not just coincidental that the students for which there are historically and consistently the least good success data in urban public education are Latino, particularly Chicano, and African American. Nor is it just a fluke that the continuance of that reality is paralleled by the historic absence in public education of such a dilemma being understood and acted on as a social and systemic quandary that requires radical change. Nor has there been clear delineation of the criteria for determining that change has come about, training needed to affect and maintain it, a process of accountability for doing so and the melding of a solid grasp of the need for that change with a commitment to achieving and institutionalizing it as a sine qua non for being employed as an educator to begin with.

Unfortunately, the prevailing way of conceptualizing in public schools about education for *Students of Color* contributes substantively to the simmering life of the issues that sustain the *Black/White Divide.* There is, for example, a sincere wish among many educators that children of all *races* be successful in school. The sincerity presides despite the fact that the categorical gaps between students of the dominant culture and students who are African Americans have existed during the duration of every teacher's career, no matter what its length. The concept of *Race,* itself, damages the prospects for ending the gaps and providing the "equal" education all educators claim to want for their students.

Given the oft evaded reality that *race* is a social, not a scientific construct, the continued use of the term by educators accrues only to maintenance of the *Divide* in school and to the continuing disparity in school "success" rates and the material and social benefits affixed to them. The problem is exacerbated by the systemic exclusion in the curricula for university and college schools of education and in public schools of sufficient analysis of the nexus between the use of the concept of *race* and the inevitable existence of racism that results. There can be no equal education when part of the enterprise for many teachers is internalized as having to figure out how to teach a *them.*

The speciousness of that thinking, when engaged in by an educator, necessarily applies to relationships with students and their families. Using *race* in education negatively impacts both sides of the *Black/White Divide,* albeit with varied intensity and specificity of results. Both sides are robbed of the opportunity to experience *Us* in another cultural manifestation in a way that would hand all involved hope for a *divide-less* future. One set of people is impacted by being categorically on the downside of the gap in indicators of success or being perceived by some who see but don't know the humans being appraised, individually or academically, as members of that academic downside even when it is not so. There are no comparable negative, summary academic appraisals and results about the upside of the *Divide*.

The concept of *race* is antithetical to ending the *Black/White Divide* in education — or in anything else for that matter. Instead, a detailed grasp of the influence of culture in teaching, learning, human interaction styles and in the structure of society and its social institutions should obviate any consideration of the concept of *race* and replace it. Each culture, including the prism it provides for social, especially interactive, perceptions, is learned and is, therefore, learnable. A focus on culture yields a recognition that the difference in people is not in how we are structured as human beings but in the social tools and styles we use to express the reality that we are exactly, historically, perennially, universally and inalterably the same. Educators could help end the *Divide*, rather than participate unwittingly or intentionally in its sustenance, if they were to celebrate *Our* identical sameness as human beings along with *Our* varied cultural mechanisms for expressing our humanness rather than focusing on *racial* differences. If the *Divide* in education is ever to end, the education and training and professional practice of teachers, administrators and school leaders must include cultural methods, other than just the ones of Dominant America, as needed. That training and professional practice must also include constant engagement of a process for seeing society through the cultural prisms of others of *us* not having been raised in it or experiencing it as you have.

In their book CULTURAL PROFICIENCY: A MANUAL FOR SCHOOL

LEADERS, Randall Lindsey, Kikanza Nuri Robins and Raymond D. Terrell write descriptively of culture and, at the same time, they are insightfully prescriptive about the institutional task to be taken on in public education if the gaps in school success by socio-cultural and economic groups are to end.

They note that "culturally proficient educators recognize that culture involves far more than ethnic or racial differences. They demonstrate an understanding of the cacophony of diverse cultures each person experiences in the school setting. Although they accept that they will not necessarily have intimate knowledge about each of the cultures represented in a classroom, school, or district, they recognize their need to learn more continually. They develop a conscious awareness of the culture of their communities, districts, or schools, and they understand that each has a powerful effect on the educators, students, parents, and community associated with that school or district."

The Need for Agreement on the Meaning of *Education* and the Distinction Between Accountability and Responsibility

The difficulty in ending the *Divide* in education is magnified by a lack of consistency in defining education itself. It is often confused with training and schooling. Training is the process by which a person provides another with an understanding about how to do something that the trainer already knows how to do, e.g., driver's training. Schooling is the process by which students are guided to become sufficiently facile in demonstrating the values of the primary culture in and for which school is established so their teachers and school administrators see it appropriate to grant them their informal stamp of approval.

Education, although it requires some training and

can be nurtured by schooling, is radically different from both of them. Education is a multifaceted and constructively functional practice. It is a process for developing a solid grasp of the existing and prospective elements of individual and social life.

The *Divide* and its destructive results are perpetuated strongly by *education* not being defined, seen and employed sufficiently as a multidisciplinary process of penetrating inquisition and curative prescriptiveness that does not require automatically matriculation in and graduation from college before it is enacted.

Education also functions to identify and formulate needed contributions to the well-being of self and fellow human beings. It is different from schooling and training and, although it is usually connected with matriculation in school, it does not require it. Nothing done in America or any other society that has constructively altered social quality and consequences was the result of those involved picking the right answer from a list of multiple options presented by someone ostensibly in possession of *all* the right answers regarding the issue(s) in question. The *Divide* will not be rendered to a bookcase for historic binders containing descriptions of social *Used-To-Bes* in America by a requisite number of students picking, for example, answer "B," rather than "A," "C," or "D" as the correct descriptor of the problem or of its solutions.

The sustenance of the *Black/White Divide* is a function of the continuance of the same kind of unresolved, fermenting, incessantly troubling and insufficiently attended to issues of second-classness that propelled the Million Man March and prompted the establishment of the Puente Project in the Hayward Unified School District and a variety of others, the Student Achievement and Learning Team (S.A.L.T.) program in the San Diego Unified School District and Adewole in the Hayward Unified School District. Given the presence of such social tinder, the best way to keep the likely fire from bursting onto the scene again is to impart to *Our* young, in all *Our* cultural iterations, the capacity to ask deeply penetrating questions about why the threat of such a fire still hangs, seemingly intractably, above all of *Us*. Educators need to pursue intensely the answer(s) about why *We* continue to conceptualize and think in ways about the threat that have altered but never ended it and about what actions, in all of *Our* cultural methodologies, will shape *Us* into an inalterable unity of purpose that will make *Our* education system the model of multiple and linked cultures needed to end the *Divide*.

That sustenance of the *Divide* is also buoyed in public education by the obdurate systemic inattention to the difference between accountability and responsibility. Accountability is a systemic and institutional process for enacting consequences for individuals for doing or not doing what is required to achieve institutional goals and have institutional values constantly ensconced in the process(es) for doing so. Responsibility is individual, not systemic or institutional. Despite the historically professed commitment, in theme and variation, of almost all teachers to "treat my students fairly" or to "treat all my children the same" and the denial of any institutional contributions to the *Divide*, there are no systemic consequences in public education for the never-ending gaps by socio-cultural groups in the indicators of academic success. Some individuals take responsibility and address the issue. Accountability for the *Divide* is still waiting to be asked to go to work in public education institutions.

Predominant focus on education as the development of skills that will enable an individual to "get a better job" reduces, ironically, the prospects for being well educated and for education having the utility it could for ending the *Divide*. That there are disparities in both employment and income by socio-cultural group is stamped often by Dominant America as a consequence of poor schools in *those* neighborhoods and of *those* parents not getting involved enough and of their children, consequently, not getting enough education. In addition to the poor schools in *those* neighborhoods, it is often implied, if not stated outright, that the insufficiency of education is the choice of *those* people, an unwillingness to do what is necessary, like *we* do, to secure the education they claim they want.

Also confounding is the insufficient grasp in *education* of the reality that children, even in primary grades, are capable of doing analysis and proposing solutions for social interaction impediments in classrooms and on playgrounds — even in neighborhoods. There is a woeful insufficiency in *education* of needed analysis and prescriptions focused on the realities of American social structure rather than just on remedying its negative effects for individuals or socio-cultural groups perceived as not yet prepared to do what is necessary for deriving the available benefits of it.

Education is not seen yet satisfactorily as a preeminent and incomparably needed means for culling out a solution for the *Divide* applicable to people irrespective of the socio-economic-cultural groups with which they identify or with which they have been classified by others. What has passed to date as education about the *Divide* is repetitious praising, with little detail, of the civil rights movement and Dr. King — mostly his "I Have A Dream" speech— but not the steadily refined analysis of a prevailing need for the movement and prescriptions for requisite social change. (There are 57 other books, speeches and essays from Dr. King that so brilliantly address the *Divide*. Students who are taught about them or hear about any of them, particularly in K-12 education, are a rarity.)

To overcome the blatant insufficiency of such education, *radical change,* i.e., alteration in the structure of the education system itself, is so very clearly needed. Accomplishing that will derive, in part, from institutionalizing inclusion of *non-dominant* cultural course content and methods of instruction. There is, though, an on-going avoidance of that requisite *radical change* that emanates, on a large scale, from the avoidance of education about it and the need for it.

Education Identity Theft —
Unsegregation not Integration

What has been offered as Education about the *Divide* has been, again regardless of intention, a characterization, in effect, of the inalterable surging-ahead nature of those of Dominant America and the incurable, lagging-behind constitution of African America. That is so despite the countless exceptions that may have been perceived by any of *Us* in America. What passes as education about the *Divide* during Black History Month says there was a civil rights movement, enacted by some courageous people, that it accomplished some of what it set out to accomplish and it is over. Period. Absent is consideration of why and where we must go next with the remaining issues. Given the prevailing perception that neither African Americans nor people of the dominant culture can be changed, regardless of the appraisal(s) of either, made by those characterized as either, whatever is proffered as education about the perceived separateness between them can produce, at best, only tolerance for what is seen as inevitable rather than rendering means for sending the issue to its merited historical grave. Dominance and subordination are learned, even if unconsciously. Being learned rather than being cemented into individual humans and humanity means the prospects for replacing them with something that serves individual humans and humanity better can be learned also and enacted instead. The absence of such education is a major element in the staying power of the *Divide* in America.

Some dysfunction in the history of public schools needs to be more clearly and widely recognized for its contribution to continuance of the *Divide.* Although the *Brown vs. The Board of Education* Supreme Court decision in 1954 was ethically and morally right, it has not been satisfactorily analyzed or communicated about in public education, in legal and legislative environments and in public generally. Then, what was called "integration" was touted as a panacea for the disparities by what was called "race" in the dominant culture's appraisal of the service provided by public schools. The perception of many was that disparity could be ended if *Black* children could be brought into previously all *White* schools. Today, 50-plus years into what was called "integration", disparity continues in the accepted indicators of student achievement. Indeed, what is more is that the "integration" misnomer is still sufficient to shield from clear public view that the disparities still exist and are a systemic problem that has been institutionalized. Rather than seeing the problem as "disparities in student achievement," it should be recognized as serious flaws in institutional focus, structure, operational and instructional methods, curricular content and professional training and productivity. However, in most school districts there is too little or no such recognition.

What was called "integration" was nothing more than *unsegregation.* On the basis of visual discernment of melanin and hair texture, students who had been disallowed enrollment in schools reserved exclusively for the children of the dominant culture were now allowed by it to attend them. An assumption related to that decision was that students who were African American, the *Negro* students, via their matriculation in the schools previously attended by only students who were of the dominant culture, would be the new beneficiaries of superior resources, including better trained and educated teachers, teachers considered better by the dominant culture because it produced them.

That *unsegregation* was confused by many for a seminal step in integration. That confusion resulted, in large part, because the act of *unsegregation* was so easily witnessed. Doing so did not require education or any special analytical talent. It was easy for residents of any municipality to recognize that students who were *Black* and students who were *White* now entered and exited the same school building, through the same door. The fact that it was occurring provided the dominant culture with the opportunity to present itself — even sincerely — as no longer segregationist. That self-attribution seemed rational to the dominant culture and those of it who ran its newly "integrated" schools.

That *unsegregation*, however, was mostly geographical and spatial, far less social and educational. Students were resegregated proportionately, not totally. To this day in high schools in America's multi-cultural communities, for example, there are consistently and proportionately more students who are of the dominant culture than African American in advanced placement courses and more students who are African American than of the dominant culture on basketball teams. Neither case is the result of the possession of superior or inferior abilities of either socio-cultural category of students. The consequences of not having gone beyond *unsegregation* show in the disproportionality of the benefits of both schooling and education. Another example, certainly, is that those of *Us* who are African American represent a much higher percentage of America's prison population than of America's college and university enrollment.

Given that the ability to learn is universal, irrespective of culture, ethnicity, gender or socio-economic status but that success data in our schools do not represent that universality, the concept of integration takes on a new significance. Integration requires *unsegregation* but is not its synonym. It is not the singular purview of geography or physical space. Integration is the voluntary coming together of coequals, for an agreed upon purpose, with agreed upon criteria for measuring its mutual utility, benefit and the appropriateness and desirability of its continuity. Integration is societal, rather than individual, marriage. As a marriage, it requires never ending efforts at constructive unity. It does not require, however, that the parties to the marriage relinquish their respective identities, including primary culture. It does require, though, an activated willingness in that primary culture to rid it of any practices or perceptions that would preclude human unity across cultural lines, e.g., dominating other socio-cultural-economic groups. Integration requires the creation of a culture of unity across the lines of the primary cultures of those involved.

Real integration in schools, like in the rest of society, is not a process for people not of the dominant culture to be assimilated into it. School integration includes developing facility with the methods prevailing in any social practice in which students are likely to become involved as citizens. It requires the practice of including cultural content throughout the curricula, not just in ethnic studies classes. It requires constant action on the recognition that culture, dominant and not, profoundly influences teaching and learning styles and that the capacity to learn is universal. It requires the employment by teachers of the varied cultural methods of students while teaching them also how to be proficient in the use of the learning and other social methods of the dominant culture until *dominance* and *subordination* are buried along with other destructive social structures and practices.

Segregation persists in public schools: it just does so without geography playing as important a role in that separation as it once did. Although there are isolated exceptions, public schools foster that partitioning through the tolerance of it. That continuing separation is a social, cultural and spiritual divorce when there never has been a marriage. It has been the dominant culture's exclusive power, both legal and extra-legal, despite many in it not choosing to exercise it, to effect that disunion. Recent political efforts in California are clear cases of perpetuating the separation. The successful effort of Ward Connerly, a recent member of the University of California's Board of Regents, to end Affirmative Action at the University of California and his failed balloted effort to officially end the use of ethnic data in public institutions are prototypes for what is, in effect, contemporary efforts to continue modern segregation. There has been no replacement of the equity lost in the expulsion of Affirmative Action. The equality that the equity in Affirmative Action had abetted was, in effect, given an institutional finger. Enrollment at the University of California plummeted for students who are African American. What was supposed to have been altered in public schools by the Brown vs. the Board of Education decision could not be followed, analyzed and constructively criticized if Connerly's effort at ending access to the data had been successful. That failure, though, neither precludes another like initiative in the near future, nor does it mean all school districts will use constructively the data available to end today's forms of segregation.

Mr. Connerly has been a "front man" in pursuit of such social actions. Indeed, the collective use of the names of all other members of the U.C. Board of Regents couldn't match the number of times Connerly's name alone has been used by the news media. That Connerly has physical features attributed to African Americans appears to have contributed to the formation of a political tactic for those on the board who agree with Connerly but do not actively pursue public opportunities for showing it. They said, in effect, "That if an African American wants these things, then certainly we cannot be accused honestly of being racist for supporting him." Connerly's actions in this case make clear that skin color and hair texture aren't automatic determinants of cultural affiliation.

The supplanting of results with self-proclaimed good intentions in the education of *Our* children of color — particularly African American, Latino and Native American — and of children who are poor, irrespective of culture or ethnicity, needs to be more widely understood in the communities in which *Our* children live, particularly by those who would educate in such communities.

That those realities have no functional inclusion in K-12 curricula is contributory to the *Divide.* Young people are involved in the multi-layered realities of that disproportionality. Yet, it is not seen in public schools as appropriate for them to be taught to apply an interdisciplinary academic approach to analysis of disproportionality in both those negative realities and in access to social benefits that would function to enhance social positives. Standardized, multiple-choice tests are not structured to measure such education and it is not seen as a needed contribution to being gainfully employable — an increasingly intense focus of schools. The focus on getting good standardized test scores and becoming gainfully employable are increasingly successful in a tug-of-war with analytical and prescriptive education for teachers' attention. Many resist the pull in the direction of the latter. Those who give analytical and prescriptive education a higher priority than focusing on getting higher standardized test scores put their careers at various degrees of risk for doing so ... even if they are providing their students a higher quality of education in the process.

Still Just A Foothold

In his 1967 book *WHERE DO WE GO FROM HERE?* Dr.

King assessed the results of the Civil Rights Movement in the 50s and 60s. He observed that " ... Negroes have established a foothold, no more. We have written a declaration of independence, itself an accomplishment, but the effort to transform the words into a life experience still lies ahead." He goes on to note, "Freedom is not won by a passive acceptance of suffering. Freedom is won by a struggle against suffering. By this measure, Negroes have not yet paid the full price for freedom. And whites have not yet faced the full cost of justice."

Does he not, despite his physical passing, speak today to the existing *Black/White Divide* and to the need for radical change in America's Public Education system so that it can be the pivotal force it should be in the creation of America's first real *Us?* Would not his *Us* be one *not* structured of *dominance* and *subordination* and never-ending requirements for and efforts at assimilation into the dominant culture by those not born into it? Would it not be, instead, a social structure founded and sustained by the foundation knowledge and belief that *We* are of all of *Our* cultures? Does he not make it clear that being *Us* requires constant learning about the ways *We* are and the pursuit of the means for solidifying and expanding them?

CHAPTER 14

SEEKING POWER VS BEING POWERFUL AND THE BLACK/ WHITE DIVIDE

Marlin Foxworth, Ph.D.

THE PERCEPTION in many countries that America is the most powerful nation in the world is matched by America's self-appraisal. Assessments of the appropriateness of that singularity of power, however, vary throughout the world. Some countries appear to ally with America out of a kinship of spirit and values, some out of fear of the consequences of antagonizing the possessor of such power, others out of a complex suffusing of both. America is variously hated and loved as those in its international relationships ride the roller coaster steamed by its power. Classic in that context are the messages to the United States coming each day from Iraq and shaped by its citizens' rise-and-plummet experiences with the U.S. invasion and occupation. YouFreeUsKillUsMaimUsHealUs Build DestroyOurPowerMakeUsHopefulLessMakeUsWealthy StarveProtectOurChildrenSlaughterThemStay...GetOut.

Parallel to that is the rising/plunging of the power coaster for those in the *Black/White Divide* who did not create it, are on the downside of it and have had to ride it.

YouOfficially Ended Slavery HatefullyKeptSubordination
InteSegregatedSchoolsPutUsDisproportionatelyInBasketball
JailCreatingLawsLiesOfFreedomTellShowUsWeGreatlyMatt
er… NotAtAll.

Hegemony and Hypocrisy —
Dominance and Subordination

Most of America's politicians and leaders justify U.S.
hegemony, in part, through a national self-perception as
the country both most committed to a belief in the universal sameness of people and possessed of the form of
government, i.e., democracy, that transforms that belief
into social practice. Most of them also never-endingly
speak of Justice and Equality as though their manifestations in America may need tweaking but do not need
consideration for radical improvement. The multiple, intermittent, relatively frequent, sometimes clandestine,
sometimes open, violent incursions by America into
countries around the globe are politically validated by it
under the rubric of those democratic values. The contradiction inherent in those invasions, i.e., killing, maiming
or injuring others — combatants, women, children — because of a threat, real or contrived, to a system that is
based ostensibly on valuing each life the same, challenges the veracity of American commitment to the universal
value of human life and to the related democratic values.
Given that the United States had military forces in over
130 countries around the globe, the insistence of President Bush (43) that Syria, for example, remove its troops
from Lebanon was riddled with the shrapnel of hypocrisy. That hypocrisy obliterated prospects for consideration of any righteousness in the president's demand,
irrespective of any rational legitimacy underpinning it.
The legal, political, power, education, culture and material hegemony of Dominant America within its borders
is no less incongruous with a belief in the worth, dignity

and universal sameness of all of us humans and with a genuine commitment to Democracy and its Justice and Equality.

The fact that America continues to be structured with socio-economic-cultural dominance and subordination and that the power inherent and sustained in that dominance is a primary mainstay of the *Black/White Divide* furnishes no less a challenge to the genuineness of that proclaimed commitment. Relativism in the investment of America's dominant culture to those values may function well in the context of commitment comparisons with some other countries throughout the world. It has, however, no constructive worth as defined through the prism of experience and history in the downside of the *Divide.*

Residing at the very top of the structural elements of our humanity is the pursuit of meaning through the interfusing in each of us of the emotional, intellectual, intuitive and spiritual. That pursuit, regardless of the vehicles we use for the journey, is fueled by what is known, even unconsciously, even if not always seen, even if individually and/or socially denied, about the universal sameness of us. The rest of what differentiates us from other life forms hasn't the same significance. With the rare exception of the lives of hermits, that pursuit of meaning occurs in a social context.

Individual human meaning in any social system is induced, in part, by accessibility to its systemic structural elements that shape quality of life. Being in a socio-cultural-economic group that has been subordinated throughout its history in that social system produces, consequently, less access to the fundamentals of the quality of life and insufficient power within the system's prevailing structure to alter that reality equitably and satisfactorily. Such, simply, is demeaning. Being an exception from the downside of the *Divide* does not guarantee perpetual access to the exceptionalism. Nor does being an exception insure that the upside of the *Divide*, the residence of disproportionately high social power, will make no rescissions to exceptions made. The consequences of "driving-while-Black" are not automatically and permanently foreclosed because one's Mercedes Benz has been paid for in full ... and legally.

Abetting Power vs Impeding Power

Human power is energy applied, sometimes mistakenly, in the pursuit of meaning. It is individual and sometimes collective in its enactment, collective and, therefore, also individual in its consequences. Individual and collective power, in any social context, variously abet or impede that pursuit of meaning. *Abetting power* derives from an inalterable conviction that the value of life is universally the same in each individual and cannot be altered by religious, cultural, socio-economic or political affiliation. Such power, at the same time, includes the recognition that while destructive, demeaning behavior, including the exercise of impeding power, can come from individuals or groups, it is the behavior and the value(s) upon which it is built that need to be opposed or attacked but not the individual or collection of individuals rendering the obstruction. Demeaning or destroying those who first have demeaned or destroyed others obviously can provide no constructive meaning. It is abetting power, like that exercised by Mohandas Gandhi and Martin Luther King, Jr., that ultimately will end the *Divide* without crushing those on either side of it when it falls.

Impeding power derives from a resolute conviction that the value of life is universally varied by religious, cultural, socio-economic or political affiliation and by the false categorization of what is called "race." The sustenance of such power and the success of efforts to pursue meaning, most often when it is defined as disproportionately high access to material benefits and the qualities of life related to them, necessitates the continuous negative interpreting, demeaning, containment, diminishing, and destruction of or indifference to the social realities faced by *them.* Categories of *impeding power* continue to provide disproportionately higher access to material benefits for Dominant America and, despite political disclaimers, lingers as a sustainer of the *Divide.* In any structure, including that which is social, there can be no sustained upside without a downside and something built into the system to keep each in its place. In any society the existence of a most powerful category of citizens depends on the existence of a least powerful category. Likewise, any social more, whether it's power, money, education, etc., requires a social less . . . unless the supply and access to it are unlimited. Such, though, is not the case in America — or any other country.

Power: Organizational Structure and/or Charisma

Human power in any society can be a function of organizational structure or of charisma and sometimes it is the blending of the two. Most organizational structures are pyramidic. Power in them is disproportionately gained via the occupation of positions that lessen in number as the top of the organizational pyramid is approached, the greatest power residing in the single role at the apex. Charismatic power derives from the capacity of an individual to attract others through the expression and/or demonstration of values to those values and to taking action calculated to establish and sustain social realities, practices and structure with those values at their base.

The most difficult manifestation of power to assess for its relationship with constructive meaning is when people capable of attracting others to the values they demonstrate also reside in a role at the apex of an institution and when, consistent with that role, they enact institutional practices that simultaneously protect a valued way of life while lessening, impeding, demeaning or even destroying another way of life or those exercising it. Is there not still the Ku Klux Klan? Are there not "spiritual" and/or religious leaders providing support for the organization's virulence?

The arduous task of ferreting out and pursuing the consistent exercise of power devoid of such profound contradiction is exacerbated when the people looking for its structure are, themselves, beneficiaries of the contradiction. Osama bin Laden, Adolph Hitler and Saddam Hussein and their followers are simple examples of incongruity in the exercise of power and its support. The evil manifested via the absolutist dictates of all three moguls is readily discernible. Unquestionably, the supporters of each provide profoundly saddening, yet classic, examples of confusion and contradiction in the pursuit of meaning. Bin Laden, Hitler and Hussein epitomize the ultimate extremes in exclusion, demeaning and violence. History has shown us that many experiencing the regimes of Hitler and Hussein opposed them at the cost of their own freedom or lives. History also has shown us that the two dictators attracted loyalists who found themselves satisfactorily included, deriving what appeared as meaning from the values both proffered and transformed to action. That, too, is clearly the case with Osama bin Laden.

Power as Indifference or Neglect

Profoundly negative social consequences don't have to be as nefariously intended and dramatically violent as those indicated above to exist. For example, the absence of actions needed but not taken by most of America's politicians, people in governmental positions of authority and by society-at-large to end the multiple and continuing displays of the *Black/White Divide* since 1619 equate to violence, regardless of proclaimed intentions to the contrary. Neglect in positions of institutional power is manifestation of institutional power. There is a multitude of classic examples of neglect or insufficiency of attention in institutional positions of power to the follow-through needed to end the *Divide* in its varied and persistent manifestations. *Brown vs. the Board of Education* in 1954 didn't get equality ensconced completely and permanently in public schools. The voting rights law in the mid 60s didn't effect completely and permanently the representation of the legitimate interests of *Us* citizens who are African American. Those inequalities persist despite the existence of what was called civil rights, also established into law in the 60s. There is the willingness of our government to recruit African Americans into the military to fight and die for this country while it allows the disappearance of needed fairness via the loss of Affirmative Action in colleges and universities for the same population. The list goes on of examples of institutional and institutionalized power and the violence, usually but not always non-physical, produced by its neglected efforts to end the *Divide.* Yet the political palaver about the importance of equality continues.

The psychological and social violence in this context separates individuals and those with whom they identify socially and culturally from a state of well-being. A state of well-being is a condition of living in which an individual and those with whom s/he identifies culturally have equal access — and equitable access when necessary — to the personal and social requisites for self-development and to the emotional, spiritual and material benefits of a social order. Individual removal from a state of well-being can be justified sometimes, e.g., imprisoning someone for having committed a crime. Removal of social-cultural categories of people despite the exceptions, from that state of well-being and/or tolerating the continuance of that reality cannot be justified. When it occurs it is violence and can only happen when there is the individual and social power, by purpose, indifference, neglect or a combination of them, to make it happen.

Justification is proffered in positions of power for ne-glecting to provide equity for American social categories perennially on the downside of the *Divide* because of a supposed commitment to equality and its requirement to treat everyone the same. However, given the structur-al function of dominance and subordination in America and its powerful contribution to the *Divide*, what passes as equality is case-by-case for those of *Us* from the down-side, applicable to exceptions who have wended their way up through most of the toughest barriers provided by the *Divide*. Yes, this means there is some justice for some individuals, irrespective of their socio-cultural-economic status. History has shown *Us*, nonetheless, that equality in such cases is not systemically guaranteed and that it may have term limits.

Change, Not Apologies and the Need for Powerful People

There is a contrariness, if not contradiction, between accepting the perennial subordination of others of *Us* in this democracy and simultaneously apologizing for its consequences. Inequality isn't ended nor is equal-ity sprung into reality by apologies. It does not work for those of *Us* from Dominant America to apologize to those of *Us* not of it for having paid little or no attention to the conditions put into and sustained in the social environ-ment and system that resulted in *them* having citizen-ship injuries. The worthlessness of only apologizing is intensified when it is followed by the insistence that *they* get immediately back into the social game and by iden-tifying *them* as the problem should *they* either not do so or decide to play a different game on more familiar, non-dominant turf. Equity is radically needed. The environ-ment has to be restructured in conjunction by those of *Us* of the social stratum that created, allowed, tolerated or helped sustain conditions in it that caused the pain and injury to those of Us that they, themselves, did not and would not have to suffer and by those of Us who did so suffer. Then a time can be chosen by the injured to get back into the game, knowing that individual skill, not social environmental structure and related conditions would determine the results.

Despite the history of ongoing courage in overcoming the consequences of systemic damage to social environment, whole socio-cultural categories of Us should not have to do so. In that sense, the exercise of power in American politics has left Us with two choices, inequality or equity. Inequality, to date, has won. Our history tells Us that those just seeking power in top level positions in the pyramidic structure of the existing social system will not be able to provide the equity needed to achieve the equality needed. Powerful people, i.e., those able to attract others to the value of equality and to participation in the constructive activism required to secure it, will be the ones who can do it. Sometimes, but not often enough, powerful people get helpfully ensconced in top-level positions in the pyramidic structure and contribute to the needed achievement of equality. Once the powerful among us have attracted Us to the successful enactment of needed equity, its effective application will produce the constructive irony of ending itself. That is so because absence of inequality negates the need for equity.

There are even more vexing examples, though, of the exercise of power that ended the prospects for pursuit of meaning for some as a vehicle for securing the prospects for that pursuit for others. Citizens of the United States admired Harry Truman enough to make him our president. His supported decision to drop an atomic bomb on Hiroshima, with a population of 504,000, on August 6, 1945 and on Nagasaki, with a population of 405,000, on August 9, 1945 destroyed life — ostensibly to protect it. Certainly all of *Us* as U.S. citizens derive constructive meaning, even in this more than half century later, from the sustenance of the democracy threatened then by the Japanese Government. Do we not, too, anticipate such meaning from the supported "War on Terrorism" being waged by President George W. Bush, et al? Has not that war, though, already killed humans in great numbers? Will it not kill more? Is that killing not done in the name of protecting life and a way of life — "our" way of life?

The actions of Truman and Bush, with sufficient support from U.S. citizenry, were to exercise the power in the role at the apex of the national structure in order to end a process of butchery of human life and the evil and surprise methods used to do so by enacting the butchery of life. Violence invites, begets and parents itself — despite the ostensible moral justification for it. Were the dead citizens, including children and other non-combatants, in Hiroshima and Nagasaki in 1945 and the dead children, non-combatants and soldiers, including American troops, in Afghanistan and Iraq since 2002 any less dead as a consequence of the identified moral purpose of the people exercising the power that killed them? Were they to be dead just until the war was over ... then rise again? Was the demeaning and heartache of the living relatives of those who were killed as a consequence of action taken in what was offered as high moral purpose — despite the lack of clarity about it in the "War on Terror" — any less so than that suffered by the relatives of those comparably killed throughout world history? Likewise, for example, are those killed in the Watts Rebellion in 1965 going to leap back up to life when power is used in America to replace the same social circumstances in Watts that have prevailed for the more than 40 years since that rebellion with equality that is, not just is talked about? Will the anguish go away from those who loved the dead when equity is used as a tactical element of a strategy to compensate for social category inequality? Yes, posing the questions is easier than answering them. Yes, the unanswered questions require the unending asking of them until they are answered. Yes, those seeking power throughout the ascendancy in America's pyramidic power structure can continue to do so without addressing the questions. No, equality cannot be made to replace inequality via the seeking of power. Yes, being clear about the distinction between seeking power and being powerful and supporting those, on or even nowhere near the pyramidic structure, who attract others to genuine equality are absolute requisites for securing and stabilizing our equality.

Human Meaning and Abetting Power

Can there be found in hindsight a clear picture of how the universal protection of life and pursuit of meaning in it might have found their way into a universal exercise of abetting power? What are the prospects for abetting power to be universally ensconced? Can meaning be pursued in a way that transcends the boundaries of social separation in their multiple iterations? If so, can it be done without obliterating the cultural and spiritual vehicles which serve in America and throughout the world as the apparatuses for framing, energizing and structuring the pursuit of meaning by All of Us? Could, for example, the trust in the teaching of Abraham and faith in God, spiritual elements held in common by Christians, Jews and Muslims, be an amalgamated instigation of unity in the pursuit of meaning without loss of spiritual and cultural integrity? Could it happen without the disbelief of some in each faith about the human legitimacy of the faith of some? How do we support the constructively powerful among us so that their capacity to attract us to Us enables us to replace the historically persistent categories of us and them with only Us?

Meaning is knowing — even without understanding — that the most elevated manifestation of humanity is not in possession of material wealth or social or organizational positions of authority or power. It is in being and in acting to recognize the universal significance of that being and to sustain it while searching for and applying its inherent, global and constructive energies to the fullest. Pivotal in the pursuit of meaning is the capacity to differentiate it from purpose. Purpose is often proffered as the social surrogate of meaning. Purpose, though, can be exclusive in the distribution of benefits, e.g., the social efforts of bin Laden, Hitler and Hussein to structure societies devoid of people with primary cultures, values and convictions they did not share. Given the universal nature of human meaning, it not only cannot be exclusive but is all-inclusive by definition. Any exercise of power that will function to end the *Divide* must be based, in part, on a clear understanding of the distinction between systematizing equality and the prevailing practice in America of providing charitable contributions to some people to help them live adequately without it.

An experience, by simultaneously resonating intellectually, spiritually and emotionally as a universal and ideal manifestation of being human, is, at the same time, intimacy with meaning and propulsion into a world of *Us*, across the border from a world of *Us-and-Them*. To live in a world devoid of *Them* makes pursuit of meaning require refinement of our collective understanding of why *We*, individually and via governmental and other institutional — even religious — praxis, do demeaning things to *Us*. Borders in this context become geographic boundaries for temporal authority to organize and protect the pursuit of meaning in its universal sameness but through the varying cultural methodologies preferred by those of *Us* residing within the boundaries. Crossing such borders, rather than being a risk of violating *Their* laws, is a matter of learning the methods *We* use for *Our* pursuit of meaning in a particular geographic, cultural and spiritual context that may be varied in some way(s) from that with which some of *Us* are most familiar. Of absolute importance to the foundation of needed social change is the grasp that, although our cultural methods may be varied, we are not.

The variables combining to allow or produce impeding power that sustains the American structure of dominance and subordination and its ongoing bolstering of the *Black/Wide Divide* need to be thoroughly understood so that a society structured of equality can be created and maintained. There needs to be an unfaltering study of humans who, by being powerful, abetted the pursuit of meaning based on the universal sameness of *Us*. Once sufficiently understood, there also needs to be a concerted effort by *Us* at institutionalizing what is found in *Our* social structure and its bedrock institutions, particularly its public schools, colleges and universities.

There needs to be a public system that attracts the abetting work of those who understand dominance and subordination as the *raison d'etre* for the *Divide* that it is. That attraction needs to be for powerful humans, not humans seeking power, who are convinced of the profound detriment of the *Divide* to America genuinely becoming a prototype of ultimate equality. This attraction of the powerful needs to be done without the requirement of being ensconced at the apex of a social or organizational pyramid. It will be critical in the process to be clear about the criteria needed to differentiate between those who are powerful and those who seek power. The task must be undertaken without the point of location at the top of the pyramidic structure being seen as the inalterable determinant of power and the social intensity, breadth and depth of its application. If, on the other hand, a functioning definition of reality includes prospects for transforming exceptions into the rule, then the universal application of abetting power to the pursuit of meaning for *Us* is more than realistic.

Inevitable Consequences of Societal Structure

Some would say that charitable organizations are the only and best hope for abetting power in our society. The difficulty with that perception, however, resides in the reality that structure, including societal anatomy, has its own inevitable consequences. That inevitability shows in the following analogy. Supposing one needed to get from the West Coast of the Continental United States to Hawaii but could get neither a needed airplane ticket nor boat ticket. It would do the individual no good whatsoever to buy the best-rated automobile in the world to make the trip. The very structure of the vehicle would, in and of itself, preclude successful completion of the trip intended.

Charity is a process for addressing the consequences of impeding social circumstances. Charity is best when addressing debilitating human conditions which are not the inevitable consequence of systematized intention in a social structure. People with a disease, for whom preventive efforts have either not been applied or have been unsuccessful, can be helped via processes for purging the disease from their bodies, ridding their biological system of the conditions that allow, maintain or produce it, lessening the debilitating effects of it, or postponing the ultimate and most devastating consequences of it. For example, it is rational to believe that charitable contributions, either singularly or in conjunction with governmental efforts, to find a cure for AIDS will help achieve the intended result. AIDS is not the inevitable consequence of American or any other social structure.

Charitable organizations in our country, thankfully, provide food for hungry people. Often the provision is most notable on Thanksgiving and Christmas. Thankfully, former President Jimmy Carter and many he has attracted to the task provide housing through Habitat for Humanity for those of us characterized as "the indigent." However, these cases of kindness are radically different from charitable efforts for ending AIDS and other diseases.

The problem with charity being used as a tool to effectively address poverty in our social structure derives from the reality that *rich* has neither definition, substance nor membership without *poor.* Theoretically, Keynesian economists suggest that stimulation of the economy and control of interest rates by the government will cause the monetary circulation in the economy to be sufficient to limit the existence of poverty. However, the current expansion of the upper class, decline of the middle class and expansion of poverty in the United States speak in tandem about the inevitability of consequences from the U.S. socio-economic structure. Yes, there are those who find ways to rise out of poverty and out of it in ghettos. Yet poverty is a constant, never ending element of America's socioeconomic structure. So too has been the racist structure of the *Divide.* There is nothing that suggests that poverty can be ended by clinically treating the poor for the disease of being poor or for being at-risk of being so. So too with socio-economic-cultural groups born into subordination, even when it is absent evil intentions of those who prosper in such a social structure. Again, the fact or quality of an intention is not the determinant of a result.

In ECONOMIC APARTHEID IN AMERICA, Chuck Collins and Felice Yeskel make abundantly clear the exclusive and exclusionary character of power at the apex of economic institutions. They point out that the 1999 ratio of average CEO salaries to average worker salaries in America's largest 300 companies was 415 to 1. Further, they show that research done in 1998 found that the " ... ratio of CEO pay to factory worker pay at 363 'large public companies' was 419 ($10,600,000) to 1 ($25,300)." Salary increases and bonuses in huge sums frequently accrue to the benefit of those at the apex of the organization where the power resides and is exercised to "downsize," "restructure" and "lay off" huge numbers of humans. In such cases, it is the power in the position at the apex of the organization, its exercise by the individual in the position and the organizational structure, including support for the apex, that combine to dehumanize. That "economic apartheid" has its parallel in the nature of the *Divide*. Powerful individuals, as contrasted to those who seek power, will not tolerate the systemic perpetuation of a socio-economic structure that produces dehumanizing disparities by socio-cultural-economic groups, something America has done economically and socially since its inception, something it has done with the *Black/White Divide* since 1619.

Compassion and Faith Based Initiatives as Substitutes for Change

From the apex of the American social pyramid comes President George W. Bush's periodically and variously chanted call for "compassionate conservatism." Conservatism is maintenance and protection of what is. Despite the multiple constructive, even phenomenal, elements of American social order and its ongoing experiment, there are facets of that social structure that yield disparities in accessibility to the proclaimed elements of the "good life." Those disparities clearly play out in multiple ways for women, people of color — particularly *Our* citizens who are African Americans and Latino Americans — and the poor. Deeply sympathizing while conserving elements of a socio-economic structure that perennially produce that for which the sympathy is being requested and offered is not a function of a powerful individual but, instead, a vehicle for seeking and maintaining power while perpetuating the demeaning of and damage to those over whom, rather than for whom, it would be exercised.

The political solicitation of "Faith Based Initiatives" often serves as a safety net for "compassionate conservatism." That is not to suggest that spiritual and/or religious organizations serve no purpose for those of Us who need the help. Quite to the contrary, the lives of so many have been bettered — even saved — by the dedicated work of such institutions. However, the call for "Faith-Based-Initiatives" that is simultaneous with the pursuit of power structured to benefit disproportionately an element of society — but not equally benefit the society in all its elements — is a result of a social system that inevitably produces the issues such "Faith-Based" organizations are given to addressing. Often these initiatives are tendered politically as proof of the caring nature of the individual in the apex of an organization. Such is like those in positions of power in tobacco companies compassionately stating their discomfort about lives lost because of smoking cigarettes. It is the power at the top of America's socio-economic political structure that precludes the heads of such companies being imprisoned for drug dealing or reckless endangerment or manslaughter or ... even murder.

Despite its many fantastic accomplishments, our social order continuously tolerates social realities like women being paid less than men for the same work, African Americans getting longer prison sentences than those of the dominant culture for the same crime, etc., etc. While the upper class is growing, the middle class shrinks, and poverty is expanding — disproportionately in communities of color. Self-proclaimed good intentions never negate negative realities. Seeking power by skillfully securing the position at the apex of a social pyramid often carries with it the practice of characterizing the system that fosters the exercise of that power as always right and good. Those demeaned by the structure are, correspondingly, characterized by so many with the power to maintain it as possessed of a problem they must overcome to allow the system to work for them. Given the inevitability of the demeaning for so many of Us by our social system, being a "compassionate conservative" is more akin to being a "compassionate thug." Being that is profoundly contradictory to being a powerful person.

The pursuit of power in the American Social System via "compassionate conservatism" and "faith based initiatives" so very often treats those of Us consistently, categorically and historically scratched from the list of primary systemic beneficiaries as though we suffer from the disease of being at-risk, reject available cures and have chosen not to pursue the benefits systemically available for the taking. The task then is to clinically treat Us for a social disease that precludes Our acceptance of the benefits of a righteous socio-economic system that would serve all well who want it to do so. Yes, individuals may not always take advantage of opportunities. However, the centuries of socio-economic inequities being visited disproportionately upon the same social categories of human beings cannot but define the issue as systemic. In effect, this power is successfully pursued and maintained by denial of systemic inequality and inequity, the substitution of self-proclaimed good intentions on the part of many in positions of power for the inevitability of divisive social results and by systemic efforts to enhance faith in a system for those who categorically have never been served justly by it.

Powerful People

On the other hand, there have been those in our not too distant historic past who have attracted others to human values that provide universal human inclusion and, therefore, universal hope and meaning. Neither Martin Luther King, Jr., nor Mohandas Gandhi sought a position at the apex of the organizations with which they worked. Those organizations were created and sustained out of human belief in and support for the values each of them spoke of and enacted. Likewise, for example, there was no organizational apex sought by Sojourner Truth, Harriet Tubman or Cesar Chavez. Simply, they were powerful individuals whose actions abetted pursuit of human freedom and the meaning in it.

Even though there are people in positions of power who are also powerful people, who attract others to valuing the universal sameness of us all, the combination is a rarity. Gandhi, King, Truth, Tubman or Chavez did not apply for the position of CEO. They did not carefully manipulate those who they hoped would follow them to garner their assistance in overcoming opposition in the pursuit of a position they sought at the top of a social/organizational pyramid. They did not submit applications for the top position in an organization. They did not have to prepare for an interview for a top position they were seeking. They did not structure negative media appraisals of those who stalked the same power and pursued the same top organizational position that would allow them to exercise it. They did not need a public information officer who could adeptly spin information about what they did or stood for so that opposition to that spinning top could be overcome constantly.

The power of King and Gandhi did not end when a bullet bludgeoned each from the earth. Although others stepped into the top positions in the organizations that were created as a result of King and Gandhi being powerful, no one attracted people to hope and meaning as they did. The task now is to find not those seeking power but the powerful in our society, the Caesar Chavezs, Mohandas Gandhis, Martin Luther Kings, Sojourner Truths and Harriet Tubmans. That process needs to intensely target our young, as well as those of us who are not, regardless of culture or gender or socio-economic status. From *Us*, then, may come the power of a universal *Us* and the rejection not of social categories of *them* but of the concept of *them* itself. Powerful people — not people seeking power — and hope are inextricably tied for *Us* all.

Individual failures are a function of universal humanness. Individual responsibility to correct those failures is rational to expect. However, the perpetuation of social, governmental and organizational structures and practices that incessantly produce the demeaning and devaluing of socio-cultural categories of people or the tolerance of it being done, despite proclaimed intentions to the contrary, beg the rise and increase of abetting power throughout *Our* country and world. Without the increase and expansion of leadership and activism of powerful people, the *Black/White Divide* will explode again ... and again ... *and* again. It does not have to be so for *Us*.

CHAPTER 15

SUNDAY MORNING: THE HOUR OF SEPARATION

Ralph Gordon

IT HAS BEEN SAID that the most segregated hour in the United States occurs on Sunday morning, the time that many Americans set aside for religious worship. Sadly, this is oh so true. Despite its tremendous potential — and its purported mission — for closing gaps between differing peoples, religious practice often follows its own road of cultural separatism. Worse yet, organized religion has been used to enforce racial segregation and to promote the perception of superiority of one ethnic group over another.

All in all, considerable progress has been made in the world of church race relations. Many houses of worship can now lay claim to congregations that span ethnic barriers to an extent. But, substantially diverse flocks are woefully in the minority — as people of color are not represented or even welcome in a preponderance of churches across the U.S. Regretfully, the converse is all too often true: Whites are frequently regarded as anomalies in African American churches — if they are present at all. At the very least, a White member and/or attendee may be seen as a curiosity or as an object of suspicion or (worse yet) derision in a Black house of worship.

I have been a member of predominantly Black churches all of my life. Even in this day and time, it is intriguing (to say the least) to see the reactions of many congregants when a White person chooses to attend our house of worship on a regular basis. If it is a White woman, the almost automatic response (primarily from the female members) is that she must be there to find and take away (entrap?) one of the Black men. If it is a White man, something more nefarious must be afoot — at least according to the wannabe conspiracy theorists of that particular religious institution.

Consider the case of a friend of mine. This White fellow has been attending our church for quite some time. Yet, it is very sad to see how many Black men and women who still do not regard him as a bona fide "brother" in the church. By now, it should be abundantly clear that this man is very comfortable and sincere in the environment of this church — especially as he makes a number of positive and quite valuable contributions. Still, the suspicion lingers for too many. One incident typified this point.

When my friend was about to give a presentation at a large men's fellowship gathering, a couple of Black men got up and exited immediately. It was as if there was nothing that they wanted to hear at that point from a White man — even if he is a fellow worshiper and an expert presenter. The departing men made the same abject and malicious decision based on skin hue that so many people of color experience as a result of racial discrimination. The men who walked out on my buddy were the ultimate losers as they missed a very sharp presentation from a hugely talented, educated and committed guy. We who stayed were the beneficiaries.

Another friend of mine is an ordained minister and preacher. He visited a church where he had been asked to give the Sunday sermon. Before he arrived at the hosting house of faith, he was told that it was a church in transition. It seems that the congregation had once been all White. Now, the membership was comprised of Whites, African Americans, Latinos and Blacks from the Caribbean. This church regarded itself "in transition." The visiting minister could see that these people felt that they were headed from one state of racial homogeneity to another. They did not feel that their present state of racial diversity was either normal or permanent. To them, ethnic separation (or segregation) was equivalent to normalcy. The racial divide was deemed to be the norm — even on Sunday morning. They looked upon racial heterogeneity to be characteristic of a transitory state. The hour of separation represented a place to which they would willingly return.

My present church is predominantly African American. It has a Latino subset, which is (perhaps) charitably known as the "Hispanic Church." The Latino group uses our church facilities for their weekly worship and other activities. The presence of this sub-congregation is reflective of the changing demographics of the East Oakland (California) community. Yet, the two ethnic groups within the church — primarily Black and Latino — rarely interact. The Thanksgiving and Christmas holidays — when food and toys are distributed, respectively — are the notable exceptions. The two congregations are essentially separate under one roof. This is an unspoken yet very real intra-church divide. I know of another Black church that rented space to a Samoan congregation. That act of generosity enabled the Samoans to lease a place to worship, even if they couldn't afford their own church edifice. Yet, the result is the same as it is with the "Hispanic Church" housed in the building of Black worshippers.

Once again, congregational cohabitation is no antidote for racial separation.

Should not a church be the place where prejudices, animosities, hostilities and even separation are melted away? Shouldn't that be a stated goal and purpose for a house of faith? Unfortunately, too many churches, in general, and far too many church members, in particular, miss the opportunity for the healing and unity which this country desperately needs. Instead of moving the nation in the direction of racial and cultural reconciliation, the houses of worship all too often perpetuate the practices and separate structures of the racial divide.

What, pray tell, is to be done?

First, people should recognize that if they worship the same God and if they are members of the same faith (or a similar one), there is a strong likelihood that they will have some significant things in common — even with those who appear to be different in skin color or language. Culture and economic status may create some differences. But, isn't that a part of the unifying message of religion: to address, recognize and reconcile just those kinds of differences and to span the seeming chasms between men and women, under a unifying Higher Power?

The main part of a church is generally known as a sanctuary: a safe place, a haven. But, to obtain the progress that is needed, perhaps we should refer to this space as a crucible: a place where we can mix the humanistic ingredients of the Creator's products here on earth. The adage tells us: "the family that prays together, stays together." Could we not stretch that saying so that it would apply to more than just blood ties: to the larger and more general family of man and woman, boy and girl — regardless of ethnicity?

In times of strife, humans have an increased tendency to reacquaint themselves with their faith. During times of peril, men and women who might have no strong religious bent are often moved to gain one. At those times of stress and strain, cultural and racial differences can diminish — in the face of a common threat or danger. This is exhibited clearly during times of mass tragedy, human conflict and natural disaster. The period following the 9/11 tragedies epitomized this. But, why should we wait for times of trouble to unite us? Why not reach across the racial divide in times of peace and calm, so that we'll be better equipped to deal with the inevitability of troubling times ahead?

Maybe those who truly wish to practice what has been preached would better serve their faith by taking action as racial facilitators. They could start by inviting someone of a different hue to their place of worship and by demonstrating to other congregants their comfort in worship, fellowship and friendship. We can go on clucking our tongues about the Sunday hour of separation. Or, we can do something about it — in a substantive way.

Let's instigate a movement toward an hour of acclimation: for our fellow believers and worshippers and for those whom we know on the other side of the racial divide — yea, even for our selves.

CHAPTER 16

SUNDAY

Marlin Foxworth, Ph.D.

U P INTO THE 1960s, the ostensible relations with God, claimed through the active religiosity in Dominant America, somehow proved impotent to banish the staying, virulence of segregation over which it had the controlling power. For the religious segregationists, disallowing *them* to attend *our* church was not recognized for its spiritual fraudulence. In effect, God had to have been seen as tolerant, at least, of segregation, not only of the church facility but also of the souls in it.

Two Nations Under God —
With More Liberty and Justice for One

Today's Sunday, despite the absence of separatist intent, is separatist effect. Given the persistence of the *Black/White Divide* and despite the language of intent proffered by our Founding Fathers, we are two nations under God, with more liberty and justice for one. There are Churches and Black Churches in America's prevailing lexicon. The latter is still spoken of in Dominant America as though it were a subset of the Church it had established. The *Black* Church was established and is maintained, though, out of the recognition that God created only *Us*, man created *Them* and *We* will create a means for collectively expressing the gladness for what God has done and the love it produces, despite what man has done. The *Black* Church came from the recognition that separateness not chosen but imposed on *Us* can only be from man, not from God. The *Black* Church stays in the spiritual strength and joy of that recognition and in the face of the modernity of that two nations under God, with more liberty and justice for one.

A particular church in the East San Francisco Bay — call it Church A — was built almost a 100 years ago. It is a magnificent edifice, a visual statement about Rome and about how "over there" and "back then" sometimes become "here and now." Its presence is an unending invitation to those living in the old, well built houses in the neighborhood of which it has been a part for so long. A school stands next to the church, bearing both its name and its curriculum for the young souls in attendance. The carpenters and masons who built the church are gone physically. What they created is not. So too with the Carpenter to whom the church is dedicated.

Bell towers rise above all else in the church's structure. The pillars and arches inside the church are a mainstay of its peaceful openness. An expansive dome is filled with the art of someone who obviously knew and was gladly influenced by the Vatican and St. Peter's Basilica. Paintings of angels and saints hover there above the altar. Many huge stained glass windows, portraying Jesus in different interactions with people, are structured into a wall in the vestibule and into those on the sides of the pews. Several ceramic pieces, depicting a group of men visiting various acts of brutality on Jesus right up to His

murder that same day, are fixed high on the walls, mostly between the stained glass windows.

Aside from clerical messages from the pulpit or in
the confessional, the dome and walls tell of the never-
ending spiritual connectedness of God, Jesus — the Son
of God — and all those angels and saints. This beautiful, tranquil, visual environment is a teacher to all who
enter the church, including the children from its school.
Jesus, as shown on the cross that is fixed on the wall
above the altar, and a couple of individuals in a few of
the stained glass windows have light brown skin. In every other stained glass window, in all the ceramic figures
and across the whole dome, Jesus, the apostles, other
individuals and all the angels and saints are "White." The
significance of this reality stems not from color itself but
from "White" symbolizing both dominance in American
society and accessibility to heaven.

A different East San Francisco Bay church — call it
Church 1 — stands in what has long been a ghetto but
is steadily transforming into a ghetto/barrio. The church
was established a couple of miles from its current location over 80 years ago. A small chapel was built at the
church's present address in 1939, a 500-seat church
in 1960 and the current 1,200 seat facility in the early
1970s. The congregation numbers over 5,000. African
Americans comprise well over 95%. Around 10 to 15 people who are of the dominant culture are members of the
church. Approximately 200 people who are Latinos are
part of the church's membership and attend a special
service done in Spanish in a nearby facility.

There is a sequence of 12 stained glass windows on
one side of the church. They show Jesus in various contexts during the three years leading up to his crucifixion.
Quotes from the bible label those pictures, saying of Jesus in the last of them that He is " ... alive forevermore."
The stained glass windows high up on the wall at the oth-

er side of the church are of people who are African American and have contributed in various ways over the last
century to the spiritual foundation of the church. Martin
Luther King, Jr., Mahalia Jackson, George Washington
Carver, Mary McLeod Bethune and more look down on
the pews. A painting of the disciple Philip baptizing an
Ethiopian is high up on the wall behind the pulpit, just
above an opening in the baptismal font. Six of the people depicted in those stained glass windows with Jesus,
including some apostles, are light skinned. Jesus and
most of the apostles in those windows and Philip and the
Ethiopian in the painting are brown skinned.

The visual art, so much a part of both churches,
speaks not only of culture and spirituality but also of the
Black/White Divide in religious institutions. Belief that
there is a spiritual life after the end of a physical one
is historically and universally a facet of religion, regardless of the culture in which it manifests itself or of how
it defines deity. Every culture is a function of learning
after birth, not a physiological function of birth. Part of
being in a culture is wanting both the people who are
the ancestors of its spiritual conviction and those who
symbolize the desired results of that conviction, e.g., life
after death, to look like you and those of the culture with
which you identify. However, despite the universal tie between culture and religiosity, there are important distinctions in how Church A and Church 1 are posited in
the *Divide.*

Social Structure and the Color of Jesus

What is the basis for almost 100% of "Church A's"
illustrations of Jesus and those with whom he lived and
worked being "White" … and staying that way? It is unlikely the decision derived from a conviction that Mary
and Joseph, the parents of Jesus, emigrated from Europe to what is now Israel, a land couched across the

Northeastern edge of Africa, and gave birth there to a light skinned child. Nor is it likely that those illustrations are an offshoot of historical testimony that that part of the world was populated almost exclusively by "White" people 2,000 years ago. Is it the result of identifying with this religion's European birthplace? Given the era in which the facility was built, could there have been ensconced in the church membership a blend of indifference and limited consciousness about others just as spiritual but colored differently? Could it be a historically sustained and perennially updated outcome of something as simple as wanting to maintain the visual history of this building? Would it cost too much or spark the ire of some congregants to alter the visual portrayal of those in heaven to reflect the multiplicity of cultures residing in the community where the church building does? Is it a product of a majority of the congregation inattentively relating to the looks of itself? Are such portrayals the historical — and possibly contemporary — consequence of the church's dominant culture visually but unwittingly contributing to the sustenance of that dominance?

What is the message to congregants or would-be congregants, of the dominant culture or people of color? Indeed, what is the message to all that emanates from perpetuating the message? What is the lesson in this to the children who marvel at the walls, wonder about Jesus, are disturbed at the manner of His death and stare in awe at the lives depicted in that dome? Is there in all this an inadvertent message to children, sent particularly from the dome and unconsciously received, about the nexus between skin color and their own spiritual worth?

What of the portrayals in Church 1? Do they not also reflect the primary cultural identification of the majority of its congregation? In that, is there not also exclusion of others, a message about the consanguinity of a specific skin color and spiritual worth? In effect, do not all the questions regarding the coloring and messages in the artwork of Church A apply to Church 1?

Herein lie differences between the two. In Church A the majority of the art inaccurately indicates the coloring of Jesus, those who supported him and those who did not. The dome of the church alleges that successfully paying the spiritual down payment and mortgage for residence in heaven is exclusively tied to being "White." The exceptions in coloration in the crucifix above the altar and in a couple of the stained glass windows still raise a question about why they are still exceptions rather than the rule prescribed by history. They also indicate, as sort of a visual and institutional autobiography, that there may have been some heightened consciousness at one time in this church about historical reality and maybe about the need to communicate perennially that people of color are co-equals in the chronicle of spiritual fulfillment.

The 12 stained glass depictions of Jesus with others in Church 1 accurately render the color of the vast majority of the population in that part of the world, at that time in history. The few anomalies could well reflect the historical reality of a minuscule emigration from Europe. Although brown skinned, Jesus and the others imaged in those windows do not have the hair texture characterized as African. The Ethiopian being baptized by disciple Philip is an appropriate exception.

What of the stained glass windows on the other wall, the ones depicting African American contributors to the spiritual existence and history of "Church 1?" Is there a message in those windows to the few who are of the dominant culture and are members of the church and to the many who are of the dominant culture who visit from other churches across the country from time to time? Is the message that spiritual contributors to the church over the last century were only African American and, by implication, will be only African American? If so, how is

Church 1 different in this regard from Church A in contributions to the *Black/White Divide?*

The differences also reside in the socio-cultural group
roles played in creating and sustaining the *Divide.* The
population that is of the dominant culture, at the base of
the founding of Church A and represented in its dome,
has always been collectively on the upside of the *Divide*
and dominant — politically, socially, economically. There
has been little or no price to be paid from within the
protective boundaries of that dominance for creating or
allowing or ignoring the subordination of groups of cultural others. Unfortunately, that reality is still seldom
or minimally, openly, publicly, insistently addressed and
communicated about by and within churches populated
primarily with people nestled in that dominance. Such
suggests, then, that perennial indifference to the historical demeaning of some of God's children in this temporal
world has no impeding significance for those exercising
that indifference on the prospects for eternal, happy residency with the same God in an eternal world. Visual
symbols are common in churches in Dominant America
that indicate that God and the sacred reside with those
born of that dominance. The fact that the ceramic figures
in Church A of those brutalizing Jesus show them all as
"White" is also inappropriate. At least in that, though, is
an indication that being "White" is not a precursor to automatic ascendancy into a status with endless reward.

The visual symbolization in Church 1 appropriately
depicts the history of Jesus and the population in the
part of the world where He lived physically. That 100% of
the people in the windows on the other wall are African
American is not a denial that anyone of the dominant
culture could contribute to the church and be spiritually
substantive. Those images, though, are of individuals
with profound spirituality, strength of character, courage, intellect, a history of individually rising above rac-

ism and its long, multiple, individual and institutional manifestations and of leading others to do the same. None in those windows is known for rejecting people who are of the dominant culture, regardless of the social and physical pummeling visited on them historically by people classified as such.

Some Failure In Christianity

Ku Klux Klan members claim faith in God, exercise religiosity and used the cross, universally the symbol of Jesus, His love for humanity and His execution by crucifixion, as the badge of its brutal, racist purpose. That speaks undeniably about religious contributions to the *Black/White Divide*. The Klan's destructive purpose is honest by comparison with the contributions to the *Divide*, particularly via indifference to it, of some other religious organizations and practitioners.

In an interview of Dr. King in Playboy Magazine in the early 60s, the interviewer indicated that "Whites" were concerned about Black Muslims. Dr. King was asked what his assessment was of Black Muslim " ... power and influence among the Negro masses?" Part of his answer described a facet of its attractiveness then but it is analytically applicable to the *Black/White Divide* up to this very day. "For the first time," Dr. King said, "the Negro was presented with a choice of a religion other than Christianity. What this appeal actually represented was an indictment of Christian failures to live up to Christianity's precepts; for there is nothing in Christianity, nor in the Bible, that justifies racial segregation."

A primary concentration in Christian Churches is on the "Word," the biographical reportage on Jesus and the behavioral prescriptions derived from it. Reading the bible is decreed as an indispensable and continuous component of being Christian and getting regularly better at it. There is usually too little concentration, however, on

Jesus as an activist. Was it not so that He chose to confront a social system — and those at the apex of it — for its demeaning of others? Did He not select individuals who were neither wealthy nor couched high in the social structure to join with Him in insisting on the treatment of each of *Us* humans as a worthy child of God? Indeed, Dr. King, in his essay, "A Testament of Hope," noted, "Jesus of Nazareth wrote no books; he owned no property to endow him with influence. He had no friends in the courts of the powerful. But He changed the course of mankind with only the poor and the despised." At various times after Jesus was tortured and executed, was the same terminal vitriol not visited on apostles of His in response to their activism and its focus on what was just and spiritually right?

Separation of Church and State and Failure to Address the *Divide*

The separation of church and state functions as religious justification for not banging away at the inequalities created and sustained by the *Black/White Divide*. The abject failure to address the fundamental, elemental issues of the *Divide* by so very many clergy and congregations without experience of the downside — or even by some who do experience it — is shielded by the pretext that religion is about spiritual life, not the political or economic. Consequently, the daily available statistics on the inequalities manifested in public education, income, health care, imprisonment, political representation, etc., ad nauseam are off the radar screen for spiritual relevancy. Statements in theme and variation about caring for "all of God's children" fashion an old substitution for addressing a social structure and system that has bludgeoned, not only with indifference but sometimes actively, some social categories of "God's children" for centuries. Ironically, some of the spiritual forbearers of contemporary religions had their physical lives ended because of their persistent opposition to social mistreatment of people with whom they were aligned culturally, socially and spiritually. Jesus, a Jew, was obviously an activist and paid the ultimate earthly price for it. Martin Luther King, Jr., a Christian, was obviously an activist and paid the ultimate earthly price for it. Why the pitiful insufficiency of others of Us in any forms of activism as taught Us by the Jesus Christians claim as the ultimate spiritual and human hero?

Those perennial realities and so many more like them create a consciousness that frequently wends its way into the pulpit in churches that are African American. From that pulpit, rather than lamentations about the purpose of the Divide to subordinate, comes faith filled and constructive insubordination and a joyful rise up and over systemic social barriers structured to keep one down. That spiritual rise is energized in part by clarity that God created only Us and out of that humans created Them. There is in the voice of so many preachers an echo of the caveat that one not do unto others what was done unto you. In that way, reciprocal hatefulness is lessened and even obviated. Any experiences with the causes of the Divide during the week make Sunday a good day to thank God for the synergy in the activism of Jesus and the Word. Sunday certainly isn't always about the consequences of the Divide. Yet, spirituality in churches that are African American is known for its applicability to the nasty here-and-now, not just to the sweet-by-and-by.

The African American Church and Unwitting Contribution to the Divide

Unwitting contributions, though, can come from churches that are African American. An article in The Oakland Tribune, Oakland, California, on August 25, 2004 provides a profound example. The headline read,

"Black religious leaders back Bush." "Citing biblical opposition to same sex marriages," the article began, "a group
of African-American pastors said Tuesday they support
President Bush for re-election." The article further implies
justification for the support: "Bush has said marriage
should only involve a man and a woman, and backed by
the ultra-conservative religious right, he has favored a
constitutional amendment to ban same-sex unions." That
buttressing of the 2004 election of George W. Bush came
with a disclaimer from a spokesman for the 19 pastors
who are African American who said, "We are not selecting
a party but a principle." That disclaimer, however, does
not negate the provision of support for a president and a
party that have provided during his tenure only one major, fully funded affirmative action practice: African American's are equally recruited, if not disproportionately so,
by the military to fight, kill and maim and/or be killed or
maimed in a war of most questionable purpose. The spirituality of those so impacted, on either side of the ongoing
confrontation, is hammered in the process. The increased
need for coffins, wheel chairs, prosthetic limbs and psychological counseling makes no discernible contribution
to ending the *Divide.*

"The church once changed society," Dr. King said in
that *Playboy* interview. "It was then a thermostat of society. But today I feel that too much of the church is merely a thermometer, which measures rather than molds
popular opinion."

The interviewer asked, "Are you speaking of the
church in general — or the white church in particular?"

The "White" Church and Contribution to the Divide

Perhaps with less intensity, but still as telling today as it was in the early 60s, Dr. King responded: "The
white church, I'm sorry to say. Its leadership has greatly
disappointed me. Let me hasten to say there are some

outstanding exceptions. As one whose Christian roots go back through three generations of ministers — my father, grandfather and great-grandfather — I will remain true to the church as long as I live. But the laxity of the white church collectively has caused me to weep tears of love. There cannot be deep disappointment without deep love. Time and again in my travels, as I have seen the outward beauty of white churches, I have had to ask myself, 'What kind of people worship there? Who is their God? Is their God the God of Abraham, Isaac and Jacob, and is their Savior the Savior who hung on the cross at Golgotha? Where were their voices when a black race took upon itself the cross of protest against man's injustice to man? Where were their voices when defiance and hatred were called for by white men who sat in these very churches?"

"As the Negro struggles against grave injustice," Dr. King continued, "most white churchmen offer pious irrelevancies and sanctimonious trivialities." A version of that today is the talk of "tolerance" and the "celebrating of diversity." Neither addresses the real issues in the structure of the *Divide*. Both shape self-proclaimed good intentions, the shields against charges of being racist. Consciousness about the ongoing results of racism has to be greatly intensified in churches with congregations that are of the dominant culture if Sunday is to be no longer a day for sustaining those results — by omission, even when not by commission.

Clergy and lay people need to structure interactive analysis of the history and continuance of the *Black/White Divide* in churches. That process must occur within the church and cross-culturally between churches. The coming together should be institutionalized in each involved church rather than simply having clergy and congregants meet with their counterparts only in an ad hoc and intermittent sort of way. It should address the linkages among culture, economics, politics, spirituality and social reality. Perspectives on the contemporary function of racism, even when they may vary greatly, need to be solicited insistently rather than just tolerated. Action to end the *Divide*, in this lifetime, must be prescribed and acted on by all involved in the process. Agreement needs to be pursued intensely on what all of us will accept as evidence that the interactive process is functioning as it must to overcome the *Divide* in each and every one of its manifestations. An analytical/prescriptive mechanism for ending the *Divide* must be collectivized, not instead of interaction and action by pairs of churches, but in addition to it. The same constructive interaction for addressing the *Black/White Divide* and other formulations of America's racism is absolutely necessary with and among the multiple other spiritual organizations and religions, even if Sunday isn't their day for energizing faith and collectivizing expressions of it.

Nothing of what Dr. King said in that *Playboy* interview seems more fitting for consideration of that challenge than this: " ... a minister cannot preach the glories of heaven while ignoring social conditions in his own community that cause men an earthly hell." The acceptance of that admonition and the enactment of the process to end that earthly hell and the brutality of the *Black/White Divide* have been entombed so long. If there is to be a resurrection of needed hope for ending the *Divide*, there needs to be an inauguration of the process to do so ... no later than next Sunday.

CHAPTER 17

MARTIN LUTHER KING TODAY

Ralph Gordon

ON APRIL 4, 1968, a bright beacon was dimmed in America. On that tragic day a mighty voice was silenced by the bullets of an assassin. On that dark day, the Rev. Dr. Martin Luther King, Jr. was shot dead on a motel balcony in Memphis, Tennessee.

In the immediate wake of the assassination, spontaneous grass root uprisings tore numerous cities apart across the nation. The media referred to these events as race riots. While the fires burned literally that weekend, and figuratively thereafter, many realized that a huge vacuum had been created in American leadership. It was not just a gaping hole in the civil rights struggle. After all, Dr. King was far more than a civil rights leader. This internationally recognized Nobel Peace Prize winner was a fighter for human rights. Moreover, he was about to put his case before the forum of the United Nations. Dr. King's intent was to put forth the argument for human rights — for all Americans — on a world platform.

Prior to that time, Martin Luther King was best known for his strong efforts and leadership in the civil rights movement, from the early 1950s and beyond. He joined others in the fight for some very basic rights in what was then a virulently segregated South. He led the battles by adopting the nonviolent principles and practices of India's legendary religious and political activist, Mahatma Gandhi. This spiritually-based form of civil disobedience took the struggle to an even higher moral level. Although a lot of people suffered and even died during these battles, many victories were won — peacefully and effectively.

The high caliber of leadership that Dr. King provided has rarely been replicated in human history: imitated, but never duplicated. This leadership void has resulted in audacious attempts to roll back many of the gains that were accomplished during those days of triumph. How wonderful it would be if Dr. Martin Luther King Jr. were still here to stand up and to step forward on many matters of concern. The great American poet and slavery abolitionist, John Greenleaf Whittier, wrote, "For of all sad words of tongue or pen, the saddest are these: 'it might have been'." We are given to wonder: What would the late, great doctor work on if he were still alive today?

Unquestionably, Dr. King would still be a general in the war for human rights for all peoples — particularly since this goal has not yet been reached in the United States of America. This is a nation that is plagued by a continuing and deeply destructive racial divide. Early on, Native Americans (the so-called "Indians") were slaughtered and moved off of their own lands. Many of these indigenous people were subsequently relegated to imprisonments called "reservations." Africans were subjugated through slavery. Chinese laborers were exploited for the building of the railroads. Mexicans saw parts of their nation swiped and then annexed to the United States — resulting in their present day designation as "illegal immigrants" when they cross the border seeking a better quality of life. Dr. King would deplore the fact that America is still not colorblind — the perspectives of the foes of affirmative action notwithstanding.

One of the things that could not occur, if Dr. King were still alive, is the continuous, devious and self-serving appropriation of his concepts and words by a movement that is diametrically opposed to what this great man stood for. With the pretense that the U.S. has already reached a state of being colorblind, these people seek to dismantle the gains that have been made on behalf of disenfranchised people of color across the land. How can this nation grow as a whole if certain of its people are continuously pushed down and left behind? Were he alive today, Dr. King would fight against those who strive to keep down the least and the lowest among us. Rev. King would stand up for the rights of all Americans — for their human rights, not just their civil rights.

Rev. King railed against America's extreme color consciousness and discrimination. He lobbied and pleaded and fought for justice for all. He envisioned a day when the color of one's skin would no longer be a barrier to his or her advancement. Under the guise of a so-called colorblind society, the anti-affirmative action forces claim to be championing the same causes as Dr. King. Nothing could be farther from the truth. But, with him absent and no one of sufficient stature, vision and clear eloquence to rebut the claims of the disingenuous ones, their audacity and plagiarism often carry the day.

Were he alive today, Dr. Martin Luther King Jr. could and would stand as a bulwark against any misuse of his words or concepts. His family has hardly risen to the task. They have shown a much greater concern for ensuring that their entities are considerably compensated for particular uses of Dr. King's words and work. It would be of great benefit for Dr. King to be here to protect and carry on his own legacy.

There are so many things that we typically take for granted: the right to ride on public transportation, without having to move to the back of the bus; the right to sit in a restaurant and receive and eat a meal, without worrying about being beaten or not served at all; the right to buy a home in the neighborhood of our choice, without the strong probability of severe harassment (including a cross burning on the lawn); the right to cast a vote, without having to run a gauntlet of illegitimate "literacy" and other so-called "citizenship" tests. Wasn't it less than half a century ago when these things were a part of the daily lives of Black Americans in many places in this country? The right to freedom from these ills was fought for and won by a generation of highly committed and decidedly nonviolent persons — they who put their own safety on the line against the forces of darkness, so that we might be privileged as we are today.

Hatred, hypocrisy and deceit may triumph for a while but not forever. Case in point ... Dr. King, a staunch opponent of the Vietnam War, would advise this country's current government that it was grossly deceitful to get us into a war in Iraq by way of a replay of the Gulf of Tonkin situation and its devious use to get us into a horribly painful, costly and deadly war in Southeast Asia. Dr. King would have a few pointed questions for the Bush II administration and its so-called WMDs, weapons of mass destruction. Isn't it strange that a country with our level of technology could not find even one of these alleged threats to our existence? Where was the connection between Saddam Hussein and the terrorists of Al Qaeda, those who despised Saddam as well? How were Americans made safer after a lawless Iraq became a magnet and a breeding ground and a haven for terrorists and their recruits?

How could we be so arrogant, short-sighted and silly as to talk about explorations on the moon and Mars when people are homeless and starving right here in America, when families are suffering from the weight of a depressed and depressing economy and when our soldiers were locked into a war for oil in a far-off land in a conflict that our military did not anticipate and was not sufficiently prepared for? Yes, Dr. King would have a few questions for the U.S. Government.

Dr. King would have asked the U.S. Government why depriving Americans of their fundamental human rights — via the shrewdly named Patriot Act and other laws and practices — was a better way of fighting terrorism than simply doing a sound job of enforcing the laws that are already on the books. Could this be better than ensuring that there was competent cooperation and less competition between the nation's law enforcement agencies (mainly the F.B.I. and the C.I.A.)? How about simply doing one's own job while not criminalizing entire segments of this country? Unfortunately, Dr. King might sadly have to welcome Arab Americans and others to the world of racial profiling — a persecution practice to which Blacks are overly accustomed. Martin Luther King would be quite busy as he would eloquently, explicitly and expertly note and combat these things today.

The fight in these times is one against forces who are often more subtle and sophisticated in their opposition to racial progress. Being a keen observer of human behaviors and tactics, Dr. King would adjust his strategies and his rhetoric accordingly. As his one-time nemesis, Malcolm X, once said: "Times change. Methods change. But, our objective never changes." Today, Dr. King would adapt his strategies but he would not moderate his stance — not until freedom, justice and equality were won for all peoples of this land.

Chapter 18

WHAT WOULD DR. KING DO?

Marlin Foxworth, Ph.D.

IMAGINE . . .

It is April 4, 1968. Spring, just two weeks old, shines its golden life onto the balcony of the Lorraine Motel. Hosea, Jesse, Ralph and Martin bask in that light and add to it with the joy in their eyes. Laughter hops up from the kidding done in their brotherhood. The thoughts of each about the work to be done again tomorrow merge and abbreviate the levity. Hope and conviction meld into the dialogue of purpose.

Yes, more is to be done tomorrow for the needed changes in the life of Sanitation Workers in Memphis. Conviction is to be established in those that hire them that the signs carried by the workers in the demonstration only seven days before meant more than the four simple words in them. What must be done to transform "I Am A Man" from words solely denoting gender to a descriptor of humankind and a call for the inalterable respect it is due? If this is for our brothers, the same is a must for our sisters.

The discussion among them continues without anticipation of interruption. Like a collective sun, their talk keeps shadows from hiding the truth. "How do we successfully stand again tomorrow with our brothers," they variously ask each other, "so the person named 'Sanitation Worker' is esteemed no differently than he or she named 'Wealthy' or 'Famous?' How ... How?" The warmth and space on the balcony shapes it as a conference center. There, wondering and talking in the light about intensifying and broadening the movement, they seed tomorrow and tomorrows.

James Earl Ray climbs to the roof across from the balcony. He, though, solicits a shadow to keep himself and the evil in his soul from the light of human respect. Hidden that way, he aims what would project his self-hatred into the life of Martin King. Convinced of being on target, he pulls the trigger repeatedly. The screaming lead carrying his hatred slams Martin down. Hiding every step from the light, James Earl Ray climbs down from his loft of hatred without being seen. He and his successful malignance hold hands and commit to more work together. Agony, fear, chaos, and anger leap together onto Martin's brothers. The call for an ambulance is yanked up out of the turmoil and made. It came. It took Martin. Hope threatened to leave with him.

Imagine ...

... it is Summer, 1970. Coretta responds to the anticipated knock and opens the door for the young reporter, an alumnus of Morehouse College. "Welcome," she says softly. "Please come in. He's waiting for you in the den. Can I get you some ice tea or something?"

"Yes, maam," Malcolm politely responds. "Ice tea

would be great." He follows her into the den, desperately
trying to hide his nervousness.

Dr. King is sitting there, looking out the window onto
the yellow-green integration of sun and leaves in the trees
on his Atlanta street. A slight scar above his left cheekbone is a clear symbol of the failed attempts in 1968 to
strike out his voice and block it's gospel from the ears of
those who would hear and act on it. He turns toward the
door at the sound of Coretta's voice. "Martin, Mr. Johnson is here."

Dr. King rises up from the couch and steps slowly toward the entrance to the den, extending his hand to Malcolm. "It's ... it's an honor to meet you," young Malcolm
Johnson stutters slightly. Looking with intense calmness
into his eyes, Dr. King says, "The honor is mine. Please
sit down. "

"I'll do my very best to be quick, Dr. King," Malcolm
offers respectfully. "I just need to review with you some of
the things you wrote and said since the Montgomery Bus
Boycott. I really want to ask you enough questions that
would probably keep us here talking for the next couple
of months ... but I'll be more focused than that. I'll just
quote some things and then ask you how you think it
applies to today. As you answer, I'll probably have some
follow-up questions too. And maybe, if we have a chance
before my time is up, we can talk about the consequences of that attack on you in 1968. I'd like to save that until
the end, though."

Dr. King's grin was the invitation to begin with the
questions.

"You opened your 'I Have a Dream' speech," Malcolm
begins, "with this: 'I am happy to join with you today in
what will go down in history as the greatest demonstration
for freedom in the history of our nation.' And you ended
it by saying that when we all have freedom ' ... black men
and white men, Jews and Gentiles, Catholics and Protes-

tants — will be able to join hands and to sing in the words of the old Negro spiritual, 'Free at last, free at last; thank God Almighty, we are free at last.' So, are you still happy about that day and do you see any indication that blacks and whites and people of various religious beliefs are increasingly joining hands in shared freedom?"

Dr. King looks back at Malcolm and does not respond for several seconds. "The joy remains," he replies slowly, "about what our collective spirit had done with us that day. There is and can be no doubt about the place we made of it for history. Yes, I am glad that we could do that. The warmth from the sun that August day was matched by the constructive warmth of that collective spirit." Dr. King pauses and looks away out the window. He gently rubs, only for seconds, the history in the scar just beneath his left eye and then turns back to Malcolm. "Spiritual winters in the soul of America," he continues, "come too easily, though. They create times on the American calendar of progress when that constructive heat lessens and even disappears. It will be our task to rekindle that spirit. It must be done, however, with a parallel purpose to the one that prompts us to rekindle the warmth in the fireplaces in our homes on a winter morning. We do so not to burn down the house but to protect us and our families from the destructive indifference of the cold."

Malcolm politely asks if he can interject another question. Given Dr. King's go-ahead, he says, "I haven't done any research on it, Dr. King, but there seem to be a lot of people around the country who feel very strongly about your speech at the March on Washington. Many would suggest that it still can serve to propel the kind of rekindling you're talking about. Don't you have faith in the prospects of your words that day reactivating the action needed to address the issues of inequality you hammered away at?"

"Yes! I have faith that the reactivation will come," Dr.

King insists. "Yet sadness still reigns about what some, including many in the news media, have made of my words that day."

"Why?" Malcolm asks in surprise. "I mean you're so honored for that speech. How could you be sad about what people think of it?"

"The frequent repetition of the words 'I have a Dream,'" he answers, "has given a significance to the fact of them ... but not to the meaning of them. The repetition makes of me a dreamer in a world where organized power almost always prefers a pragmatist. The silence about what continues to damage human hope, about the bellowing contradictions in that to the equality on which this country was said to have been founded and about the refusal in positions of power to engineer a society with a foundation structured genuinely of that equality are, themselves, powerful continuing statements. And that silence and refusal harmonize a warning that says, 'beware of those who would ask you to join them in pursuit of the unrealistic because it cannot be achieved. So ... that narrowness of focus, coupled with silence about it ... in government, in other places of power, in colleges and universities, in churches continue to preach to us that a dream transformed into a reality with the same substance is impossible."

"Excuse me," Malcolm interjects as amenably as he can, "isn't that the way life is?"

"It is not," Dr. King responds with uncharacteristic bluntness. "Let me explain." He turns for only seconds toward the sun lit trees framed by the den window and then faces Malcolm again. "These silent admonitions to avoid the unrealistic are prescriptive —not descriptive of life's possibilities and demands. The unified will of people can create change, even if some would have thought it to be unrealistic, even if some in positions of power would attempt to block it. Yes, the prevailing political perspective is that the holding of hands — not only spiritual hands, but political, economic and educational hands — of the 'black men and white men, Jews and Gentiles, Catholics and Protestants' is unrealistic. So, too, would it be considered unrealistic with respect to us pursuing such holding of hands with Muslims, Buddhists and others of God's children in a multitude of spiritual practices. Faith demands of those who have it that they join hands, not only with others of the same faith but also with those who are not. So doing is a statement without a word spoken. It says that all of us are God's children and, therefore, no one of us can be of lesser value. Regardless of varied pigment in our hands, or the price we pay for the soap to wash them, they all clasp exactly the same way. If this country does not reengage an unrealistic movement to become a united one, the fact of that failure will be its downfall."

A clock there on the wall behind Malcolm ticked piercingly through the short lull.

"Those who murdered Jesus," Dr. King says more slowly and softly, "would have thought it to be unrealistic for Him to rise up after dying and move, by himself, a huge stone that blocked the entrance to the cave where he had been buried. He did. He … did! We can do what we must and even laugh at being told that it is unrealistic."

Silence sways back into the room again for seconds. Malcolm, knowing there was nothing left to be said about being realistic, asks, "How broadly can the term 'one' be defined? Throughout the years you have spoken of the racism in white communities. How do you see being 'one' with such people?"

"Becoming 'one,'" Dr. King answers immediately, "again necessitates getting people to understand that it is not undoable. Being one is simultaneously a social goal and a human reality that already exists. Let me see if I can clarify that. Wait just a minute … my son Dexter and I were talking the other day about what I had said after the murder of four of our little girls at the 16th Street Baptist Church in Birmingham. He gave me a transcription of those words. Let me see if I can find it."

He reaches into a stack of papers on the edge of the table next to the couch. "Here it is," he says, after paging through some documents. "I was then and am now thoroughly convinced of the accuracy of what I said. Let me read it: 'Death comes to every individual. There is an amazing democracy about death. It is not aristocracy for some of the people, but a democracy for all of the people. Kings die and beggars die; rich men die and poor men die; old people die and young people die; death comes to the innocent and it comes to the guilty. Death is the irreducible common denominator of all men.'"

"The undeniable sameness of us at the end," Dr. King says while putting back the document from which he had read, "in its physiological structure as well as in its inevitability, is so only because of the inalterable sameness of us at the beginning. That the heart of each of us beats and one day does no longer has symbolic significance equal to its physiological magnitude. The death of each of us," Dr. King continues, pointing first at Malcolm and then back at himself, "is the termination date for our quest for meaning. It is that pursuit of meaning that makes of each of us a human being. The meaning of life is known through the integration of mind and emotion and spirit. It is the discovery that even though each of us is possessed of imperfections we are no less created in the image of God than anyone else."

"Wait ... please," Malcolm asks. "You are saying that all of us are the same. But our society today says we are different. I don't need to tell you about what statistics show us of the differences in social and economic realities between black people and white people. How is that the case if we are all the same?"

Dr. King responds instantly. "There is nothing inherently wrong with material possession. It is an element of life on earth. What is wrong is the sustenance of a social system that makes pursuit of the material top priority, the sustenance of a social system that substitutes the pursuit of material benefits for the meaning and purpose God has asked us to pursue, the sustenance of a social system that for centuries has made access to the means of securing the material separable by human coloration. In making us people, God granted us coloration. Variance in coloration is not variation in humanness or in the needs that come from being human. The only difference in the structure of humanness is in those things that the eye can see. And the eye can see only what is on the surface. Color is superficial. Human need, faith in a social system that it will be met, hope, spirituality, love, joy and passion for justice, are structural elements of humanness, the substance of its depth. The eye cannot see that. Only the heart and soul can."

Dr. King stops fleetingly to sip his tea while Malcolm quickly thumbs through pages in a binder on his lap. He finds a few that he wants, places them on top of the binder cover and looks back at Dr. King. Leaning to return the glass to the table, Dr. King continues to make his point. "Our task remains. We must come to understand why our individual and national energies are so devoted to securing the material and why, when we deem others to be not like ourselves, we are so willing to tolerate, if not actively pursue, limiting or ending their capacity to do the same. Even though that destructive willingness can exist in any social group, we have to be clear about why it is that only one such group can turn it into a social, political, economic and, therefore, historic and futuristic reality for others of us in America. 'Making it' in America is now more than ever defined by the amount and assessed value of our material possessions and of the square footage of privately owned space in which we live and keep those things. The price and labels of the cloth with which we cover our bodies and of the automobiles we drive are unfortunately the badges of achievement increasingly idealized in our society. The loss in that to us as humans is so great! It is so great because this is a temporary life, one of secondary importance. The next life promises a community structured of oneness. There will be no poverty in that life. Not living in that community will be a function of choice rather than a consequence of not having been offered the key needed to open a gate. There will be no system that promulgates the dominance of any earthly culture over any other one. 'Them' will not exist in the vocabulary in that life because there will be only Us. And yes ... I am saying we can achieve this heaven on earth."

Malcolm pulls up one of the documents he had put atop the binder and says, "The day you were given the Nobel Peace Prize in Oslo, Norway, you said, 'I refuse to accept the idea that the 'isness' of man's present nature makes him morally incapable of reaching up for the eternal 'oughtness' that forever confronts him. I refuse to accept that man is mere flotsam and jetsam in the river of life that surrounds him. I refuse to accept the view that mankind is so tragically bound to the starless midnight of racism and war that the bright daybreak of peace and brotherhood can never become a reality.'

"That seems to be what you were getting at just seconds ago," Malcolm says. "I am curious to know if I am right about that. And ... you had written something about the tie between racism and economic injustice. I believe it was in one of your articles. Please forgive me but I can't remember which one. Anyway ... is there a connection among 'isness,' 'oughtness,' racism and economic injustice?"

Dr. King continued to face Malcolm, pondering what

he had just asked. "I believe I wrote that in "Pilgrimage to Nonviolence," an article I did for a series in *Christian Century* on things that influenced a change of mind. In this case I was addressing what brought me to my conviction about the purpose and need for nonviolence. Getting back to your question ... yes, there is a reciprocating sustenance between racism and economic injustice. The partnership between the two functions like a marriage of poisons. Born of it are so many children of 'isness.'"

Malcolm shifts a little on the couch and leans back. "How so?"

"Gaps by race in the benefits of America's economic structure have existed every second, in every century since its establishment. The never-ending unwillingness of most of us in America to actively oppose that injustice is a clamoring statement that those gaps are just the way it is. The gaps persist even as the economy ebbs and flows. Despite the tokenism we have for the 'sameness' of us all in America, despite the moral, social and spiritual 'oughtness' for collective action to end those economic injustices, there is never sustained, prolonged, collective effort, across the land, in every community, in every state to do so."

"But, Dr. King," Malcolm interrupts insistently, "your perception about what needs to be done with America's economic structure notwithstanding, this is the best economic system in the world? Wouldn't you agree?"

"It is the best, Malcolm, but for those to whom it provides the most. If amassing and maintaining profoundly unequal high material wealth for a small percentage of a human population is the definition of best, it is the best. If killing people around the world because their beliefs or actions may threaten the lessening of material advantage to that small percentage in America that has it is the definition of best, it is the best. If having the staying power to limit access to that material advantage for certain elements of a society is the definition of the best, it is the best. If maintaining and modernizing itself over centuries and maintaining and modernizing the disproportionate access to its benefits is the definition of the best, it is the best ... However, the poverty it creates and maintains cannot justifiably be labeled as the 'best poverty!' The insufficiency — even absence — of education and health care that are constant for so many in this society are not the 'best insufficiencies or absences.' The loss of hope for so many in this system cannot be justified as the 'best loss of hope.'"

Silence captures the room and blares for a few more seconds. Malcolm drops his pen. He bends over, picks it up and places it along with his note pad on the table next to him. He doesn't know what to say or ask for the moment.

Dr. King's eyes and smile seem to pull some more of the light and warmth of the sun back into the room. "So," he starts up again, "If 'Best' is to be determined, however, by all of us having housing, clothing, education, consistent access to meaningful employment, the material benefits that shape this society's collective perception of a 'good life,' transportation, nutritional and medical basics of life, freedom from being assaulted by some who do not share our skin color or our beliefs or methods of expressing our spirituality, then this system is not the 'best.' There continues to be a phenomenal distinction in the life of a rich person in America and that of any other person. There continues to be a phenomenal distinction between the prospects for access to that 'good life' for the white man and for people who are not white, for the black man specifically.

"Excu ... excuse me, Dr. King," Malcolm interrupted. "This is embarrassing ... but I need to take a break. Would you mind directing me to the bathroom? I think," he smirked, "that ice tea was a bit much for me. I'll be right back so we can stay on point."

"Not at all. Regardless of where we are in this economy," Dr. King said with a wide grin, "we all need to use such commodities. Go through that door. Turn left in the hallway and go to the third door on the right. While you step out, I'm going to look for something I read that might be helpful."

Malcolm walks a little uneasily through the door and Dr. King steps out toward his office. He comes up to a wide, Cherrywood bookshelf just behind his desk and begins dragging his finger along the rows of books, skimming the titles, until he stops at one, pulling it off the shelf. He starts the process again, drawing down another hardcover and then a couple more. He grazes rapidly through the pages of each, finding the folded down page corners he was looking for and putting some paper clips there. He turns back toward the door. Coretta stands there. She spreads her arms part way, palms up, tilting her head a bit — all to shape a wordless question about the quality of the exchange with the young journalist.

Dr. King grins a little and winks. "He's a good man," he confides. "He is where he is on his road of discovery."

Coretta smiles back. "Don't be too much longer, now, Martin. You need some rest." He nods and strolls back to the den. Malcolm is waiting there, himself looking out the window into the peaceful synchrony of sun and trees.

"My that's beautiful," Malcolm says, glancing at Dr. King and then back at the trees. "Thanks for the break. Where were we?"

Dr. King holds up a book, putting the other ones on the table in front of him, and swings smoothly back into the dialogue. " In what he had written so many years ago, near the turn of the century," Dr. King begins again, "W.E.B. Dubois so wonderfully summarized our today, without physically being here today." Waving the closed book back and forth slightly toward Malcolm, Dr. King, says, "He simply wrote,

'The country is rich, yet the people are poor.'"

Malcolm asks, "May I butt in?" A nod from Dr. King tugs out Malcolm's next question. "I don't necessarily doubt the cogency of what you read. But ... isn't there also individual responsibility? All of poverty can't be caused only by those who are wealthy."

"You are correct," Dr. King acknowledges. "However, carrying out individual responsibility in an effort to become permanently ensconced in the system does not guarantee that it will happen. It does not happen most for the black man — no matter how long and how hard we have tried. The failure to try is, indeed, the responsibility of the man who did not. The consistent failure of a social order to honor those efforts, to recognize them for their sameness with efforts of the white man, is a failure of the system and of the people with the power to keep it in place. Yes, the system also effects the denial of access to some who are white. But ... the denial is longer and deeper and wider for the black man. History has shown us that reality every single day since black people became the first and only people forced to come to this land. A denial by the economic system of the white man is denial of him as an individual. The denial by the economic system of the black man is denial of us as a people. The exceptions of the white man being denied and of the black man making it have been used as justification of the system and of the inequalities it inevitably produces. Our white brother should not be denied needed access to what is needed for material survival, health or prosperity. The white man can suffer individually from the economic flu. That flu, however, has always been an epidemic where the black man lives. Yet," Dr. King calmly but very pointedly injects, "it is unfortunate the struggle to bring justice to that system is not firmly ensconced in black communities."

Malcolm asks for clarity.

"Although the income gap exists between black and white America," Dr. King explains, "the structure of the gap exists within black America as well. There are those among us who have stepped their way up into the system. Often, though, it is done without remembering what it was like at the bottom of the steps. It is done without grasping that an invitation to the visible porch of exception is never the same as being invited into the house or having equal access to the material necessary to build one just as big next door. Without recovering from that loss of memory, the black man can continue to unintentionally contribute to that epidemic inequality. The time and emotional, spiritual and social energy needed to insistently and non-violently change the system and the inequalities it continues to produce is spent more on overcoming those consequences than on ending their causes. Without recovering from that loss of memory ..."

Malcolm politely holds up his hand to ask Dr. King to pause. He does. "Can you blame the black man, Dr. King, for trying to make the system work for him just like it does for white people?"

"No. I cannot," he answers. "Yet ... the absence of focus on altering the system as it is may well prove to be social suicide. We cannot and must not forget that the structure of this economic system has more staying power than the percentage of black men who may rise up in it — and benefit most from it. The history of relationships between White America and Black America makes it clear that the reality that wealth is not unlimited will powerfully energize opposition to systematic equal distribution of it. If the material benefits in our country, for example, are shared by those of us who are not white in a proportionate match with our percentage of the total population, the history of advantage to whites would be over. The present power structure in America — hopefully not one of the near future — would actively resist that equality while denying that it was being done. Equality and advantage have never been neighbors. Indeed, they have lived in different and segregated communities. So too for wealth and poverty. When equality is present its opposite cannot be. If we do not successfully address the widening inequality cemented into America's economic system we will certainly come to a time when there will be a small number of men who possess enough wealth to send poverty everywhere cascading to the early hell it deserves but who will not do it. What then will be the means for resisting the temptation to remain silent so that at least access to that porch of exception will not be lost? And should silence and the mere pursuit of survival not be enough to sustain us, will what happened in Watts five years ago repeat itself all over the country? And if it does, will there be a final result? And if there is a final result for the black man, will it be equality or intensified subjugation?"

"There are those, Dr. King," Malcolm contends, "who would wonder if you are suggesting that communism is the way to go. How would you respond to that?"

"No! I am not advocating communism," he retorts. "A quick appraisal of what we've seen of it, in the Soviet Union, in China and throughout the world, makes clear that citizens were left out or put down in that social and political structure as well. People who opposed that system too vociferously were killed for doing so. That is the case today as well. But throughout America's history, those of us who are the ancestors of slaves and who have fought destructive practices stuck in our social system since slavery were often threatened or injured or killed for doing so. There is still in America fear among many that loss of advantage would result from the equality we demand.

"What we must structure is not a system that disallows differences in constructive social, including material, results of the system as long as those differences are a function of individual choice and do not alter the essentials of an equal quality of life. Our individual interests in the material vary. There are those of us who want to buy fancy shoes — and want to be able to get new ones rather than waste the time needed to repair the soles of the old ones. There are those of us who want decent shoes — and want to be able to spend time needed to attend to our souls. We must build a system in which equal access to its benefits is never varied by the race of the individual seeking them and in which there is no race with the singular power to systemically deny that equal access to humans not of it. The differences of us as individuals are the creative gifts of God, the tools that come forth from the amalgamation of our strengths and weaknesses, insightfulness and ignorance. Any systematic difference in the treatment of us that fashions the social lifting of those in a dominant category and the social indifference visited on others of us who are not is the theft of life by the devil."

Malcolm rubs his forehead like he was trying to massage away either painful confusion or the pain of understanding — or both. His eyes stay pinned on the floor briefly until he gently swings them back up toward Dr. King so they can introduce what he needs answered next. "There were even fellow Christian clergy," Malcolm presses, "who vehemently opposed both your analysis of racism and injustice, including economic injustice, in America and what you proposed to do about it. Many others, frankly, consider their criticism of you as legitimate. How do you see it?"

Dr. King reaches over to the table again and brings up another book, THE TREASURED WRITINGS OF KAHLIL GIBRAN. Malcolm waits quietly while Dr. King quickly riffles and then slowly thumbs through some pages. "It was Kahlil Gibran," he begins in a moment, "who so succinctly addresses for me the behavior of some Christian ministers who render the opposition you mention. He wrote, 'You curse Judas because he sold his Master for a few pieces of silver, but you bless those who sell Him every day. Judas repented and hanged himself for his wrongdoing, but these priests walk proudly, dressed with beautiful robes, resplendent with shining crosses hanging over their chests. You teach your children to love Christ and at the same time you instruct them to obey those who oppose His teachings and violate His law.

'The apostles of Christ were stoned to death in order to revive in you the Holy Spirit, but the monks and the priests are killing that spirit in you so they may live on your pitiful bounty ... Your souls are in the grip of the priests, and your bodies are in the closing jaws of the rulers." Dr. King closes the book. Both he and Malcolm say nothing. Malcolm looks down again at the floor and then out the window into the light.

"I understand," Malcolm slowly, gently responds. "But some would say that spiritual life and material life are separate. If some of them heard what you just said, they'd say you're merging them together is simply a matter of trying to sell your philosophy so that you can get back on some kind of speaking circuit. I'm not saying that ... but some certainly would. What do you think?"

"Wait a moment," Dr. King politely admonishes Malcolm and reaches over to the table where he had laid his books. "Here it is," he says after picking up another one and only seconds more of page turning. "It is Gibran again who clarifies the issue more simply and better than I. He wrote in *THE PROPHET*, 'And a merchant said, Speak to us of Buying and Selling. And he answered and said: To you the earth yields her fruit, and you shall not want if you but know how to fill your hands. It is in exchanging the gifts of the earth that you shall find abundance and be satisfied. Yet unless the exchange be in love and

kindly justice, it will but lead some to greed and others to
hunger.'" Then, while closing the book and putting it on
the table with the others, Dr. King adds, "Is that not our
America today, Malcolm? Let it be thought that my intentions are only self-interested. But should we not ask why
it is that our brother Kahlil, who is no longer here for
such a circuit, knew so long ago what is so troubling today? Why can we not see that our "exchange" is without
the needed love and the results continue to be greed for
some and hunger for others? Must we not see that? Must
we not also see that our process for exchanging those
gifts of the world is without justice and stays powered by
greed and protected by the greed of the powerful? Must
we not see that the absence of love will, in turn, power
how the hungry in America and around the world see
what we have become as a nation? Will that not trigger
tomorrow, or the day after or the next year or the decades
after that, responses equally without love ... maybe even
with violence as its ultimate absence?"

Malcolm asks, with a touch of frustration, "Despite all
that you have pointed out about inequality in our economic
system, don't you think the economy is steadily improving
in its distribution of wealth — even across racial lines?"

"For 351 years, racism," Dr. King offers back, "has
plowed steadily along the moral roads of this country's
life from a social enclave of straight-forward bigotry to
a nation with the systematic but unadmitted exclusion
of many in it who are yet called 'citizen.' In light of that
reality, insistence on continued travel down the highway
of gradualism is worse than an ill-advised traffic advi-
sory in stormy weather. It is tantamount to hailing a National Cab and having it take us in the wrong direction
on a busy and slippery one-way street. A violent crash is
inevitable. Those who survive it will likely be bitter. We
have had all the driver's training we need to travel the
full distance safely, without another single delay. But will

we? We may have only until tomorrow morning to decide to do so because the next day we may run out of fuel and the engine may shutter and shut down. What happens to those caught in a bus trying to evacuate people from a village of hunger when the unchecked and unantici- pated consequences of maximized greed plummet down on them like Hurricane Bigotry? Will we drown because we must swim too far, without rest? While sinking the last time, will we wonder about the love of God for us? Will we starve to death because even if we make it to dry land there will be nothing to nourish us when we get there? Will our souls be the only survivors because there is nothing available on that land to heal the damage done to our bodies? Will we ...

Dr. King stops talking and turns slowly to look out again at the trees and the sun that had just begun its good-bye for the day. The remaining light coming through the window sparkles in the water that had risen a little in his eyes. Then, with no book in front of him, he says, "My teacher, Mohandas Gandhi, taught the mind of my soul about the love without which there will be no change. 'I know,' he said so many years ago, 'this cannot be proven by argument. It shall be proved by persons living it in their lives with utter disregard of consequences to them- selves.'" Turning back toward Malcolm, he says, "I'm tired. I've enjoyed our exchange. Is there anything else I might address before we call it a day?"

Malcolm tucks several pages of notes back into the pocket of a leather folio. He replies, "Yes. There are sev- eral more questions I would ask but I really don't want to overstay my welcome. There is one last question, though. I am a little uncomfortable with it. So please bear with me ... People are sort of wondering about the reduction of your visibility since the attack on you a little over two years ago. No one I've talked to questions your commit- ment nor the profound influence you continue to have on all of us. It is common knowledge that you've written a lot and that people around the world want to hear you speak more about nonviolence and its value for us all. Many people even know that you give most of the money you earn from your books and speeches to advance the non-violent efforts in America and other places. Could you fill me in a little bit, in any way you could, about your life since that attack?"

"Let me see," Dr. King muses. "The change really started after being shot ... four times." He passes his fingers gently over his left cheekbone. "You see this scar. That bullet grazed me. What you can't see are the three scars on my left side. I was unconscious for three days after that shooting. I awoke in the hospital and immediately saw Coretta sitting next to the bed. Tears were angling down from her eyes. That moment we began to talk, again, about longevity having its place and we decided that I needed to heal physically before returning to the work we were doing with Southern Christian Leadership Conference. Well, the healing has taken place. I have not announced it yet but I will be returning to our active work a week from next Thursday and ..."

Imagine...

CRYING IN THE PARK.

I could not help it ...

Taunting embarrassment that
Sometimes begged the ether
To hide my face
From those of so many
Who passed by me ...

With wonder in their eyes
About what was in mine.

My heart, though, could not accept
And did not want
My eyes to hear
The command that day ...

The one to get real ...
And know that the death of a body
Crushes its soul and
What it would have taught.

Crying ... there on the park bench
While reading the love of Martin
King of Us
And the history
That gave birth
To Malcolm's "X,"
I knew I would be
Rejecting the beckoning
To a safe, prosperous house
On Realism Road.

Yes ... the glistening of my own eyes
Would light the path they walked
And warm the river
I must swim to my soul.

CHAPTER 19

WHERE DO WE GO FROM HERE ... AGAIN?

Marlin Foxworth, Ph.D.

THAT THE MANIFESTATIONS of the *Black/ White Divide* have taken on some subtleties over the last half century has not, obviously, ended the continuous existence of the *Divide*. That is so because their destructive consequences remain fixed in place. Equally apparent is the persistent insufficiency of constructive activity in America's corporate, educational, governmental, social and, even, most spiritual institutions to address, overcome and replace the issue with a social order structured with the equality we Americans claim but yet do not have. There is no such thing as partial equality.

Dr. King was comprised of a mesh of virtue and flaw like the rest of Us humans and like the American Society We created centuries ago and have tweaked and sustained since. Yet, through the light he so brilliantly shined on humanness, he envisioned, astutely and thoroughly articulated, penned and consistently enacted what he knew had to be done to transform equality from ink and sound to substance. He showed, to both those who love(d) him and those who hate(d) him for it, the contradictory snags in Our societal mesh. With the strength of his soul, heart, intellect, voice and the muscles in his legs, he exposed the contradistinction of America's internationally communicated self-appraisal as the world's preeminent historical and contemporary practitioner and symbol of equality and justice, on the one hand, and, on the other, its tolerance for and enactment of demeaning and brutal treatment of some humans across the world, including its own on the downside of the *Divide.* In his book, *WHERE DO WE GO FROM HERE: COMMUNITY OR CHAOS?*, those contradictions are addressed in great detail. Can the realization that Dr. King is with us, despite the absence of his body, be merged with a sufficient number of kindred spirits keenly aware of the distance We have yet to travel to equality?

Will We continue to be misled by economic, governmental, religious and social gradualism and the insufficiency of education about them? Will We continue to leave unchallenged the pretense that *partial* and *equality* are unified descriptors of genuine Democracy? Will We continue to be bilked of hope by the inveterate substitution of proclaimed good intentions for honest political challenges of the *Divide* by most who ask for Our vote? Will the savings account for that hope soon be overdrawn? Will the elements of the *Divide* coalesce in a way that adds, in effect, a kind of spiritual uranium to the racist manifestations of Dominance and Subordination and produce a social explosion unlike any America has seen within its borders since the Civil War? Or will We end the *Divide* and replace it with a unity structured of an Us inalterably convinced of universal human sameness and perennially radiant about a society with culturally varied means for demonstrating it? To do so, will We soon find and put to unceasing constructive use the amalgamated intellectual brilliance, ethical commitment and spiritual power of so many Americans, even many not experiencing the bludgeon of the *Divide*, who hate it but not the people on either side of it? Will the people so engaged open and keep open the door to enlightening self-criticism about either having made unwitting contributions to the *Divide* or having not done enough to dismantle it? If so, can that ignite a hope-filled renewal of efforts to answer Dr. King's question? Indeed, where do we go from here ... again?

The Trip to Where We Need to Go

The trip to Where We Need To Go From Here must be taken on a bus that is spiritually framed by that same unshakable conviction about indestructible human sameness, propelled by Our multiple cultural cylinders and fueled by inalterable collective and individual commitment to reach that Land of Equality. The process of establishing "community" rather than "chaos" demands both focused mapping for the trip to that land and the willingness to travel the risky road, an edifice of twists, turns and hidden cross-paths, to get there. Many obstacles plummet deep shadows onto that road during the day and, because it has so few streetlights, it can't be seen easily at night. Any of Us who would get on the bus must know that some who oppose our taking the trip will try to force Us off the road or scatter social and political nails in front of the bus at each blind curve along the way. Those who would rotate into the driver's seat for the trip must know they may be more intensely targeted along the way for daring to sit in clear view through the biggest window on the bus while they take responsibility for changes in speed, take a firm grip on the steering wheel and watchfully curve the bus to where the purpose of the trip can be fueled along the way.

There needs to be intense talk on the trip about talk itself. Both history and context give meaning to words that perpetuate the *Divide* while humming the opposite. If a *Land of Equality* is to replace the *Divide*, what has kept it from being so for centuries, including language, must be identified and faced down. Slavery, segregation and its present, usually less blunt, often just beneath the surface but persistent modifications need to be assessed for the conceptual and value base they have in common. Given that values are what humans act on and talk is the vehicle for justifying the action, appraising language that sustains the *Divide* will be both a critical first step and ongoing requirement for the insistent work We must do at each bus stop along the way. Talk is powerful! Words with one meaning on the surface and another just beneath it are full time sustainers of the *Divide*.

Addressing Politics and Politicians that Sustain the Divide

Obviously, both major political parties can be counted on to use language intended to secure the votes of African Americans when doing so may be an indispensable variable in winning an election, securing support for legislation or minimizing opposition to it. We need to ingest regular, heavy doses of Political Ginkgo to help separate, sharply and consistently, what is election time or ongoing political Equality-Talk from words that combine to heartening Our commitment to action needed to achieve that Equality and make it permanent. We also need to construct a socio-cultural-economic-political hearing aid to pinpoint for Us the very moment when substance is poured into an election campaign blender so that a political smoothie about the *Black/White Divide* can be offered for consumption instead of nutritional food for thought about ending it. We need to be able to tell the difference between campaign talk of hope and hopeful talk about a campaign to end the *Divide*.

Although an intuitive assessment of what is said

about the *Divide* is profoundly important, it is insufficient by itself. There needs to be what is analogous to a set of "Nutrition Facts" about talk given out for consumption about the *Divide*. We need to be able to spot a sugar substitute for the real thing when we've been given a political cookie baked in the oil of good intentions. We need to determine what will be the equivalent of a healthy "Serving Size" in political environments when We hear about equality. We need to know what is too much political fat, sugar, carbs and calories and when there isn't enough protein for equality to maintain its needed health in the diet of Our daily social practices and environment.

Getting to that equality will require an ongoing assessment of the consequences to societal health of accepting a Spin Diet as though it provides real nutrition. We should no longer swallow claims of equality at times and in circumstances when there isn't any?

Any organization that would serve Our society and/ or benefit from it, including materially, should clearly communicate how it defines equality and what results from an examination of itself for insufficiencies in needed contributions to it. There should be periodic and public communication from organizations about needed corrections they will enact and what they will accept as evidence that the corrections have functioned as intended. When they do not, there should be communication about that reality and about the next genuine steps in the corrective process.

Race Isn't, *Culture* Is

Constructive responses need to be fashioned and regularly applied to representatives of organizational, institutional and governmental agencies when there is talk of races, because there aren't any. Racial Tolerance, despite the sincerity of many who support it as an ideal social practice, needs to be recognized for the distraction it provides from focusing on the *Divide*. There is no need to develop tolerance for something that isn't. There should be steady insistence, instead, that the focus be on racism and its varied iterations. It must be made clear that the concept of race is the foundational propulsion of racism. Us-And-Themness, It's-Just-The-Way-It-Is-Itis, Let's-Be-Realistic-ism, dominance/subordination and the indifference and violence, physical, psychological and spiritual, that sustain them are powerfully influenced by the concept of race and belief in its reality.

Those of Us who would lead must realize and act on the reality that the separateness we may say we do not want cannot be ended without ridding ourselves of the concept of race because it functions to maintain it. To continue focusing on race, race relations, racial pride and the like may result in being perceived as well intentioned but will contribute nothing to ending the *Divide*. This admonition to discontinue the focus on race should not be taken in any way as a recommendation to discontinue the gathering of what is called "Racial Data." Those data, although misconstrued as representative of races, are most useful, instead, for identifying the social, governmental and institutional manifestations of racism — again, regardless of whether or not it is intended. (Perhaps such figures should be called "Data on Racism" until it no longer exists.) Yes, those statistics are useful for indicating social realities that We, in our various cultural iterations, need to address actively. It is more important in this context, however, that those data be recognized as manifestations of failures in our social structure to obviate the cause(s) of any distinction by culture in access to social benefits. Such numbers, when objectively obtained, need to be used to regularly and consistently identify the social-governmental-institutional materializations of Us-And-Themness. Those data must be used to guide the focus for that collective, constructive activism on firmly replacing the *Divide* with Us.

Race isn't. Culture is. Those of Us who would effect the economic, sociological, political and spiritual overcoming of the *Divide* must focus on culture. It can be learned. Race can't be. Those who would lead need to be able to see the multifarious elements of the *Divide* through the cultural prism of those of Us who experience its profoundly negative consequences. Choosing to learn of the consequences without that direct experience will not be the same as the inevitable learning that derives from facing them. Learning without that direct experience, however, in tandem with learning resulting from it, is infinitely more hopeful for collaboratively contributing to the end of the *Divide* and constructing that social system purposefully focused on enhancing the human — not just material — benefits of and for Us.

Social programs generated in the dominant culture for showing compassionate concern for *those* people in that other race and their suffering cannot contribute to ending the Divide. That is so because the suffering of *those* people, particularly due to realities like disproportionate and perpetual poverty, for which the compassionate concern is programmed, is shaped variously and inevitably by the same socio-cultural-economic system from which that compassionate concern is ostensibly expressed. Racial Tolerance for *those people* is, in effect, despite whatever sincerity is in it, social deviousness. Racial Tolerance is tantamount to tolerance for elephants that fly. It is a focus on something made out to be hugely consequential that doesn't exist instead of focusing on what does: a society with multiple cultures and a social system with dominance and subordination as determinative elements of their stratification. The material contributions of compassionate conservatism to the survival of those for whom the compassion is exercised needs to be exposed constantly for its duplicity. Rushing someone to the hospital who has been beaten severely merits respect. How meritorious is the provision of the transportation, though, when the person driving either rendered the beating or, by ignoring it, was complicit in it and denies having been so?

Social Monikers and the Divide

There needs to be an end of the use of color or culture qualifiers in a way that separates the fulfillment of a social role from a "colored" or non-dominant cultural fulfillment of it. For example, there are no "African American Authors." Yes, there are authors who happen to identify themselves as African American. The fact of being African American does not, in and of itself, alter the complexities and demands of being a prolific and popular writer. The fact of being African American neither limits nor obviates the need to structure language and its flow in a manner that strongly attracts people to the words written. Reference to such an author as an "African American Author" makes that person a subset of being an Author, something not quite the same as an Author. Maya Angelou, for example, happens to be a human who so very obviously is pridefully, spiritually, socially, intellectually, affectively and effectively committed to being African American. So, reference to her as a human being who happens to be African American and an Author is a legitimate way to describe constructive social reality. Media leaders, their reporters and newscasters and those who would lead, govern or teach need to be confronted with the distinction between the application of culture as a prideful element of self-identification and its use as dehumanizing spin — even when done unintentionally. Those who persist with the spin need to be faced publicly — as often as necessary — for their contributions to the *Divide.*

It must be made publicly clear that the moniker "minority" has no numerical significance in the terminology of the *Divide*. It does not matter presently if a voter who is African American votes with 50% or more of the voting citizenry. Nor does it matter when no socio-cultural group, including people who are traditionally called "White," comprise 50% or more of the population in any municipality or state. In both cases, human beings who are African American are labeled by Dominant America as *minorities*. The consistent use of the term "minority," as a "racial" designation, as a substitute for the "Not-White" color qualifier, is an unwitting descriptor of America's brand of "Democracy." If one with skin pigmentation other than "White" can never be anything but a "minority," what does that portend in a society that prides itself on always having the "Majority Rule?" Those in and with access to America's circles of dominant social power need to be confronted about the subordinating function and undemocratic contribution to the *Divide* in that contradiction. If We are to finally reach the equality We seek, "Majority" and "Minority" are to be used only as reference to having taken a position with more than or less than 50% of a participating population on the issue or candidacy before them for consideration. Use of the term "Minority" in any other way states, in effect, "you and yours must remain subjugated to the perennial control of the dominant, i.e., "White" culture." Such control is the primary and prevailing effect of the *Divide* and demands — and should be met with — Our intense intolerance.

The Need for Organized Response to Historic, Political Deception

Although such subjugation over the last half-century has reduced, while increasing in subtlety, its prospects for re-intensifying have not been obliterated. The cessation of elected and other public officials publicly calling people "nigger" doesn't mean the virulent treatment of those of Us citizens who are African American has ended.

The harmful treatment of citizens in Oakland, California who are African American by a group of Oakland Police, the "Riders," makes the point. The officers in question were not found to have harassed and threatened those of Us who are of the dominant culture in Oakland's upscale neighborhoods. The number of votes cast by citizens who are African American but somehow lost during the 2000 and 2004 Presidential Elections makes the point. Had those votes somehow not been "lost" would the outcome of those presidential elections have been different? The abject silence of the President and anyone on his staff about that assault on Democracy makes the point. The slow presidential and governmental response to the plight of people, mostly African American, devastated by Hurricane Katrina makes ... the ... point! The ending of Affirmative Action at the University of California and the statistics on enrollment that followed make the point. The diminutive number of efforts at addressing the systemic contributions in public schools to the disproportionately low success data for those of Us who are African American makes the point. That obstinate reality that the people who do engage in those corrective efforts are exceptions to the rule and never sufficiently supported by those who rule makes the point. The absence of any intense, thorough governmental-legal action to end the disproportionately high imprisonment and prison sentence lengths of those of Us who are African American makes the point. And ... makes the point. And ... makes the point. And ... And ... And ...

Those of Us who would end the *Divide* need to organize a constant request — demand, if necessary — of data from both governmental and other public-serving institutions, e.g., public schools, to determine what, if anything, they are doing to perpetuate or end the *Divide* themselves. Those demands need to be in writing and a record kept of them. The response or lack of same for the requests for data will be telling about the interest or disinterest in ending the *Divide* of the agencies, institutions and organizations and the people in them from whom the data were requested. The responses need to be periodically communicated in local and, when appropriate, national media.

Talk of America being the Melting Pot in which society's many cultural ingredients have gladly relinquished their discrete identities and merged into inseparable oneness is food left on the counter too long at *Chez Politique*. Consuming it may taste great but doing so has helped create and sustain the illness of enduring inequality in America's social body. The body faces, then, the convulsing of throwing up as a painful means for starting a cure. A constructive process of food inspection would be better so that what would plague the body could be identified for its challenge to health and be thrown in the garbage disposal of political lexicon before the damage it invariably creates produces another convulsion.

Those who would talk in socio-institutional-political venues as though the American Melting Pot is a reality and/or contend that some of Us ought to travel the assimilationist path need to be seen for contributing to the maintenance of the *Divide* and for accepting a society structured of Us-And-Themness. Such contributions would be so whether made through ignorance or devious intention. Given the existence to date of a dominant culture in America, only one actual meaning has been promulgated by that Melting Pot pretentiousness. In effect it is this: if chocolate and vanilla are put into an American made Melting Pot, it will be structured in a way that transforms chocolate into vanilla. The taste and gladness chocolate had provided historically will be lost.

Understanding the historic deceptiveness of the Melting Pot concept must also be part of public education. Even kindergarteners can understand that when two substances with the same structure but visually discernible differences in their surfaces are merged in a melting pot both will lose their initial identity and together produce a third one. Neither one of the substances, however, would be stripped of its identity and made to take on the identity of the other. In America's Melting Pot, however, one would be made to take on that of the other.

The significant, discernible differences between the humans on either side of the *Black/White Divide* are not in humanness but in the *human* experiences on both sides. Those plagued with the denseness and/or destructive purpose that preclude them getting that, need to be kept from political office through a process of ethical, collective activism. That process, however, needs to be watched for its prospects for making a perennial *Them* of those of *Us* so infected. It is the behavior resulting from the denseness or exclusive and destructive purpose that needs to be kept from effecting the negative, separatist consequences in what should be a leadership role. To attack the person to be kept from office rather than the separatist consequences of that ignorance or pernicious purpose clearly risks reinforcing the *Us-And-Themness* We would claim to oppose. All of Us on either side of the *Divide* have the capacity to choose to respond constructively to destructive behavior in an effort to preclude its effect(s) and continuance.

Those who are clear about the *Divide,* its elements and the resultant contradiction to Democracy and who work constructively to strip the *And-Themness* from social structure and function need to be propelled into office regularly by collective activism. That propulsion needs to be fueled consistently or it cannot work. Organizing that action will require clarity about what We will accept as evidence that a prospective candidate could lead the Old, partial Us over the *Divide* to an Equal Us. The prospective candidate's record of actively addressing the *Divide*, as opposed to just talking a little about it during election time, must be a major element of evidence. There must also be clarity about what the criteria are for assessing the effectiveness of addressing the *Divide* by an individual once put in office. Should those criteria not be met, that activism must be engaged to replace the person in the next election. Watchfulness must be exercised every ... single ... day during a term in office. Help for ending the *Divide* must be provided voluntarily for anyone in office who is clearly working to do so.

The words of racism and the words used to spin them away from the social confrontation they merit are tantamount to non-physical bullets. The damage and death they visit on Our social body have to be carefully assessed. The primary focus of the assessment needs to be on the shooting done from the arsenal of social dominance. It has to be decided what weapons with social-armor-piercing word-ammunition have been triggered at the *Them* residing outside the walls of that dominant social fortress. Who was wounded and killed and who is likely to be targeted again has to be made clear. Return fire has to be identified and stopped even though its consequences can't be as devastating. Doing unto others what they do unto you ultimately makes you what you have opposed. The media need to be consistently and analytically monitored for use of language that is, in effect, racist ammunition.

Identifying *Them* vs Self-Identification

The role of language in both self-identification and the identification of others of Us in this society needs to be tugged up to the surface of Our collective social consciousness. Self-identification, not stratification by the

dominant culture and a subordinate value and categorization so many in it place on a skin pigmentation, is a
powerful determinant of being *African American*. Ward
Connerly, a past member of the University of California
Board of Regents, has helped to make that clear. Despite
having the melanin and hair texture attributed to being
African American, he has stated that he is not from Africa and is, therefore, not African American. His efforts on
the Board of Regents to obliterate needed means to address the racist effects in public education confirm that
self-appraisal. Self-identification as African American is
most often coincident with skin color which, however,
cannot be justifiably employed as a singular and automatic indicator of the identification. There are countless
people identified as African American, by people who are
and people who are not, who are possessed of what is
seen as requisite skin pigmentation and hair texture but
who do not choose that self-identification. Being African
American is not chosen instead of being human. Nor is it
proffered antithetically to being American. It is selected
as a human means for manifesting a primary and constructive affiliation with human beings with comparably detailed experience in a society stratified by color.
People who are African American must be seen for the
human self-identification made and for the positive human, rather than *racial*, contributions to the multifarious elements of life and its quality in a land of Us. Those
who would lead Us need to object publicly to any use of
the African American identification as a subset of being
a *Real American*.

Joyful self-identification as African American merits
respect as a demonstration of humanness. Respectful
acknowledgement of those of Us self-identified in that
way, even by those of Us not identifying ourselves the
same, merits recognition as a joyful manifestation of human respect. However, the absence of any consideration

in Dominant America to hyphenate or provide color or culture qualifiers to self-identification needs to be recognized for its subsidy to the *Divide.* Why do those of the dominant culture not employ self-identification as "European-American" or "White American"? It is simple: any qualifier added to self-identification contradicts its deduced significance when one perceives one's own dominant social stratum as the unrivaled and superior representative of American Society. Those who would end the *Divide* need to understand and oppose the practice of so many in the dominant culture of subliminally characterizing citizens who are African American as being of lesser human and/or social magnitude. The reality is that the dominant culture has the power not only to *them-label* but also to maintain the labeling practice as part of America's social lexicon. That is so even though not all in Dominant America would have it be so. It is more than a superfluous distinction to state that there were "African American votes" lost in the presidential elections, as contrasted to "votes lost of citizens who are African American." The former makes a subset of the vote and subtly suggests a lesser significance of its loss. The latter does not. That use of language that minimizes the significance of those not of Dominant America needs to be confronted for the energy it provides America's societal stratification.

At the same time there can be no doubt that those of Us who choose self-identification as African American can do so as a means of trumping a negative history of subordination by rising above it with a positive personal and collective history. It is a means for saying, "You may continue either or both your conscious efforts or unconscious practices to subjugate me and mine but We will rise above it no matter what you do, how long you do it and what form it takes! You may characterize me and mine as second-class but We won't accept such classification — even for a second!"

Identification of others as "White," when done as either conscious or unconscious stratification of those in a social category as historically and presently oppositional and/or demeaning to one's own, needs to be understood as a descriptor with a base in reality in African American experience. Yet coordinated, constant, unrelenting, constructive confrontation of the historically oppositional and demeaning social structure and practices would tender hope for Equality when incessant talking about "White People" has not. Additionally, employing "white" skin pigmentation as a single assumptive indicator of racist opposition is as inappropriate as the summary and racist appraisals derived by skin gazing from the loft of Dominant America. There are, in fact, people who appear *White* but who are aware of the privilege into which they are born and who are active — some powerfully so — in opposition to the racist structure of this society.

America and Castes

There can be no end of the *Divide* without clarity that castes are not just social categories in countries like India or Pakistan. The AMERICAN HERITAGE DICTIONARY's definitions of "caste" include the following: "A social class separated from others by distinctions of hereditary rank, profession, or wealth." ROGET'S 21ST CENTURY THESAURUS includes the following as substitute terms for "caste:" "lineage, position, race, rank, social order, standing, station, status, stratum." The dominant culture has ranked those of Us who are African American in all of the ways indicated above. It has done so over the centuries of language transformation from "Slave" to "Colored" to "Negro" to "Black" to "African American." Nor, over all that time, has "nigger" been relegated by Dominant America to an American Societal Dictionary of Dead Caste-Like Talk or a Bigot's Thesaurus of Ended Language. (The use of the term "nigger," for and by those of Us who are African American, is often done jokingly and even endearingly. Such use remains a classic example of cultural strength applied to transfigure what has been imposed as a negative to a positive. The work of the late John Ogbu, Ph.D., delineates, in detail, that transforming process.) The overcoming of the *Divide* cannot occur without acknowledgement of the caste-like status imposed on communities that are African American. Here, as with other language elements of the *Divide*, the exceptions to that caste-like stratification must be seen for their confirmation of the rule. Social confrontation of the *Divide* has to make it clear that there can be no end to the *Divide* as long as exceptions to subordination in it are proclaimed as indicators that its persistence is only a function of those who choose not to rise up and step over it or lack the ability to do so.

Getting Clear About *Diversity*

Celebrations of diversity need not be stopped. Consideration of diversity as racial and human difference does. What does it portend for a democracy and its prospective quality when the cultural categories within it are considered as inalterably separable and, in effect, ranked by the dominant culture for their significance in the social order it controls? What does it say about the level of advancement of a democracy when, from the loft of the dominant culture, *they* are recognized for alacrity in musical show business and *we* run the economy, when *they* are praised as professional athletes but *we* own the teams, when *they* are disproportionately in prison and *we* are disproportionately the heads of corporations, when *they* are so often imprisoned longer than are *we* for having committed the same crimes, when *they* are to attend the schools for which *we* create the curricular content and determine the cultural methodolo-

gies for teaching and learning, when *we ... they, we ......*
they, we .... they, we ....
.. they .... division
ad infinitum?

The activist focus needs to be based, in part, on the clarity that the diversity needing celebration is in the form of the cultural methodologies used to demonstrate our identical human sameness. Call and response is not methodologically identical to silent attentiveness in church. Both, however, are about a relationship with God. "Whasup?" is no less a greeting and statement of caring than is "How are you doing?" Angrily referring to someone as an individual who cohabits frequently with mothers is not differently demeaning than calling that person the son of a mother dog. Soul music is no more or less a cultural preference of the humans who would sing it and hear it than is rock and roll for the humans who would sing and hear it. Trafficking drugs on the streets of a community is no more or less contemptible than bilking the coffers of a corporation and, by so doing, damaging the lives of people connected to the organization. Despite dominant culture jargon, a *black lie* is no more untruthful or significant than a *white lie.*

There must come to our societal surface the reality that celebrating diversity, despite the sincerity of those of Us who do so, has been to date also a substitute for recognition of and action to end diversity in access to the benefits of America's social structure. There need not be fear about loss of social benefits in a democracy structured of equality for all in it, in all the cultures of it. There will be fear, however, that change to a democracy so structured, one in which equality is a hardbound fact, will result in reduction of existing, disproportionately high privilege for some. That fear is rational because it will. There need not be fear, though, about loss of primary culture. Just as any of Us can have more than one friend to whom we are equally loyal and just as such loyalty does not need to be internally conflicted, loyalty to a primary cultural Us and a national Us need not produce a competition with debilitating and separating individual and social results.

Those who would lead Us, however, need to spend time carefully anticipating the specifics of the feared loss. If Diversity is seen as equally significant but varied methods for showing human sameness rather than unequal human variation, what loss of privilege will derive for the people advantaged by the latter? Will that loss of advantage be seen as deprivation of rights? If seen that way, will the response rekindle a social environmental melding of Orwellianism and McCarthyism? Just as Dr. King and Malcolm X were targeted for their insistent opposition to the *Divide,* will those doing the same today have the same done to them today? Part of the needed activism must be to develop a preparedness for legally confronting extra-legal manipulation of law designed to block challenges to disproportionately high privilege for those who have it and tolerate some perpetual denial of privilege for those who don't. Better to anticipate such and have it not occur than to not anticipate it and have it occur.

Needed Activism, Leadership and Leaders

Where we go from here with respect to those kinds of issues and the language used to cloud them requires a collective analysis of what is needed in governmental and extra-governmental leadership roles. Almost always what we get for candidates varies from people who talk a good game but have little history of addressing the *Divide* to candidates who talk a reasonably good game and have no history for addressing it. The *Divide* is perpetuated when either wins. The task is not to wait for leaders who would intensely address the *Divide* but, rather, for us to seek them out and help shape their preparedness to lead.

Wherever America goes from here will be determined in great measure by whether or not dominance and subordination remain a part of our social structure and its system. Our country allows those of Us not directly impacted by the negative results of social structure and praxis to determine what, if anything, is done about them. The title of Lani Guinier's book, THE TYRANNY OF THE MAJORITY, is fittingly on target in that regard. If the majority of voters determines every outcome in an election but is not impacted by a negative social reality for which a curative initiative has been balloted, the result can easily be that the initiative is not passed and the damage of the human beings needing it remains in perpetuity. For example, there is a disproportionately high number of people of color who live in neighborhoods adjacent to freeways. Consequently, they are exposed disproportionately to toxic fumes. An initiative to address the issue could be voted down by a majority of voters who do not live in the community and may not have even driven through it. The resulting perpetuation of such human damage is, then, simply attributed to the tenet of Democracy that "the majority rules." Such is a classic case of being a double minority: 1) A category of people who are not of the dominant culture and, consequently, considered by it to be a "minority"; and 2) being of a group of participating citizens adding up to less that 50 % of people determining the outcome of the initiative. Given the disproportionate distribution of poverty on communities of color and the disproportionate positioning of poverty in the least healthy environments, the toxic fumes in this context are both physical and political.

Unless the *That's-Just-The-Way-It-Is-Itis* is excised from the political process, the social damage deriving from the above example and comparably destructive social realities will again merge with a collective sense of having had enough of it — again. When will it blow? How often must

it blow? Will the pattern continue for social upheaval occurring in communities that are predominantly African
American about every 20 years or so? When will the dominant axe of indifference come swinging down — again?
We need to find leaders who have the interest, knowledge
and capacity to structure Our social process in an inclusive way that rationally precludes the need for social
rebellion? We need to boost those with that leadership
potential who are already in public office but have not
stepped out strongly enough, particularly when such is a
consequence of fear about losing the next election. While
looking for and supporting prospective leaders, We need
to create some. We need to make sure they understand
that a Democracy has two choices when it touts itself as
relentlessly committed to justice while tolerating the multifaceted absence of it for so many of its Own. It can look
honestly within itself and end the hypocrisy or end up
ending itself because it didn't.

Collective activism must make sure those who are in
or are pursuing social leadership roles, in public office
and not, are committed to making real the definition of
Equality as existence of sameness in human worth and
access to societal benefits and the absence of fixed categories of *Them*. Any society pursuing Democracy can
have temporary categories of *Them* that result from siding
with the minority of participants on any given issue. That
themness is contextual, affixed to the particular issue,
e.g., voting for a loosing candidate in a presidential election. Beside the issue not turning out as desired by *them*,
there is no loss in existing social benefits or reduction in
access to the process(es) for attaining them. However, any
society with a structure having historically fixed socio-
cultural-economic categories of *Them* with diminished
social benefits and access for their attainment has chosen to limit its pursuit of Democracy ... even if claiming
preeminence in the endeavor. Such is the case in America

despite the denial in venues of power that it is so.

That activism must establish criteria by which the existence or absence of Equality in any social context is to be determined. Every candidate for office needs to be questioned about whether s/he sees any condition of inequality and what s/he plans to do about it. If inequality exists within the boundaries of authority for the position on the ballot but the candidate denies or spins around it, every constructive, collective effort possible needs to be enacted to straighten the candidate out or skillfully oppose her/him. Better than having to engage in that oppositional activism is doing the searching necessary for finding the right candidate long before any election. It is one thing to seek the "Black Vote" during a campaign and then to do nothing about the *Black/White Divide* when elected. It is better to actively address the cruel, destructive inequalities of the *Divide* and fail than to use the *Divide* like a pimp would use a prostitute to gain political voting lucre and then do nothing about the issues once that check is deposited. It has been four decades since Dr. King and Malcolm X were murdered for daring to address the issue as vehemently and intelligently as they did. The activism needed must make it clear why their contributions to defining and ending the brutal *Divide* still are more pertinent today than are the collective contributions of both major political parties and most people in government office, including the presidency. Biographical history may inspire but it can never be enough by itself to spring and sustain transformative social action. How many more years or worse, decades, must we hear annually about a magnificent dream without having one Ourselves? That activism must be carefully analytical about what there is in Our national sense of self that precludes intensive consternation about the talk of Equality surpassing its presence?

Equality should not be taken as the absence of distinctions in constructive human contributions and skills. The pressure and demands on the head of an organization, for example, will most often be more intense and consequential than those on her/his assistants. Some variation in material compensation for the two roles, therefore, can be rationally justified. However, treating the people fulfilling those roles with varied human respect because of differential appraisal of the significance of the roles cannot be justified. Nor is there justification for material compensation for the work done by both leaving one with a secure future, based on objective assessment of the quality of life offered by America, and leaving the other without it. Nor is there justification for variance throughout a nation's history in socio-cultural access to any social roles, including governmental ones. The history of prospects for one of Us who is African American becoming President of the United States is calculated, on both sides of the *Divide,* as unrealistic is clearly indicative of the need for activism focused on correcting the persistence of such fathomless inequality. Just as Rabbi Michael Lerner was told so often that his advocacy for a Palestinian State was unrealistic, largely because he is a rabbi, there are so many among Us who comparably assess the prospects for ending the *Black/White Divide* as unrealistic. Just as Rabbi Lerner responded to that admonition regarding his advocacy for a Palentinian State, We too must respond to the comparable admonition that ending the *Black/White Divide* is *unrealistic*. With respect to ending the *Divide* and creating a *United States,* it's time fo US, too, to stop being realistic.

Dr. King was murdered because the values evidenced in his activist behavior threatened the continuance of privilege for the upside of the *Divide*. Malcolm X's experience in Mecca ended his social perspective that "Whites," by definition, were automatically the enemy? That change in perspective, rather than being antithetical to the principles of Islam, resulted in him being seen as a threat to the preeminent power and control of Elijah Muhammad in the Nation of Islam and, consequently, antagonized some of its members. They killed him.

As long as he remained a separatist, he was spoken of on the other side of the *Divide* as a social irritant but quietly accepted by some there for his contribution to the *Us-And-Themness* needed to fuel the *Divide*. Then there was the post-Mecca switch of his focus from separatism to unrelenting insistence on ending the ebbing and flowing subordination of humans to the multifaceted virulence of racism and on powering the transmigration of equality from being trapped in the dictionary of social pretense to nationally experienced fact. From this came his inking on the roster of real threats to the *Divide*. Had he not been murdered by those who twisted the spiritual soundness of Islam as justification for doing so, there is doubtless likelihood that Malcolm would have been Xed by some other kindred spirit of James Earl Ray. Where we go from here has to include an organized consciousness that although the activist confrontation of the *Divide* must be non-violent, the responses to the activism will not always be, particularly as its successes mount and inequality tumbles down hill. Speculation can be endless about what changes might have occurred in America had Dr. King and Malcolm X lived. It will be so very important to anticipate responses that would trigger the same kind of speculation for any who would lead as we ratchet up the pursuit of equality. One way to reduce the prospects for successful and "final" assault on leadership will be to spread it like a virus of love. Too many would have it and none experiencing its constructive effects would want it to end.

"As legal slavery passed," noted Julian Bond, Chairman, National Board of Directors, NAACP, "we entered into a permanent period of unemployment and underemployment from which we have yet to emerge." Effective, intense activism on eradicating both the permanency of that period and any prospects for its resurgence will undoubtedly be bludgeoned with perverse "legal" and extra-legal obstacles. Indeed, any challenge to the unequal distribution of privilege, particularly in its material manifestations, will be taken by those advantaged by it as a threat to them and to America's social system — yet another prospect for resuscitation of McCarthyism. However, it is fortunate that, unlike labor in today's American economic structure, justice and equality cannot be off-shored ... to a place where it would be cheaper to produce them. Achieving them will require intensified, ethical, non-violent activism ... again.

Equity is an attractive concept on the upside of the *Divide* but almost always when it is defined as the worth of a commodity on the market being greater than what is owed on it. Given that there is no human *Can't* locked into any socio-cultural group, a supply of Equity is a must wherever there is the absence of Equality among such groups in access to the benefits of a social system. Exceptions to that access are indicative of their prevailing opposite. Inequality promulgated by a confederacy of dominant social practice and indifference cannot be excised from the structure of America's social body via the use of equality-talk as the scalpel for curative surgery. Nor will the social medicines of compassionately conservative, faith-based initiatives function any better to remove the cancer of inequality from Our social bodies in the downside of the *Divide*. Besides, the co-pays demanded by HMOs (Hope Minimizing Organizations) for treatment of fractured or lost hope are rising — after being too high from the start.

The venues and specifics of the elements of inequality for socio-cultural groups need to be identified in every town, city, county, state and the District of Columbia in this nation. In each place, the people who would transform equality from talk to action need to specify for those in positions of power what provisions of equity are necessary to overcome each identified manifestation of inequality, what will be accepted as evidence that the equity set in place is working and the circumstances under which equitable corrective action will no longer be needed. While physical violence in response to effective activism should be anticipated, it should also be made clear that perpetuating a social system with inequality structured in it, along with social and governmental unwillingness to enact the equity to end it, is violence in and of itself. Just because those of Us on the downside of the *Divide* are almost never lynched anymore doesn't mean you will never see Our hope hanging lifelessly from the Tree of Social Stagnation.

Inattention and indifference on the part of people who are in public office to the *Black/White Divide* and the inequality it perpetuates need to be seen as violation of the Constitution-of-Us. Attention to the *Divide* only during election time needs to be recognized as a breach of that constitution as well. There is a difference between actively damaging, even killing, someone and turning your back while someone or something else does it. However, culpability for the human damage or death that ensues exists for either behavior. Active confrontation of the *Divide* requires making publicly clear the political, social organizational and governmental manifestations of such inattention and indifference. The unwillingness to own up to it should ignite careful plans to remove those in denial from office and/or actively oppose their organizations. Political conviction for the crime of indifference to the *Divide* and the lives it damages, the quality of life it attenuates and the hope it bludgeons needs to be met with the sentence of removal from office, by any legitimate, legal, ethical and open way possible.

It is time that conservative social and political practices are analyzed regularly in every social and governmental venue for what they conserve. It is one thing to conserve social structure and practice that caters to a privileged, dominant element of society while consistently demonstrating inaction and, consequently, indifference to ending inordinate poverty in communities that are African American. It is a part of that conservation to insist on not only maintaining but also expanding the privilege and material benefits for a social stratum for and by whom the system was created. As in other stops along the *Divide*, denial of bad intentions or the presence of self-proclaimed good intentions regarding America's economic structure continues to divert attention from its unending contribution to the *Divide*. It would be another thing for the conservation to be of manifestations of equality that had ended that long-standing privilege and dominance and had structured avoidance of the redistribution of them to any element of Us. The conservation of a socio-governmental practice that provides needed equity in a constant effort to overcome the *Divide* and its dominance and subordination is one that justifiably could transform radical leaders to conservatives. Given the history of conservatism in America, it is ironic that it could be transmogrified by constructive, radical political action — its historical enemy. America's prevailing economic structure has to be publicly recognized and challenged for its constant contribution to the *Divide*.

The Need for Radical Change

It is time that liberal social and political practices are analyzed regularly in every social and governmental venue for what they liberalize and for what cannot be accomplished by doing so. The unintended contributions of liberal politics to bolstering the *Divide* must be surfaced more clearly. It is one thing, for example, to establish and fund a governmental program designed to help people become gainfully employable, even when the resultant hiring of all involved doesn't reach 100%. It is another to not oppose or sustain by indifference or inaction a socio-economic system that tolerates disproportionately high unemployment and the related material want in communities that are African American. Poverty as an ongoing reality for any socio-cultural element of Our society needs to be a cause of non-violent national disturbance and transformative action. Powerfully demanding such action is necessary because incommensurate poverty in communities that are African American has been the case throughout the lives of any of Us who must face it and throughout the lives of every ... single ... generation ... in ... America ... before ... Us!

Radical change is a must if that historical reality is to be removed from America's social structure. The time for national recognition of the message in conserving and justifying a socio-economic system with the belief that anyone not doing well in it has only her/himself to blame is long overdue. Yes, there are individuals in any and every socio-cultural group who have not and do not do what is necessary to materially sustain themselves. There is not the remotest justification, however, for the disproportionate poverty in communities that are African American being considered the function of any one or a combination of ineptitudes of individuals who are poor and live there. How many communities have to be assessed before the plummeting of poverty on communities that are African American is seen for his persistent reality in American social structure? Will We get it if we are collectively analytical about Akron, Atlanta, and Austin? Will it be necessary to add Baltimore, Bangor, Baton Rouge, Boston and Brooklyn to Our analytical enterprise? Will it take adding Charlotte, Chicago, Cleveland, Columbus, Columbia, Corpus Christi, Dallas, Dayton, Detroit, Durham, Grand Rapids, Greensboro and Hartford to the task? If that isn't enough, maybe We should consider Indianapolis, Jackson, Kansas City (x 2), Lansing, Lexington, Little Rock,

Los Angeles, Louisville, Manchester, Memphis, Meridian, Miami, Milwaukee, Minneapolis, Mobile, Nashville, Newark, New Haven, New Orleans, New York City, Oakland, Oklahoma City, Peoria, Phoenix, Pittsburgh, Portland (x 2), Providence, Raleigh, Richmond (x 2), San Francisco, Seattle, Spokane, St. Paul, Syracuse, Tacoma, Trenton, Washington D.C. and Winston Salem? Will We have to add more before the analysis of the obvious becomes the force for change it must become?

Those of Us who would lead the confrontation of the *Divide* must make it abundantly clear in the socio-political turfs in which we are active that the centuries old persistence of poverty in communities that are African American is a function of racism as effect. Historic and contemporary denial of that reality has been met too long with tolerance from multiple social sources, in myriad materializations. It has to stop! Good intentions alone have not been good — ever — at effecting, as ostensibly intended, the end of poverty and its asymmetrical presence in such communities! That has to stop! Conservatism has functioned to maintain a system despite it never having been fair for those without the requisite power of dominance to benefit greatly from it. Liberalism has reduced the contemporary breadth and depth of poverty but not the persistent fact of it. Neither conservative nor liberal socio-political practices have ever confronted America's socio-economic system for the inevitabilities of its structure. Facing the reality that rich and poor each require the other for its existence is so very long overdue. Facing the reality that dominance and subordination are the pivotal determinants of the socio-cultural disparities of wealth and poverty is so very long over due.

A call for radical change in America's socio-economic structure isn't a thinly veiled push for communism. It does, however, necessitate a national look at how the structural elements of American society, including racism, reduce, often radically, access to America's material and other social benefits for those of Us historically on the down s(l)ide of the *Divide.* The identical structural sameness of all humankind includes INDIVIDUAL differences in the capacity to access the benefits of a socio-economic system. It does not include perennial differences by socio-cultural group in access and receipt of those benefits. If that occurs, it is a function of a social system. It is not an inevitable consequence of the structure of humanity in any of its cultural formulations. Why must we continue with a socio-economic structure that is developing an increasing number of people who will never be able to spend their income for a year and an increasing number of people who cannot afford food for themselves and/or their families for a day? An income of a $1,000,000.00 a year produces $2,740.00 a day. Ten days' savings, even after taxes are deducted, can buy an awfully nice car. How does one benefit, though, from saving poverty? What is the social investment benefit over the long haul for a socio-economic system with such profound differences in the distribution of material benefits? Given that the arithmetic of those differences shows them widening, how long until there is another social explosion? What will it take for all of Us to get that drug trafficking in poor communities, while being immoral and inexcusable, is so often a matter of accepting and internalizing America's intense interest in the material and creating a smaller economic system to pursue it because the doors to the larger system seem locked?

The continued failure to look at the issue of poverty and its manifestations in communities in this land that have a history emanating from conquest, colonialism or slavery is a continued contribution to the explosiveness of the *Divide.* Rather than a system that increasingly favors those already benefiting materially the most, consequently perpetuating the continuance of both wealth and poverty, a system constantly producing a much narrower range of material well-being is needed. The content of that material well-being, what will be accepted as evidence that it is cemented in place and, if it is not, how corrective actions are to be set in motion need to be carefully delineated by Our social leaders and government. Those of Us who would press against the racism and related poverty in America's socio-economic structure need to be clear that doing so will be met with powerful opposition from those benefiting most from the system We would challenge. Some opposition will also come from people on the downside of the *Divide* who see making such a challenge as unrealistic. The reasons and logic in support of that perception will be numerous. Again, maybe it is time to stop being realistic!

The Need for Real Education to End the Divide

Public education is doomed if its worth continues to be determined by whether or not student scores on standardized tests continue to rise. How many more times must it be shown that the scores on such tests are largely determined by zip code? Having the highest test scores means neither that the schools with them are the best or the schools without them the worst. They mean neither that the students in the schools with the highest test scores are the smartest nor that the students in the schools with the lowest scores are the dumbest. Inferences throughout America are drawn from those test scores about the worth of teachers, schools, and the productive possibilities for students in them. Consequently, negative appraisals are drawn like metal to powerful magnets in schools in communities on the downside of the *Divide*. Yes, there are large numbers of students who are African American and live in poor communities who are doing well academically. Such still too often and inappropriately percolates surprise. Those success numbers are not yet considered in public education as indicative of academic capabilities in communities that are African American being just as strong as in other communities. Nor are those numbers seen appropriately as evidence that equity is needed to increase them.

The education praxis established by the dominant culture is for the dominant culture. The absence of exclusive intention does not preclude the use of unequal practices and disparity by socio-cultural groups in results. Yes, irrespective of primary culture, students need to learn and adapt to the methods of the system in power. No, irrespective of power, such a system is not structured well to meet the needs of students not of the dominant culture. Such students have to adjust to the methods, curricular content and history of the culture for which the schools were created and are maintained. Such requires an additional task for students deeply embedded in a primary culture other than the one at the foundation of the school. Students of the dominant culture must go to school and learn academic disciplines. Students of another culture, most particularly if it has a history of being segregated — formally or informally — from the dominant culture — must go to school and learn the curricular content and adapt to the cultural methods of the dominant culture. They must also adapt to the assumptions and ignorance about them of some who are in charge and not of their culture.

Although it has been damaged in recent years, there is a long history of liberal practice to provide additional assistance to students who have migrated to the United States. That assistance is righteously based on the reality that students can be precluded from learning what they otherwise might without having equal access to the dominant methods and curricular content of America. It is a rational assumption that not having lived in the dominant culture humanly impedes sufficient facility with its methods, including language. That assumption does not contain an element of belief that absence of needed facility is really a function of inalterably minimized capacity for it. There is only token surprise when students having come into Our country being non-English Proficient become thoroughly English Proficient after having been provided the means and the time for that to occur.

There is very little comparable appraisal, however, of the weightiness of insufficient familiarity with the multiple manifestations of cultural dominance for Our students living in impoverished communities that are African American. Such communities, Our ghettoes, are nearing 400 years of existence. Where in our social system is the needed recognition of that? Those of Us who would lead in the collective effort to end the *Divide* must confront constructively America's public and private education institutions and systems for the duplicitous practice of cultural accommodation for humans migrating here but not for those of Us living here, those of Us whose ancestors were forced to come here to begin with. We must confront the social and political support for ending efforts at minimizing the consequences of that duplicity, e.g. the removal of affirmative action from the University of California system. We must tug to the surface of Our social consciousness that such an action not only denies complicity with the history of racist separatism but also says, "The problem is yours! Get over it. Do something about it. Or live with it!" *Us-And-Themness* indeed! The flawed effort in the Oakland Unified School District to consider the efficacy of Ebonics in the education of Our students who are African American died because of lack of sufficient support, planning and inclusion. The courage of those who led in the effort needs to be rekindled in an ignition of a much more strategically sound agenda.

Simultaneously Facing The Divide In Two Ways

At the same time We are intensifying the confrontation of the *Divide*, We need to radically change Our appraisal of the task. We need to act simultaneously in two ways that appear contrary: 1) We must face the *Divide* as though it will never end and that Our very survival will require ceaselessly vaulting over it and teaching all of Our own to do the same and to teach the same; 2) We must face the *Divide* as though there can be no doubt that its replacement with an Equal Us will happen in Our lifetime.

The task before Us will have multiple requirements, some that will show their faces only around the curves in the road along the way. Critical among those requirements is that we don't reciprocate the divisive idiocy of America's history. Simply, people who are of the dominant culture are not the issue. The social structure of dominance and subordination is. The undue privilege given people who are of the dominant culture and born with varying degrees of security into that dominance is. Once constructively faced with it, many good human beings born into the privilege have seen and will see its divisiveness and the history of human havoc it has wreaked. Such human beings have gladly become Us and willingly taken on the risks of having done so. More will.

The confrontation of the *Divide* will have a better chance of failure if it only takes on traditional methods for doing so. We need to be organized in groups without organizational names and permanent locations. Consider the following as a process. Ten people, who know each other and have a reciprocal sense of respect, come one night into the same room. Each is asked to take five minutes to delineate what s/he sees as the most powerful and destructive elements of the *Divide*. There is no dialogue in the process, only listening and the careful taking of notes. A specific amount of time is set aside after each presentation for clarifying questions to be raised. A content analysis of the notes is done after the meeting. The categories of biggest concern are determined by assessing both the intensity and frequency with which they came up during the session.

A second meeting is held. In this one the issues of biggest concern are communicated. That is followed with each of the 10 indicating what s/he feels most passionate and confident about doing to address the issue. A plan of action is delineated and criteria for determining its effectiveness in taking on the issue are established before people go home. For example, one of Us is to arrange for a public meeting, either formal or informal, at which people are invited to discuss an identified issue. Another of Us is to contact various media to inform them about the pending meeting. Another of Us is to take notes at the meeting to be clear about the responses to the issue discussed. Another of Us is to write an op-ed piece for the local press about the results of the meeting's discussions. Another of Us is to take advantage of a relationship with a public official who might be able to have the item officially agendized for action. Another of Us is to come to the meeting simply to assess the audience and appraise the response to the expression of concern about the issue as it shows in eyes and voices and gestures and cultural style. Another of Us is to make sure five additional and trusted people come and participate in the meeting. Another of Us ... etc. ... etc. ...etc. ... until the issue is handled in a way that meets the criteria established for success.

Group and self-criticism will be key to having the issue handled in a way that meets the success criteria. Then ... the next issue is to be taken on and the practice is to be expanded, if and as needed, into more groups, with more people, without the groups being named and without necessarily identifying group leaders to officially take on the role. Ties with existing groups, e.g., NAACP,

Urban League, religious institutions, women's organizations and cultural organizations need to be expanded as trust in doing so is clearly established. A multitude of activist elements need to shape the variegated process that non-violently and ethically will bring the inequalities, racism and the *Divide* they created and sustain to their grave. Anyone given the opportunity to participate but who sees the goal as unrealistic needs to be confronted with two essential questions. Should America be the richest country in the world despite the material, social and spiritual history of its virulent *Divide?* Or should it be the best country it can be because of an unfaltering commitment to the establishing and keeping of an *Equal-Us?* The answer to the questions will be, in effect, either a turning and walking away or the clasping of Our hands.

Rather than being seen as catapulting *Us* into a United State, Our efforts may well be seen as a threat to the elitism of the supposed United States. Whatever We face in the process, We must stay on ...

THE ROAD TO US
by Marlin Foxworth

The shadows born of the marriage of trees and sun
Do what they always have
Since that first chorus of loving musts
Was sung in the harmony of creation ... and people ...
And time ... and God.

In the caress of these shadows —
Sometimes done in collaboration with kindred dusk —
The gifts of creation — of Us and to Us —
Are embraced and thanked and shielded,
If only for needed moments,
From the destructive rays of hatred
Or worse —
From the poison fumes
Of a Human Divide
Born of indifference.

As a neighbor waiting for a knock on the door
And the request for the warm guidance it always grants,
Sun is not lost
In the caress of these shadows.
It stands by them
Nodding always in the direction
Where the road to Love widens and rises.

"See," it says to those resting in the shade,
"There is the road to US,
The one true path to the village
Where the only bridge toll
For entrance
Is the cost of never calling another
"ONE OF THEM."

A GLOSSARY OF TERMS USED IN THE BLACK/WHITE DIVIDE

Marlin Foxworth, Ph.D.

ACCOUNTABILITY: A process for institutionalized answerability and consequences applied to individuals for the actions they've taken or not taken that are either required or disallowed by the organization that created the roles the individuals are filling. It contains due process procedures. It is different from responsibility.

ACTIONS OF BIAS/BIGOTRY: Negative, destructive actions, including violence, physical and/or psychological and social, taken against people perceived by the perpetrator(s) as having inalterable affiliation with a socio-cultural category seen by the perpetrator(s) as unworthy of respect. Most often committed against individuals or groups without knowing the human(s) toward whom or against whom the action is taken and without knowing and understanding well or at all the social circumstances and influences they experience.

ASSIMILATION: Relinquishing of one's primary cultural identity and taking on a different one consequent to perceiving that doing so will enhance one's security and prospects for a productive social future. An often unspoken unequal requirement for what is called *equality* to be approximated even though not secured. As such, a contradiction in a country claiming *equality* for all.

ATTITUDE: Verbal and/or physical posture, consonant with self-idealization, which an individual takes to symbolize what s/he believes s/he would do about a given issue when not having to face it or being called on to do so.

CASTE: A classification of citizens, other than the dominant one, locked historically into a location in a society's hierarchy. Although the reality is denied in the United States, subordinate or caste-like positions exist, primarily for people whose ancestors became part of American Society by virtue of conquest, colonialism or slavery. Native Americans, Latinos — most particularly of Mexican Ancestry — and African Americans have been forced throughout American History into caste-like or subordinate social roles. (Definition influenced by the works of the late John Ogbu, Ph.D., Professor of Anthropology, U.C. Berkeley) As is the case with class, individual exceptions exist in countless numbers, to being inalterably locked into caste-like or subordinate roles. Those exceptions, however, are seen by some in American Society's dominant stratum as proof that there are no caste-like categories in American Society.

CLASS: A classification of citizens, which is the inevitable consequence of an economic system, structured in such a way that material wealth and the access to it are disproportionately distributed. The disproportionate distribution exists as a consequence of "rich" and "poor" each requiring the other for its existence. "Middle Class," in turn, needs the other two categories for its definition and existence. The lowest class, epitomized by poverty, is disproportionately visited upon people of color, particularly those in caste-like social categories, i.e., those resulting from a history of conquest, colonialism or slavery. The middle and upper class are disproportionately people of America's dominant culture.

CONSERVATIVE: In American society, its politics and social structure, conservative means what the term implies: to conserve, to keep in place, a social structure and its mechanisms for disproportionately distributing its material and other social benefits to the dominant social stratum. A social perspective maintaining that not equally gaining the benefits of the social system, e.g., money and privilege, is the primary, if not sole, responsibility of the individual and not the consequence of the social structure. It calls for compassionately caring for those people in non-dominant, i.e. not privileged, social categories while abjectly refusing to take any responsibility for the conditions creating their existence and denial of equality.

CULTURAL CONFLICT: The establishment and maintenance of distrust for those of a cultural group other than one's own consequent to either having been demeaned, threatened and/or attacked, politically or physically or socially, presently and/or historically by that group or having developed a negative appraisal of it from the perception(s) of it provided by members of one's primary culture.

CULTURE: A set of human experiences, varied in detail and nuance from other sets of human experiences but never any more or less human than them, that fashions human interaction methods and styles, e.g., language, and which shapes the prism through which we see our prospects for meaning, respectful social treatment and constructive social benefits in any society and its institutions, e.g., public schools, and from which we conclude the appropriateness for group affiliation.

CULTURAL IDENTITY: Cultural identity is, like all human identity, a sense of social kinship created by human experience filtered through a historical collection of nuanced social encounters and practices that serve as determinants of the appropriateness and desirability for group affiliation. Such identity is first universally human identity. The socio-cultural component of that identity is a function of the variance in that social experience.

DENIAL: An often passive and subtle manifestation of bigotry and/or discrimination, operative through disclaimers that individual and/or institutional discrimination against cultural/ethnic groups exists. It is a means for substituting professed good intentions for the discrimination experienced by others. It obviates self-examination and functions as a means for passing intergroup prejudice and discrimination to oncoming generations of the culture exercising the denial. It also functions as a prompt for ongoing, negative, reactive group appraisals from those in socio-economic-cultural categories against which the denial has been applied.

DESEGREGATION: Unsegregation. The act of those in a dominant culture to remove the geographical space separating members of the dominant culture from those in a non-dominant or subordinate culture in public institutions, e.g., public schools, by creating the prospect for visual discernment of people of varied skin pigmentation entering and exiting the facility through the same door. The term is socially and politically but inappropriately used as a synonym for "integration" and, therefore, serves, intentionally or otherwise, to shield from clear public view the maintenance of an institutionalized

dominant-subordinate social, political and economic relationship. It is different from integration.

DIVERSITY: Perception of people in social groups as the
result of differences in one or a combination of our varied
skin pigmentations, hair textures, languages, cultures
and "races." Given that such variety is inevitable, this
definition leads to the belief that we can never be one
people and the goal of social relations becomes nothing
more than peaceful coexistence. "Celebrating" diversity is
a stated goal in the historically, woefully insufficient effort
to overcome the negative social — include economic —
consequences of group separateness inevitably resulting
from America's societal structure.

DOMINANT CULTURE: Historically, the culture group with
the majority population from which came, consequently,
the foundation values upon which a society's public institutions, economy, primary language, social responsibilities, practices and obligations and hierarchy of power
and privileges are established and through which, in
turn, its hegemony is maintained even when the culture
is no longer numerically the majority, e.g., those of the
dominant culture ("White") in California at the beginning
of the 21st Century.

EDUCATION: Education is a multifaceted and constructively functional practice. It is a process for developing
a solid grasp of the existing and prospective elements of
individual and social life. It produces the means for developing the capacity for multidisciplinary, penetrating
inquisition and curative prescriptiveness to constructively analyze personal and social issues unsolved and
to achieve goals that would be their antithesis, e.g. rising
above racism and ending the *Black/White Divide*. Education also functions to identify and formulate needed

contributions to the well-being of self and fellow human beings. It is different from *schooling* and *training* and, although it is usually connected with matriculation in school, it does not require it.

EQUALITY: The sameness in human worth and in the corresponding human treatment, including institutionalized governmental, legal and social praxis, for enacting it. The absence of fixed categories of *them*. It does not call for pretense that each of us has identically the same individual characteristics and talents anymore than saying each of us is the same height and weight. It does depend, though, on the inalterable conviction that human worth is based on the fact of humanness, not on the appraisal, via a sliding scale of value, of an individual's alignment or characterization with a socio-economic-cultural group. The antithesis of inequality and the absence of inequity.

EQUITY: A concept of fairness inextricably tied to justice. Variously needed and structured institutional compensation for the deductions in equality resulting from a social system, including one structured of dominance and subordination. Affirmative Action is an example of equity. The process by which systemic blockages are removed to make sure individual success and failure are both systematized and institutionalized equal opportunities. The social balance needed to address the absence of equality resulting from the chronic disparity in the access to the benefits in a society.

ETHNIC GROUP: A subset of a culture. In effect, a culture-within-a-culture.

GOOD INTENTIONS: In the context of the *Black/White Divide*, *Good Intentions* are a long standing governmental, individual, political and social substitution for ending racism and its ongoing, historic effects. In the context of the *Black/White Divide*, it says, in effect, " I want what is best for all my fellow citizens and I am not a racist. Consequently, there is no contribution to racism for which I am responsible. The fact that racism exists is someone else's responsibility."

HYPHENATED-AMERICAN: The attachment of a label of ancestral and/or primary, current cultural affiliation of American citizens to the term "American," e.g., African-American. Such a hyphenated term can function as self-identification and identification with a primary culture. That hyphenation also is used, primarily in Dominant America, as an indicator that, unlike itself, a given sociocultural group is a sub-set of American classification. You will find very little communication from Dominant America with which it classifies itself as a social subset, i.e., "White-Americans" or "European-Americans".

IMMIGRANT: Someone coming more or less voluntarily into an environment dominated by a culture different in various degrees from her/his own. Such includes humans who come not necessarily because they want a new country but because to stay in the country in which they had been living would be too politically and/or economically and/or socially problematic and/or unacceptably dangerous.

INDIFFERENCE: The powerfully destructive presence of absence. The absence in indifference becomes part of everything it condones. It deducts useful, even necessary, energy and focus from the social dynamism and magnetism imperative for transforming what is into what should be. It is a driving element of today's racism.

INTEGRATION: The voluntary coming together of coequals, for an agreed upon purpose, for an agreed upon time,

GLOSSARY

339

with agreed upon conditions and criteria for measuring the mutual utility, benefit and the appropriateness and desirability of its continuity. It is a societal, rather than individual, marriage. As a marriage, it requires never ending efforts at constructive unity. It does not require, however, that the parties to the marriage relinquish their respective identities, including culture. Integration is a social, political and economic state of unity of all people in a society, in all their cultural iterations, who choose to participate. Integration in schools is not a process for students of other cultures to assimilate into the dominant one. It is the practice of including both cultural content of all involved throughout the curricula, not just in ethnic studies classes, and of employing the appropriate and needed cultural methodologies to teach them. It requires constant action on the recognition that culture, dominant and not, profoundly influences teaching and learning styles but not the capacity to learn. The latter is universal. It is different from *desegregation*. Integration is not yet a functional element of American Society.

LIBERAL: A social perspective that both justifies the primacy of the "American Way" and acknowledges imperfections in it. An approach to pick from what is seen as an available number of options for addressing the consequences of those social structure imperfections in the "American Way." A liberal response offers a Western Medicine kind of social remedy: a prescription that will end some ailments, reduce or obliterate the symptom(s) of more serious infirmities locked into the body, and, hopefully, reduce or slow negative consequences even if there has been no final determination of the cause(s) of the ailment."

LIBERATION: The replacement of a socio-economic-political practice or structure which produces and supports oppression and subordination of socio-cultural categories of people with social practices and structure founded in equality that unifies people and obviates social inequality in all of its manifestations.

LOVE: The purposeful action of contributing to the state of well-being of another or others. Love is not an emotion but is most often accompanied by one, e.g., joy.

MINORITIES: Socio-cultural groups of people not of the dominant culture. A label ascribed to such groups deemed by the dominant culture to have cultural and societal perspectives, characteristics, histories and methods of less significance than those it ascribes to itself. "Minorities" exist in American society even when there is no numerical, cultural or social "majority," e.g., in California where the dominant culture, i.e. European-Americans, are less than 50% of the population. Consequently, the term is used in a way that is contrary to the numerical meaning of "majority and minority" in the context of democratic social practice, i.e. when a *majority* is more than 50% of the voting population selecting, for example, a candidate for office or approving a proposed binding social initiative brought before it for approval, and a *minority* is less than 50% of that population voting for that candidate or initiative. The existence of "Minorities" in this context is the result of the dominance of a socio-economic-cultural group, e.g., European-Americans, regardless of whether it is a numerical majority.

OPPRESSION: "The systematic and pervasive mistreatment of individuals on the basis of their membership in various groups which are disadvantaged by the institutionalized imbalances in social power in a particular society. Oppression includes both institutionalized and/or socially normalized mistreatment, including instances of violence. It includes the invalidation, denial, or the non-recognition of the complete humanness (the goodness, uniqueness, smartness, powerfulness, etc.) of those who are members of the mistreated group." (Definition by Ricky Sherover-Marcuse, *Unlearning Racism Workshops*)

PEOPLE OF COLOR: Human beings with recent ancestral origins in Africa, Asia, Latino Countries, Native Americans and others with no self-identification with *White* (read *Dominant*) America.

RACE: A social, not a scientific construct, based on the perception that discernible physical characteristics like skin pigmentation and hair texture are the symbol of inalterable and irreversible separation of humankind into groups, each with social characteristics which are correspondingly, inalterably and irreversibly affixed to it and which are not manifested in individuals not of the group. Given that it is a social concept, it is a manifestation of stereotyping in and of itself. Research has shown again and again that there is one race, the Human Race, and no others exist.

RACISM: The belief that there are races and the social and institutional practices that perpetuate the social separation that inevitably derives from the concept. Racism is the effect of such separation regardless of intent. A social tool for maintaining a dominant position in a dominant/subordinate social structure. A function of the belief that "Race" is a physiological phenomenon from which inevitably result behavioral, intelligence and ability differences by "racial" group and corresponding and justified social stratification and unequal access to and distribution of the benefits deriving from a social structure.

RADICAL: A perception that social change requires alteration in social structure based on the recognition that structure, independent of intentions, has its own consequences. A changed structure produces change(s) in its consequences. Although radical change can mean total replacement, it can also mean replacing faulty components of a societal structure that historically and unceasingly damage those of socio-economic-cultural categories that did not create the structure, are not equally included in it and have insufficient power, within its current boundaries and through its prevailing rules of operation, to change it. Radical change can do in a social system what heart bypass surgery and hip-replacement surgery can do to a body. After the surgery is successfully concluded, the body still functions but it now serves or serves better what it should have but had not or had not well enough before, with no loss of service to any other parts of the body.

RESPONSIBILITY: An individual choice of answerability for the effect of one's actions or inaction. It is different from accountability.

SCHOOLING: The process by which students are guided to become sufficiently facile in demonstrating the values of the culture on which the school is established for their teachers and school administrators to grant them their informal stamp of approval. Graduation ceremonies are partly about that. Schooling is sometimes confused with but is different from education and training.

SEGREGATION: The demeaning and socially damaging practice, a power prerogative of only a dominant culture, of separating people into socio/economic groups, usually done in American Society via categorization by discernment of combinations of skin pigmentation and hair texture attributable to what is called a "Race." In the centuries from its onset until approximately the 1960s, it was a dominant culture practice (although not accepted or condoned by all in it) of intentional, blatant, often legal, boldly — even violently — enforced physical, geographical, institutional, economic and political separation forced on people of color in, for example, housing, neighborhoods, public entities like schools and places of worship, places and types of employment and in access to and roles in government. Since the 1960s, despite it not being legally and boldly enforced, the separation still exists, still creates great human damage but is not as readily discernible. For example, despite the fact that our public high schools have been desegregated, there is a disproportionately high number of students who are of the dominant culture in Advanced Placement courses and a disproportionately low number on the basketball team and a disproportionately low number of students who are African American in Advance Placement courses and a disproportionately high number on the basketball team. Neither "high" or "low" is the inevitable consequent of something inherent in a "race." For obvious reasons, the consequences of inequality in that disproportionality has its most profound negative impact on students who are not of the dominant culture, e.g., students who are African American.

SOCIAL STRUCTURE: A societal framework and its socio-architectural value-design. Social structure has inevitable consequences for people in a society, sometimes even despite the intentions of the people who live in and lead that society. For example, attainment of wealth is an ideal goal in America's social structure. Since wealth is not unlimited, attainment of it necessitates corresponding lack of attainment of it, no matter how hard someone works. Any high degree of material wealth in a category of America's society necessitates a corresponding lesser amount of it in other categories of the society, despite the claims of being a *land of equality.*

STATE OF WELL BEING: A condition of living in which one has equal or, as needed, equitable access to the personal and social means for self-development and for security in a social system and access to its benefits.

STEREOTYPE: The summary characterization of individuals in a social and/or cultural group different from one's own, usually done through visual discernment, which concludes that each of the individuals of the *other* culture has the same behavior(s), characteristic(s) or trait(s) — or lack of same. For it to take place, stereotyping requires ignorance about the individual(s) being characterized on the part of the individual(s) doing so. In theme and variation, stereotyping is concluding that "they all ... (Fill in the blank.)"

TOLERANCE: A relative of good intentions. It is the capacity one develops to withstand what s/he cannot stand or does not like, e.g., learning how to avoid getting angry at the fool next door who plays her/his radio too loud and on the wrong station until 2:00 am. Its application as a social practice is most destructive when it is taught to our young as a means for graciously putting up with socio-cultural categories of *Them*, e.g., another *race*. It also functions as an indication of the belief that socio-cultural separateness is a prominent element of American Society that is not likely to go away.

TRAINING: The process by which a person is provided with the needed understanding and capacity to do something that the trainer already knows how to do, e.g., driver's training. It is different from education and schooling.

VALUE: A belief, with an internalized and corresponding sense of its correctness, upon which an individual would act when seeing the need to do so and/or when called upon to do so. It is different from attitude.

VIOLENCE: That physical and/or psychological process by which an individual is involuntarily separated from a state of well-being. It is done by an individual or collection of individuals on behalf of self and/or a group with which affiliation and self-identification is made, against another individual or group, resulting from the belief that one has the right to deny a state of well-being to others and from the denial that the right to a state of well-being is the function of birth only, irrespective of any other condition or criteria.

WORKS CITED

Angelou, Maya. *POEMS*. New York, New York: Bantam Books, A Division of Random House, Inc., 1986.

Bailey, Chauncey. "Black Religious Leaders Back Bush." Oakland, California: *Oakland Tribune*, August 25, 2004.

Bell, Janet Cheatham, ed. *FAMOUS BLACK QUOTATIONS*. New York, New York: Warner Books, Inc., 1995.

Cobbs, Price, M.D. and William Grier, M.D. *BLACK RAGE*. New York, New York: Bantam Books, 1968.

Cobbs, Price, M.D. and Judith L. Turnock. *CRACKING THE CORPORATE CODE*. New York, New York: AMACOM, a division of American Management Association, 2003.

Collins, Chuck and Felice Yeskel. *ECONOMIC APARTHEID IN AMERICA*. New York, New York: The New Press, 2000.

Foxworth, Marlin, Ph.D. "Putting Spirituality in Public Schools." New York, New York: *Tikkun Magazine*, November, 1998.

——. "Segregation Knows No Limit [editorial]." *Valley State Sundial*, Northridge, California: San Fernando Valley State College (now California State University, Northridge), October 19, 1962.

——. "Housing Closed to Negro [article]." *VALLEY STATE SUNDIAL*. Northridge, California: San Fernando Valley State College (now California State University, Northridge), October 19, 1962.

Gibran, Kahlil. *THE PROPHET* [1923]. This edition New York, New York: Alfred A. Knopf, Inc., 1980.

——. *THE TREASURED WRITINGS OF KAHLIL GIBRAN*. This edition Edison, New Jersey: Castle Books, 1975.

Guinier, Lani. *THE TYRANNY OF THE MAJORITY*. New York, New York: The Free Press, A Division of Simon & Schuster, Inc., 1995.

Hansberry, Lorraine. *A RAISIN IN THE SUN*. New York, New York: Random House, 1959.

King Jr., Martin Luther, *A TESTAMENT OF HOPE: THE ESSENTIAL WRITINGS AND SPEECHES*. San Francisco, California: HarperSanFrancisco, a Division of HarperCollins Publishers, 1986.

Kochman, Thomas. *BLACK AND WHITE STYLES IN CONFLICT*. Chicago, Illinois & London, England: The University of Chicago Press, 1981.

Lerner, Rabbi Michael and Cornell West, Ph.D. *JEWS AND BLACKS*. New York, New York: G.P. Putnam's Sons Publishers, a Grosset/Putnam Book, 1995.

Lewis, David Levering. *W.E.B. DuBOIS: BIOGRAPHY OF A RACE*. New York, New York: Owl Books, A John MacRae Book, Henry Holt and Company, 1994.

Lindsey, Randall B., Kikanza Nuri Robins and Raymond D. Terrell. *CULTURAL PROFICIENCY: A MANUAL FOR SCHOOL LEADERS*. Thousand Oaks, California: Corwin Press, Inc., 2003.

Merton, Thomas. *GANDHI ON NON-VIOLENCE*. New York, New York: New Directions Publishing Corporation, 1981.

Ogbu, John Ph.D. *MINORITY EDUCATION AND CASTE: THE AMERICAN SYSTEM IN CROSS-CULTURAL PERSPECTIVE*. [A Carnegie Council on Children Monograph] Academic Press, 1978.

Satel, Sally. "Medicine's Race Problem," *POLICY REVIEW* (Online),http://www.policyreview.org/DEC01/satel.html

Sherover-Marcuse, Ricky. *UNLEARNING RACISM WORKSHOPS*. [Personal Communication]

Shreeve, James. "The Greatest Journey," *National Geographic Magazine*. Washington, DC. March, 2006.

Smith Sr., Rev. Dr. J. Alfred with Rev. Harry Louis Williams II. *ON THE JERICHO ROAD*. Downers Grove, Illinois: InterVarsity Press, 2004.

Stampp, Kenneth. *THE PECULIAR INSTITUTION — SLAVERY IN THE ANTE-BELLUM SOUTH*. New York, New York: Vintage Books, 1956.

Verdin, Tom, "Census: Whites Not the Majority: State Shift in Numbers a Symbolic Milestone." (Associated Press), Hayward, California: *The Daily Review*, August 30, 2000.

Whittier, John Greenleaf. The poem *Maud Muller* from ONE HUNDRED CHOICE SELECTIONS. Philadelphia, Pennsylvania: Penn Publishing Co., 1897.

Wright, Richard. *NATIVE SON.* [1940] New York, New York: Harper and Row, 1966.

The American Heritage Dictionary. Boston, Massachusetts: The Houghton Mifflin Company, 1992.

ROGET'S 21ST CENTURY THESAURUS. New York, New York: Bantam Dell, A Division of Random House, Inc., 2004.

About the Authors

MARLIN FOXWORTH, PH.D. has a B.A. in Journalism, a M.A. in the Psychological Foundations of Education and a Ph.D. in Education. In his lengthy experience in urban education administration, he has done one elementary principalship, a high school vice-principalship and four high school principalships. He has filled several district administrative roles, including being the Interim-Deputy Superintendent in the Oakland Unified School District, and three Superintendencies in California districts: Rialto Unified School District: Hayward Unified School District; and Milpitas Unified School District.

Marlin has taught from the first grade straight through to courses for people pursuing their masters degree in education. He has done multiple adjunct teaching jobs at a variety of colleges and universities: University of Phoenix (Current, Masters of Teacher Education courses at campuses through the San Francisco Bay Area); California State University, Hayward (now Cal. State University East Bay); San Francisco State University; St. Mary's College; University of La Verne, United States International University; National Hispanic University; and East Los Angeles City College.

Also of tremendous importance in his background is the learning garnered from his intense involvement in the civil rights movement of the 1960s.

Marlin's writing has appeared in *Tikkun Magazine* and the *Oakland Post.* He is currently at work on a new book about culture conflict in education.